Artificial Intelligence for Business

Artificial Intelligence for Business

What You Need to Know about Machine Learning and Neural Networks

Doug Rose

✦Addison-Wesley

Boston • Columbus • New York • San Francisco • Amsterdam • Cape Town
Dubai • London • Madrid • Milan • Munich • Paris • Montreal • Toronto • Delhi • Mexico City
São Paulo • Sydney • Hong Kong • Seoul • Singapore • Taipei • Tokyo

Editor-in-Chief: Mark L. Taub
Acquisitions Editor: Malobika Chakraborty
Development Editor: Chris Zahn
Managing Editor: Sandra Schroeder
Senior Project Editor: Lori Lyons
Production Manager: Aswini Kumar/codeMantra
Copy Editor: Gill Editorial Services
Indexer: Erika Millen
Proofreader: Betty Pessagno
Cover Designer: Chuti Prasertsith
Compositor: codeMantra

Many of the designations used by manufacturers and sellers to distinguish their products are claimed as trademarks. Where those designations appear in this book, and the publisher was aware of a trademark claim, the designations have been printed with initial capital letters or in all capitals.

The author and publisher have taken care in the preparation of this book, but make no expressed or implied warranty of any kind and assume no responsibility for errors or omissions. No liability is assumed for incidental or consequential damages in connection with or arising out of the use of the information or programs contained herein.

For information about buying this title in bulk quantities, or for special sales opportunities (which may include electronic versions; custom cover designs; and content particular to your business, training goals, marketing focus, or branding interests), please contact our corporate sales department at corpsales@pearsoned.com or (800) 382-3419.

For government sales inquiries, please contact governmentsales@pearsoned.com.

For questions about sales outside the U.S., please contact intlcs@pearson.com.

Visit us on the Web: informit.com/aw

Library of Congress Control Number: 2020947363

Copyright © 2021 Pearson Education, Inc.

Cover image: yucelyilmaz/Shutterstock

All rights reserved. This publication is protected by copyright, and permission must be obtained from the publisher prior to any prohibited reproduction, storage in a retrieval system, or transmission in any form or by any means, electronic, mechanical, photocopying, recording, or likewise. For information regarding permissions, request forms, and the appropriate contacts within the Pearson Education Global Rights & Permissions Department, please visit www.pearson.com/permissions.

ISBN-13: 978-0-13-655661-9
ISBN-10: 0-13-655661-2

ScoutAutomatedPrintCode

For Jelena and Leo

Contents at a Glance

	Foreword	xv
	Preface	xix
PART I	**Thinking Machines: An Overview of Artificial Intelligence**	**1**
Chapter 1	What Is Artificial Intelligence?	3
Chapter 2	The Rise of Machine Learning	19
Chapter 3	Zeroing in on the Best Approach	35
Chapter 4	Common AI Applications	45
Chapter 5	Putting AI to Work on Big Data	53
Chapter 6	Weighing Your Options	61
PART II	**Machine Learning**	**65**
Chapter 7	What Is Machine Learning?	67
Chapter 8	Different Ways a Machine Learns	83
Chapter 9	Popular Machine Learning Algorithms	95
Chapter 10	Applying Machine Learning Algorithms	115
Chapter 11	Words of Advice	125
PART III	**Artificial Neural Networks**	**129**
Chapter 12	What Are Artificial Neural Networks?	131
Chapter 13	Artificial Neural Networks in Action	143
Chapter 14	Letting Your Network Learn	155
Chapter 15	Using Neural Networks to Classify or Cluster	169
Chapter 16	Key Challenges	175
PART IV	**Putting Artificial Intelligence to Work**	**179**
Chapter 17	Harnessing the Power of Natural Language Processing	181
Chapter 18	Automating Customer Interactions	193

Chapter 19 Improving Data-Based Decision-Making 199
Chapter 20 Using Machine Learning to Predict Events and Outcomes 207
Chapter 21 Building Artificial Minds 219

           Index 231

Contents

Foreword xv
Preface xix

PART I   **Thinking Machines: An Overview of Artificial Intelligence** 1

Chapter 1   What Is Artificial Intelligence? 3
            What Is Intelligence? 4
            Testing Machine Intelligence 6
            The General Problem Solver 8
            Strong and Weak Artificial Intelligence 11
            Artificial Intelligence Planning 14
            Learning over Memorizing 15
            Chapter Takeaways 18

Chapter 2   The Rise of Machine Learning 19
            Practical Applications of Machine Learning 22
            Artificial Neural Networks 24
            The Fall and Rise of the Perceptron 27
            Big Data Arrives 30
            Chapter Takeaways 33

Chapter 3   Zeroing in on the Best Approach 35
            Expert System Versus Machine Learning 35
            Supervised Versus Unsupervised Learning 37
            Backpropagation of Errors 38
            Regression Analysis 41
            Chapter Takeaways 43

Chapter 4   Common AI Applications 45
            Intelligent Robots 45
            Natural Language Processing 48
            The Internet of Things 50
            Chapter Takeaways 51

Chapter 5	Putting AI to Work on Big Data	53
	Understanding the Concept of Big Data	54
	Teaming Up with a Data Scientist	54
	Machine Learning and Data Mining: What's the Difference?	55
	Making the Leap from Data Mining to Machine Learning	56
	Taking the Right Approach	57
	Chapter Takeaways	59
Chapter 6	Weighing Your Options	61
	Chapter Takeaways	64
PART II	**Machine Learning**	**65**
Chapter 7	What Is Machine Learning?	67
	How a Machine Learns	71
	Working with Data	74
	Applying Machine Learning	77
	Different Types of Learning	79
	Chapter Takeaways	81
Chapter 8	Different Ways a Machine Learns	83
	Supervised Machine Learning	83
	Unsupervised Machine Learning	86
	Semi-Supervised Machine Learning	89
	Reinforcement Learning	91
	Chapter Takeaways	93
Chapter 9	Popular Machine Learning Algorithms	95
	Decision Trees	99
	k-Nearest Neighbor	101
	k-Means Clustering	104
	Regression Analysis	108
	Näive Bayes	110
	Chapter Takeaways	113
Chapter 10	Applying Machine Learning Algorithms	115
	Fitting the Model to Your Data	119
	Choosing Algorithms	120
	Ensemble Modeling	121
	Deciding on a Machine Learning Approach	123
	Chapter Takeaways	124

Chapter 11	Words of Advice	125
	Start Asking Questions	125
	Don't Mix Training Data with Test Data	127
	Don't Overstate a Model's Accuracy	127
	Know Your Algorithms	128
	Chapter Takeaways	128
PART III	**Artificial Neural Networks**	**129**
Chapter 12	What Are Artificial Neural Networks?	131
	Why the Brain Analogy?	133
	Just Another Amazing Algorithm	133
	Getting to Know the Perceptron	135
	Squeezing Down a Sigmoid Neuron	138
	Adding Bias	141
	Chapter Takeaways	142
Chapter 13	Artificial Neural Networks in Action	143
	Feeding Data into the Network	143
	What Goes on in the Hidden Layers	145
	Understanding Activation Functions	149
	Adding Weights	151
	Adding Bias	152
	Chapter Takeaways	153
Chapter 14	Letting Your Network Learn	155
	Starting with Random Weights and Biases	156
	Making Your Network Pay for Its Mistakes: The Cost Function	157
	Combining the Cost Function with Gradient Descent	158
	Using Backpropagation to Correct for Errors	160
	Tuning Your Network	163
	Employing the Chain Rule	164
	Batching the Data Set with Stochastic Gradient Descent	166
	Chapter Takeaways	167
Chapter 15	Using Neural Networks to Classify or Cluster	169
	Solving Classification Problems	170
	Solving Clustering Problems	172
	Chapter Takeaways	174

Chapter 16	Key Challenges	175
	Obtaining Enough Quality Data	175
	Keeping Training and Test Data Separate	176
	Carefully Choosing Your Training Data	177
	Taking an Exploratory Approach	177
	Choosing the Right Tool for the Job	178
	Chapter Takeaways	178
PART IV	**Putting Artificial Intelligence to Work**	**179**
Chapter 17	Harnessing the Power of Natural Language Processing	181
	Extracting Meaning from Text and Speech with NLU	183
	Delivering Sensible Responses with NLG	184
	Automating Customer Service	186
	Reviewing the Top NLP Tools and Resources	187
	NLU Tools	189
	NLG Tools	190
	Chapter Takeaways	191
Chapter 18	Automating Customer Interactions	193
	Choosing Natural Language Technologies	195
	Review the Top Tools for Creating Chatbots and Virtual Agents	196
	Chapter Takeaways	198
Chapter 19	Improving Data-Based Decision-Making	199
	Choosing Between Automated and Intuitive Decision-Making	201
	Gathering Data in Real Time from IoT Devices	202
	Reviewing Automated Decision-Making Tools	204
	Chapter Takeaways	205
Chapter 20	Using Machine Learning to Predict Events and Outcomes	207
	Machine Learning Is Really about Labeling Data	208
	Looking at What Machine Learning Can Do	210
	Predict What Customers Will Buy	210
	Answer Questions Before They're Asked	210
	Make Better Decisions Faster	212
	Replicate Expertise in Your Business	213
	Use Your Power for Good, Not Evil: Machine Learning Ethics	214
	Review the Top Machine Learning Tools	216
	Chapter Takeaways	218

Chapter 21	Building Artificial Minds 219	
	Separating Intelligence from Automation 221	
	Adding Layers for Deep Learning 222	
	Considering Applications for Artificial Neural Networks 223	
	Classifying Your Best Customers 224	
	Recommending Store Layouts 225	
	Analyzing and Tracking Biometrics 226	
	Reviewing the Top Deep Learning Tools 228	
	Chapter Takeaways 229	
	Index 231	

Foreword

Approximately two decades ago, when I first started to explore artificial intelligence (AI) and machine learning (ML), these technologies were, for the most part, confined to academic institutions. In the past few years, we have seen a major leap in the field as AI and ML have begun to be used successfully in real-world applications, such as driverless cars, targeted advertising, prediction of rare diseases, and so on. Three major factors are behind this development: the availability of big data, improvements in processing power, and development of advanced ML algorithms. Today even a mobile phone is capable of running sophisticated ML algorithms in real time. These technological achievements introduce considerable opportunities for researchers and nonexperts to learn, use, and deploy customized ML solutions for their specific needs. Flexible software libraries are being made available for public use, and the models can be built in the cloud, which makes them an even more accessible solution.

Unfortunately, the simplicity and availability of software libraries hide the complexities of ML solutions. On the other extreme are math-heavy books that reveal and revel in the complexities of ML but in a language that only experts and researchers can understand. What have been lacking are books and other credible content that tell the wonderful story of AI and ML in an easy-to-understand format. This book, *Artificial Intelligence for Business: What You Need to Know about Machine Learning and Neural Networks*, fills that gap, serving as a bridge for nontechnical executives to understand AI and ML and use these technologies to solve their business problems.

I have published many research papers in international journals and conferences in the field of AI and ML. I thought this book would be one of those reviews that I do as part of my academic service. However, after reading Chapter 1, "What Is Artificial Intelligence?", I could tell that the tone was different. It was clear that Doug knows his audience, and he wants to tell a simple yet compelling story. His goal was to attract everyone to this fascinating world of AI and ML without overwhelming or frightening them with the mathematical jargon. As data science becomes more pervasive than ever, we need such efforts to introduce the field of AI and ML to everyone and expose them to the possibilities they create in our world of ever-accelerating change.

The book is divided into four major parts: Thinking Machines: An Overview of Artificial Intelligence, Machine Learning, Artificial Neural Networks, and Putting Artificial Intelligence to Work. In Part I, Doug dedicates a chapter to explaining AI fundamentals, beginning with its history. A basic understanding of the evolution of AI and what AI can and cannot do is essential for grasping the possibilities and limitations. Doug goes on to explain the fascinating notion of strong and weak AI, the power of combining AI with big data, and the ensuing challenges. He spends considerable time explaining fundamental concepts of the field, including expert systems, data mining, supervised and unsupervised learning, backpropagation of errors, and regression analysis. This part of the book also emphasizes the major applications of AI, such as intelligent robots, natural language processing (NLP), and the Internet of Things (IoT). By the end of this part, readers' minds already will be busy thinking up new ways to harness the power of AI and ML to enhance their business.

Part II dives deeper into the core concepts of ML, illustrating the concepts with numerous examples that enable readers to relate ML to the specific business problems they want to solve. This part introduces readers to specialized ML disciplines, such as semi-supervised learning, reinforcement learning, ensemble learning, and popular algorithms, without exposing them to heavy mathematics but through the use of examples and analogies. Exposing beginners to different models of ML is key to expanding their lateral understanding of the field and is something this part does well. In particular, the archery analogy used to describe the bias-variance trade-off is an incredible explanation of this challenging concept.

Part III is dedicated to neural networks. This is the most challenging part because literature on neural networks without major mathematical equations is scarce. However, Doug starts off nicely by providing a brain analogy while differentiating the brain from neural networks. He then explains the perceptron and activation functions and how they work by providing simple calculations to make readers understand the processing power of the fundamental unit of a neural network. The current research in deep learning has given rise to complex and large neural networks. However, by giving readers a fundamental understanding of a single perceptron's form and function, Doug prepares readers to tackle the more challenging concepts surrounding modern deep neural networks, which may have thousands of such entities.

Because beginners often struggle to understand concepts such as backpropagation, gradient descent optimization, and the cost function, Doug presents these ideas succinctly with examples from everyday life in Part IV. He connects neural networks with the ML concepts already learned in Part II. This approach helps readers make sense of different ML concepts and their relationship to each other and to neural networks in solving different challenging problems. This part ends by identifying key challenges, providing guidance on choosing the right type of data and tools, and explaining the importance of taking an exploratory approach.

I highly recommend this book to beginners in the field of AI and ML. Even if you have no background in mathematics or statistics, you will find the book easy to understand. This book is also a good read for many ML practitioners and data scientists, who may want a refresher on certain key concepts. I am sure, after reading this book, you will be filled with new ideas and be eager to further explore the fascinating field of AI and ML. This is the purpose of this book, and Doug met that goal. I wish Doug and this book all the best. It is an honor and a privilege to be associated with this book.

—Dr. Shehroz S. Khan
University of Toronto

Preface

For thousands of years, people have been fascinated with artificial intelligence (AI). In ancient mythology, the Greek god Hephaestus was so skilled with his hammer that he built a giant bronze mechanical man called Talos to protect Europa in Crete from pirates. Thousands of years later, in 1817, Mary Shelley grappled with AI when she wrote *Frankenstein*. Even more recently, the classic 1927 futuristic film *Metropolis* featured the robot named Maria who cared for the children and ultimately drove the city to rebellion.

While myths and science fiction have stirred the imagination to consider the potential (and potential horrors) of AI, philosophers have struggled to define the very nature of human intelligence. In the 1600s, Thomas Hobbes famously wrote that our "reason is nothing but reckoning." He concluded that we are just the sum of our memories, suggesting that maybe these memories could be coded to mechanical intelligence.

A few centuries later, in the 1960s, the philosopher Hubert Dreyfus criticized this idea of mechanical intelligence, writing several books on the subject. One of the most famous was *What Computers Can't Do: A Critique of Artificial Reason*, which was first published in 1972. His key argument was that our unconscious human instincts could never be captured with formal rules.

Movies like *The Terminator* warn us about how easy it might be to create an intelligent network like Skynet that could extinguish our species through a simple binary miscalculation. Silicon Valley celebrities have argued whether AI will be our greatest achievement or the ultimate cause of human extinction.

Mythology, science fiction, and philosophy make the topic of AI fascinating. However, when you start to look at how artificially intelligent machines do what they do, it's hard to be sure whether to scream or yawn. On the one hand, some displays of AI are extraordinary. It's amazing to take a ride in a self-driving car. On the other hand, most modern AI focuses on classification. You have a machine classifying millions of photos, videos, or audio files. That's not the kind of technology that motivates you to build an underground bunker or start smashing robots.

Certainly, AI has enormous potential. But we tend to like to judge things based on their performance, not their potential. So far, AI has performed well. The availability of massive data sets over recent years has given machines new food to find out more about us and the world in which we live. Machines are able to identify patterns in data that humans can't perceive and would probably never think to look for. But there's still an enormous gap between this level of performance and human intelligence.

There's also an enormous gap between the threats posed by AI and human nature. Certainly, AI carries practical and ethical challenges. But the first round of the challenges will be less about the ethical implications of creating sentient beings and more about our responsibilities to each other. Think of it as less like *The Terminator* and more like the 1981 cult classic *Escape from New York*. When the movie came out, unemployment among 16-to-24 year-olds males was at 84%. It imagined New York as a compassionless, lawless urban jungle that had to be converted into a prison. Our ethical obligations to each other will dog us long before any existential threats from rogue robots.

The first challenge posed by AI will almost certainly be how to support the people whose skills will be obsolete through automation. What will we do with the tens of millions of truck drivers, cabdrivers, retail workers, machine operators, and accountants? They won't all become programmers, yoga instructors, personal trainers, YouTubers, and artists.

It's much more likely that these socioeconomic challenges with automation will eventually eclipse our concerns about machines outsmarting humans. It won't be about a supercomputer taking control of a robot army and turning it against the human race. Instead, it will be about the automated burger flipper that took your nephew's job at Steak and Shake. After all, he may have needed that job to help pay for college.

You should be aware of these challenges as you start to think about the impact of AI. But this book isn't about grappling with these socioeconomic challenges. It's about opportunities. Specifically, it's about business opportunities. To find the best business opportunities, you need to better understand AI as a *tool*.

If you think about it, some of the top businesses didn't succeed because they were first to market. Apple didn't build the first music player. Google wasn't the first search engine. These companies succeeded because they understood the scope of the tools and technologies and how to apply them to current and future business needs.

This book is about getting you on that path. You'll get a high-level overview of the different technologies under the umbrella of AI. Throughout the book you'll see examples of how to apply this technology to different business opportunities. Once you better understand the tools, you'll be in a much better place to create long-term strategies for a new or existing business.

The business opportunities are too diverse (and as yet to be discovered) for a simple list. My hope is that you will understand the full scope of the technology and then be able to apply it to the opportunities in your organization or even to start a new business.

This book is organized into four parts. Part I is an overview of AI. Part II expands on this overview and deepens your understanding of machine learning. Part III goes into *neural networks*—computers that simulate the structure and the function of the human brain through the use of layers of interconnected artificial neurons. Finally, Part IV covers some common tools for using AI to help your business. This area has grown in popularity in recent years due to the increasing availability and decreasing cost of computer storage and processing and accessibility to massive data sets.

In Part I you'll look at some of the early theories that drove the design of the first intelligent machines. Most of these theories start with an attempt to understand human intelligence. What does it mean to be intelligent? Is it our ability to connect symbols to concepts? Our creativity?

You'll see the struggle that early computer scientists had with trying to create the first intelligent programs. At first, many computer scientists focused on symbolic reasoning. They figured that if they could get computers to understand our symbols, it would help them better understand our world. So they created systems that identified letters in our alphabet, digits, and different graphical representations like stop signs and question marks.

These early ideas still influence AI today. This symbolic approach gave rise to expert systems. These systems went through countless if-then statements to simulate thinking and decision-making; for example, if you see *A*, then make an "ah" sound. If you see a stop sign, then stop. Each of these decision points had to be painstakingly programmed into a computer.

In the 1990s, expert systems were the dominant form of AI. Companies used these systems to help make medical diagnoses, approve or reject loan applications, or find a good stock pick. The computer would go through long lists of if-then statements. So for a loan you might have an expert system that goes through a predefined list, such as, "If they have a credit history, then check for missed payments." "If they missed payments, then how many payments were missed over the past year?" "If they missed more than 10 payments in the past year, then reject this loan application."

As you can imagine, these lists can get pretty long. You need a human to try to imagine every possible if and then. A really complex task could result in a *combinatorial explosion*—so many different possibilities that it's nearly impossible to come up with all the different combinations.

As computer programmers encountered these limitations, they started to revisit the idea of machine learning (ML). ML has actually been around since the early 1950s. It was used to create programs that could beat a human player at checkers. These checker programs were extremely innovative. The machines could come up with their own strategies and learn from their mistakes. Even these early computers were sophisticated enough to learn how to beat a human player.

ML was a huge leap from programmed instructions and if-then statements that merely simulated the very human process of thinking and making decisions. Part II of this book takes a deeper dive into ML to reveal how it changed the rules of traditional software development.

With ML, the machine no longer needs to be explicitly programmed to complete a task; it can pour through massive data sets and create its own understanding. It can learn from the data and create its own model, one that represents the different rules to explain relationships among data and use those rules to draw conclusions and make decisions and predictions.

With ML, you might feed a machine all the data on the different inventory it takes to build a car along with blueprints for every car ever manufactured. After pouring through this data, the machine begins to understand certain things about what it means to be a car. It knows that cars need wheels, doors, and a windshield. There might be thousands of different kinds of cars, but the machine creates a model to identify all of them.

To enable machines to create these models, programmers have developed numerous advanced ML algorithms. A *machine learning algorithm* is a mathematical function that enables the machine to identify relationships among inputs and outputs. The programmer's role has shifted from one of writing explicit instructions to creating and choosing the right algorithms.

To take ML to the next level, computer scientists came up with the concept of an *artificial neural network*, the topic of Part III of this book. Artificial neural networks are patterned after the structure and function of the brain. The machine contains a web of interconnected artificial "neurons," each of which contains an ML algorithm. These neurons make decisions based on inputs from other neurons, the strength of the connections to those other neurons, and the deciding neuron's own algorithm and internal bias.

The artificial neural network was inspired by the way biological neurons work in the human brain. As humans, we learn new things and create memories based on increasing the strength of the connections between these nerve cells.

Modern artificial neural networks can create ML systems consisting of billions of these neurons. Such a complex network has tremendous power to find patterns in massive data sets. You can feed data into such a network, and it will create a model to better understand the larger patterns. For example, you could feed millions of images of dogs into your neural network and let it self-adjust and create its own model of what it means to be a dog. That model might not match how humans think of dogs. It may not identify dogs by looking at their shape and color or their ears and nose. Instead, it identifies statistical patterns of the different dots (pixels) in the images of the dogs. In a sense, the neural network develops its own understanding of "dogness." This way it can learn to correctly identify a dog even if it has never seen this particular dog before.

As you can imagine, the predictive power of neural networks has a wide variety of practical applications and enormous business potential. If you're in finance, neural networks can spot trends in the market to help you make trades. If you're in pharmaceuticals, you might have a neural network look for characteristics of existing drugs and compare them to new compounds. If you're in retail, you might look for patterns in what customers buy to figure out what they're likely to buy next.

Many large companies are already using neural networks for voice recognition, transcription, and digital personal assistants. For example, if you subscribe to Netflix, the system recommends movies and shows based on what you've watched in the past. Amazon uses neural networks to make targeted product recommendations and to power its personal digital assistants, including Alexa.

But you don't need to go that big to reap the value of neural networks. Think about the data in your organization. Then think about some of the patterns that would be valuable to see in your data. If you can quickly come up with valuable patterns, then AI is probably a good fit for your organization.

If you have no experience with AI, it is probably best to read this book from start to finish. By reading the chapters in Part I, you'll develop the fundamental understanding of ML required to tackle more complex topics. If you are more familiar with AI, then you could potentially start with Part II.

As you read, keep in mind that the ultimate purpose of this book is to get you thinking about the challenges and problems in your business or your area of expertise that AI and ML can help you overcome or solve. Think about the data you have, and imagine what you could possibly extract from that data to overcome a specific challenge, solve a specific problem, or answer a specific question. After all, without your very human ability to ask questions and imagine possibilities, AI and ML are useless. The power, as it has always been, is in the combination of our creativity and our tools.

Acknowledgments

Thanks first to all the organizations that have given me the opportunity to work with their talented teams, including Home Depot, Cox Automotive, Cardlytics, Genentech, and the Center for Data Intensive Science (CDIS).

Thanks also to the University of Chicago. The students in my classes at UChicago provided great feedback, and answers to their questions are weaved throughout this book. I also have online courses as a companion to this book on LinkedIn Learning. LinkedIn is one of the finest organizations I've ever worked with, and their highly skilled employees made creating these courses both fun and interesting. Special thanks to Steve Weiss, Yash Patel, and Scott Erickson for planning, editing, and filming these courses.

This book would not have been possible without the help of quite a few people. Joe Kraynak did a terrific job editing the book. John Haney created all the wonderfully whimsical illustrations. And Shehroz Khan provided outstanding technical feedback and excellent guidance. I'd also like to thank the editors at Pearson, including Kim Spenceley, Chris Zahn, and Karen Davis.

Special thanks also to my wonderful wife, Jelena, who is always my first (and most brutal) editor. She patiently read through my first drafts while sitting in the corner of my son's karate dojo. Finally, thank you to my son Leo for being my inspiration. Please keep writing. My greatest hope is that one day I'll simply be known as Leo Rose's dad.

About the Author

Doug Rose has been transforming organizations through technology, training, and process optimization for more than 25 years. He's the author of the Project Management Institute's (PMI) first major publication on the agile framework, *Leading Agile Teams*. He is also the author of *Data Science: Create Teams That Ask the Right Questions and Deliver Real Value* and *Enterprise Agility for Dummies*.

Doug has a master's degree (MS) in information management, a law degree (JD) from Syracuse University, and a BA from the University of Wisconsin–Madison. He is also a Scaled Agile Framework Program Consultant (SPC), Certified Technical Trainer (CTT+), Certified Scrum Professional (CSP-SM), Certified Scrum Master (CSM), PMI Agile Certified Professional (PMI-ACP), Project Management Professional (PMP), and Certified Developer for Apache Hadoop (CCDH).

You can attend Doug's lively and engaging business and project management courses at the University of Chicago or online through LinkedIn Learning.

Doug works through Doug Enterprises, an organization with an office in whatever city he lives. Currently that's in Atlanta, Georgia, where he spends his free time either riding a stationary recumbent bike or explaining the Marvel Universe to his son.

For more about Doug, visit his website at http://www.dougenterprises.com.

Part I
Thinking Machines: An Overview of Artificial Intelligence

1   What Is Artificial Intelligence? 3
2   The Rise of Machine Learning 19
3   Zeroing in on the Best Approach 35
4   Common AI Applications 45
5   Putting AI to Work on Big Data 53
6   Weighing Your Options 61

1

What Is Artificial Intelligence?

In this chapter:

- Defining *intelligence* and *artificial intelligence*
- Tracing the early history of artificial intelligence
- Recognizing key limitations
- Differentiating strong and weak artificial intelligence

In 1955, Dartmouth professor John McCarthy coined the term *artificial intelligence* (AI for short) as part of an academic grant to assemble the first AI conference—the Dartmouth Summer Research Project on Artificial Intelligence in 1956. The goal of this conference was to get computers to behave in ways that humans would identify as *intelligent*.

At the time, computers were taking up whole floors in office buildings, yet they had less processing power than most modern smart watches. Making these computers intelligent was quite an ambitious goal, and conference participants soon bumped up against the limitations inherent in the hardware at the time. They made little progress toward creating the machine equivalent of a human brain.

The most lasting contribution from this grant was the term *artificial intelligence*. It ignited everyone's imagination and inspired journalists, writers, academics, and computer scientists to envision a futuristic world in which machines would think like humans. Had Professor McCarthy come up with a different name, this conference, in all likelihood, would have faded into memory. Thanks to McCarthy's choice of words, however, *artificial intelligence* has continued to fuel the imagination and drive progress toward creating intelligent machines.

Unfortunately, the concept of AI and the prospect of machines displacing humans in the workplace are frightening to most people. Just imagine if the first personal computers had been called *artificial employees*. Workers would have panicked as soon as the first PCs arrived at their office. Personal computers sound *personable*. Artificial employees would have threatened to take their jobs!

Likewise, the term *artificial intelligence* sends shivers down the spines of many people who rely on their intelligence for their jobs. This can include professionals such as lawyers, doctors, and analysts. They might all imagine a day when they're supplanted by computerized counterparts.

To alleviate some of the fear surrounding AI, it is important to separate the term from the technology. While the term evokes images of sentient and perhaps omniscient machines supplanting humans, the technology is more subdued. You won't see a mechanized version of the human brain any time soon. As a technology, AI is merely any system that exhibits behavior that could be interpreted as human intelligence, such as winning a game of chess against a world-renowned chess master.

What Is Intelligence?

The dictionary definition of *artificial intelligence* is the capability of a machine to imitate intelligent human behavior. Determining the meaning of *intelligence*, however, is the greater challenge. Although we all agree that intelligence has something to do with knowledge and the ability to reason, human intelligence seems to go beyond that to include consciousness or self-awareness, wisdom, emotion, sympathy, intuition, and creativity. To some, intelligence also involves spirituality—a connection to a greater force or being.

To further challenge our ability to define *intelligence* is the fact that human intelligence comes in many forms. Whereas some people are highly intelligent in the field of mathematics, others excel in art, music, politics, business, medicine, law, linguistics, and so on. Some people may excel in academics, whereas others are skilled in trades or have a higher level of emotional competence. And although people have tried to develop a single standard for measuring intelligence, such as the intelligent quotient (IQ), such standards are skewed. For example, a typical IQ test evaluates only short-term memory, analytical thinking, mathematical ability, and spatial recognition.

Without a reliable standard for measuring human intelligence, it's very difficult to point to a computer and say that it's behaving intelligently. Computers are certainly very good at performing certain tasks and may do so much better and faster than humans, but does that make them intelligent? For example, computers have been able to beat humans in chess for decades. IBM Watson beat some of the best champions in the game show *Jeopardy*. Google's DeepMind has beaten the best players in the 2500-year-old Chinese game called Go—a game so complex that there are thought to be more possible configurations of the board than there are atoms in the universe. Yet none of these computers understands the purpose of a game or has a reason to play.

As impressive as these accomplishments are, they are still just a product of a computer's special talent for *pattern matching*—extracting information from its database that enables it to answer a question or perform a task. This seems to be intelligent behavior only because a computer is excellent at that particular task. However, we rarely attribute human characteristics to other machines, such as boats that can "swim" faster or hydraulic jacks that are "stronger" and can easily lift a car above a mechanic's head.

In many ways a game is a perfect environment for a computer. It has set rules with a certain number of possibilities that can be stored in a database. When IBM's Watson played *Jeopardy*, all it needed to do was use natural language processing (NLP) to understand the question, buzz in faster than the other contestants, and apply pattern matching to find the correct answer in its database.

Early AI developers knew that computers had the potential to excel in a world of set rules and possibilities. Only a few years after the first AI conference, developers had their first version of a chess program. The program could match an opponent's move with thousands of possible counter moves and play out thousands of games to determine the potential ramifications of making a move before deciding which piece to move and where to move it, and it could do so in a matter of seconds.

AI is always more impressive when computers are on their home turf—when the rules are clear and the possibilities limited. Organizations benefiting most from AI are those that work within a well-defined space with set rules, so it's no surprise that organizations like Google fully embrace AI. Google's entire business involves pattern matching—matching users' questions with a massive database of answers. AI experts often refer to this as good old-fashioned artificial intelligence (GOFAI).

If you're thinking about incorporating AI in your business, consider what computers are really good at—pattern matching. Do you have a lot of pattern matching in your organization? Does a lot of your work have set rules and possibilities? This work will be the first to benefit from AI.

Testing Machine Intelligence

Alan Turing was an English computer scientist who famously took part in decrypting the enigma machines that the Germans used to communicate during World War II. After the war, he set his sights on early computers. In particular, he was interested in how machines might be able to think.

In a 1951 paper, he proposed a test called the *imitation game* that was based on a Victorian parlor game. In the game, a man and woman sat in one room, and their *interrogator* sat in another (Figure 1.1).

Figure 1.1 Imitation game

The interrogator would ask the man and the woman a question. Then the team would pass back their answers in a written note. It was up to the interrogator to decide if each written answer came from the man or the woman. In an added twist, the man tries to fool the interrogator, whereas the woman tries to help.

Now, to a modern ear, this game sounds dreary and misogynistic. But to Turing, this was an excellent foundation to test a machine's intelligence. He imagined an updated imitation game where the man was replaced by a machine (Figure 1.2).

Figure 1.2 Turing test

Then the interrogator would ask both the woman and the machine a question and get back their answer in a written note. If the interrogator was just as likely to pick one or the other, then the machine must be seen as intelligent. This game was later known as the *Turing test*.

This test sparked a lot of curiosity in an "imaginable machine" even though it came out a few years before McCarthy even coined the term *artificial intelligence*. Even after nearly 70 years, this test still sounds intriguing. Imagine if you could ask a machine a question in your own natural language and get a response that is indistinguishable from that of another human?

That being said, most experts agree that the Turing test is not necessarily the best way to gauge intelligence. For one, it depends a lot on the interrogator. Some people might be easily fooled into thinking that they're talking to another person. It also assumes that AI will be similar to human intelligence. You would assume that a machine would be able to have a decent conversation before it started performing an advanced task such as searching for new drugs or accurately predicting global weather patterns.

Yet the Turing test still inspires a lot of innovation. Companies still try to create intelligent chatbots, and there are still NLP competitions that attempt to pass the test. It seems like modern machines are only a few years away from passing the Turing test. Many modern NLP applications can accurately understand the majority of your requests. Now they just need to improve their ability to respond.

Yet even if a machine can pass the test, it still seems unlikely that that same machine would be seen as intelligent. Even if your smart phone can trick you into thinking you're talking to a human, that doesn't mean that it will offer meaningful conversation.

The General Problem Solver

One of the very first attempts at AI was in 1956. Allen Newell and Herbert A. Simon (Figure 1.3) created a computer program they called the general problem solver. This program was designed to solve any problem that could be presented in the form of mathematical formulas.

Figure 1.3 Newell and Simon

Courtesy Carnegie Mellon University Libraries

One of the key parts of the general problem solver was what Newell and Simon called the physical symbol system hypothesis (PSSH). They argued that symbols were the key to general intelligence. If you could get a program to connect enough of these symbols, you would have a machine that behaved in a way similar to human intelligence.

Symbols play a big role in how we interact with the world. When we see a stop sign, we know to stop and look for traffic. When we see the word *cat*, we know that it represents a small furry feline that meows. If we see a chair, we know it's an object to sit in. When we see a sandwich, we know it's something to eat, and we may even feel hungry.

Newell and Simon argued that creating enough of these connections would make machines behave more like us. They thought a key part of human reasoning was just connecting symbols—that our language, ideas, and concepts were just broad groupings of interconnected symbols (Figure 1.4).

Figure 1.4 Interconnected symbols

But not everyone bought into this idea. In 1980, philosopher John Searle argued that merely connecting symbols could not be considered intelligence. To support his argument against the claim that computers think or at least have the potential of someday being able to think, he created an experiment called the Chinese room argument (Figure 1.5).

Figure 1.5 The Chinese room argument

In this experiment, imagine yourself, an English-only speaker, locked in a windowless room with a narrow slot on the door through which you can pass notes. You have a book filled with long lists of statements in Chinese, a floor covered in Chinese characters, and instructions that if you're given a certain sequence of Chinese characters you are to respond with the corresponding statement from the book.

Someone outside the room who speaks fluent Chinese writes a note on a sheet of paper and passes it to you through the slot on the door. You have no idea what it says. You go through the tedious process of looking through your book and finding the statement in response to the sequence of Chinese characters on the note. Using the characters from the floor, you paste together the statement to a sheet of paper and pass it through the slot to the person who gave you the original message.

The native Chinese speaker who passed you the note believes that the two of you are conversing and that you're intelligent. However, Searle argues that this is far from intelligence because you can't speak Chinese, and you have no understanding of the notes you're receiving or sending.

You can try a similar experiment with your smart phone. If you ask Siri or Cortana how she's feeling, she's likely to say she's feeling fine, but that doesn't mean she's feeling fine or feeling anything at all. She doesn't even understand the question. She's just matching your question to what are considered acceptable answers and choosing one.

A key drawback of matching symbols is what's referred to as the *combinatorial explosion*—the rapid growth of symbol combinations that makes matching increasingly difficult. Just imagine the variety of questions that people can ask and all the different responses to a single question. In the Chinese room example, you'd have an ever-growing book of possible inputs and outputs, which would take you longer and longer to find the correct response.

Even with these challenges, symbol matching remained the cornerstone of AI for 25 years. However, symbol matching has been unable to keep up with the growing complexity of AI applications. Early machines had trouble matching all the possibilities, and even when they could, the process took too much time.

Strong and Weak Artificial Intelligence

John Searle didn't just create the Chinese room argument. He also pointed out that you can think of AI in two different ways. He called them strong and weak AI (Figure 1.6).

- With strong AI, a machine displays all the behavior you'd expect from a person. If you're a *Star Trek* fan, this is Lieutenant Commander Data. If you prefer *Star Wars*, then this might be C3PO or R2-D2. These artificial beings have emotions, a sense of purpose, and even a sense of humor. They may learn a new language just for the joy of learning it. Some computer scientists refer to strong AI as general AI—a broad intelligence that doesn't apply only to one narrow task.

- Weak (or narrow) AI is confined to a narrow task, such as product recommendations on Amazon and Google in response to the keywords a user enters. A weak AI program doesn't engage in conversation, recognize emotion, or learn for the sake of learning; it merely does whatever job it was designed to do.

Figure 1.6 Strong and weak AI

Most AI experts believe that we're just starting down the path of weak AI—using AI to answer factual questions, provide directions, manage our schedules, make recommendations based on our past choices and reactions, help us do our taxes, prevent online fraud, and so on. Many organizations already use weak AI to help with narrow tasks, such as these. Strong AI is still relegated to the world of science fiction.

You can witness weak AI at work in the latest generation of personal assistants, including Apple's Siri and Microsoft's Cortana. You can talk to them and even ask them questions. They convert spoken language into machine language and use pattern matching to answer your questions and respond to your requests. That's not much different from traditional interactions with search engines such as Google and Bing.

The difference is that Siri and Cortana behave more like human beings; they can talk. They can even book a reservation at your favorite restaurant and place calls for you.

These personal assistants don't have general AI. If they did, they'd certainly get sick of listening to your daily requests. Instead, they focus on a narrow task of listening to your input and matching it to their database.

John Searle was quick to point out that any symbolic AI should be considered weak AI. However, in the 1970s and 1980s, symbolic systems were used to create AI software that could make expert decisions. These were commonly called *expert systems*.

In an expert system, people who specialize in a given field input the patterns that the computer can match to arrive at a given conclusion. For example, in medicine, a doctor may input groupings of symptoms that match up with various diagnoses. A nurse inputs the patient's symptoms into the computer. The computer can then search its database for a matching diagnosis and present the most likely diagnosis to the patient. For example, if a patient has a cough, shortness of breath, and a slight fever, the computer may conclude that the patient probably has bronchitis. To the patient, the computer may seem to be as intelligent as a doctor, but in reality all the computer is doing is matching symptoms to possible diagnoses.

Expert systems run into the same problems as other symbolic systems; they ultimately experience combinatorial explosions. There are simply too many symptoms, diagnoses, and variables to consider when trying to diagnose an illness. Just think about all the steps a doctor must take to arrive at an accurate diagnosis—conducting a physical exam, interviewing the patient, ordering lab tests, and sometimes ruling out a long list of other illnesses that have similar symptoms. Imagine all the possible ways a patient could answer each question the doctor asks and all the various combinations of lab results.

These early expert systems also had a serious limitation—the real possibility that given certain input, the system would be unable to find a match. You have probably experienced this on various websites; you input your search phrase, and the site informs you that it found no match.

Even with these drawbacks, the symbolic approach was a key starting point for AI and is still in use today, typically with some modifications (as you'll see next).

Artificial Intelligence Planning

Early expert systems started to disappear in the late 1980s, but the symbolic approach remained. Today, you see it in what's called *artificial intelligence planning*—a branch of AI that employs strategies and action sequences to enhance the computer's ability to match symbols and patterns.

AI planning attempts to solve the problem of combinatorial explosion by using something called *heuristic reasoning*—an approach that attempts to give AI a form of common sense, thus limiting the number of patterns the program has to match at any one time. This approach is sometimes referred to as *limiting the search space*.

Imagine heuristic reasoning applied to the Chinese room experiment. You could use heuristic reasoning in an AI program to limit the possibilities of the first note. You could set it up so that the program expects a message like "Hello" or "How are you?" or "Do you speak Chinese?" to limit how far the program has to search to match the pattern.

The drawback is that if the program doesn't receive the anticipated input, it then has to search the entire database for a match as well, which requires additional processing. For example, suppose the first note asks, "Do you know how to say purple in English?" The program must first rule out the anticipated messages and then search the entire database, or what AI planners refer to as the *entire search space*.

AI planning is common with navigation systems such as Google Maps. You enter your location and your destination, and the system finds the shortest, fastest route. It still uses a symbolic approach that relies on lists, and Google must gather the data to create those lists. It does so by pulling data from numerous sources, including satellite and aerial imagery; state, city, and county maps; the US Geological Survey; its own Street View cars; and from users who contribute their own map information. All this data is carefully vetted and then stitched together to create highly detailed maps. Google Maps also extracts current traffic data from local highway authorities to help route drivers around accidents and backups.

Unlike early symbolic systems, Google Maps uses heuristic reasoning to limit its search to a certain geographical area based on the location and destination you enter, and it can provide detailed directions, such as whether to turn left or right at a given intersection without having to search through its entire database of symbols and patterns.

Even though it's considered old-fashioned AI, symbolic systems and AI planning are still used in many new projects. It performs well in systems that have predefined symbols and patterns. You can see this with driving directions, but it also works with contracts, logistics, and even video games. If you're considering a new AI project, don't be quick to dismiss the benefits of good old-fashioned AI. Newer approaches may not be the right fit.

Learning over Memorizing

There's a big difference between memorizing and learning. Imagine that you were looking at the eight images in Figure 1.7. You would probably quickly recognize that these are eight different breeds of dogs.

Figure 1.7 Eight breeds of dogs

Now imagine I showed you the picture in Figure 1.8.

Figure 1.8 Another dog

Would you know what it is? How would you know? You'll notice that it's not exactly the same as any of the pictures in Figure 1.7.

So that means that you've *learned* something about dogs. You might not know *what* you've learned, and you probably have trouble describing *how* you learned it's a dog, but chances are your human brain was able to make the connection.

On the other hand, computers are far better at memorization. So you could program a computer to memorize those eight dog illustrations. Then if you show the computer one of the eight, it could quickly make a connection. But it's much more difficult to have a computer learn. It could easily fumble on this ninth image as it tries to find the perfect match.

Symbolic AI is about memorizing and matching these different symbols. So a symbolic system could easily memorize the eight dog illustrations and make exact matches. But if it couldn't find an exact match, it cannot give an answer. You also could certainly create a symbolic system that translates written text from different languages. A machine could memorize millions of different typed words and phrases. The challenge is that it wouldn't really be learning a new language. It would just be a digital version of an old-style language phrasebook.

You've also seen that you can use expert systems to match your input to some preprogrammed scenario. Yet these symbolic systems will always be confined to the system's own memory. It will only know what it's programmed to know, so these systems rely on humans to *seem* intelligent. They could respond with canned phrases and memory storage. But these symbolic systems will fail when they encounter any new or unforeseen symbol (Figure 1.9).

Figure 1.9 Encountering a new symbol

So the big challenge going forward is trying to make AI more *generalizable*. Instead of matching memorized symbols, newer machines will look for features and patterns to create abstract models. These models have the potential to help these machines learn. That way they can better handle new items that the machine might not have seen. If it's just predicting well on what it already knows, it's just a simple act of memorization.

Humans have evolved to be very good in both memorization and generalization. We use memorization to quickly fetch information on how to act in a familiar terrain or domain. Generalization is our human ability to use our prior knowledge to work well in unseen or unfamiliar situations. For us, survival is the key, and that is what we try to optimize all the time.

For machines, this is missing. That's why it's essential to identify the criteria a machine needs to optimize to generalize the knowledge it learns so that it can perform well in the present or future.

Chapter Takeaways

- *Artificial intelligence* is the capability of a machine to imitate intelligent human behavior.
- Early AI is pattern matching; it enables machines to imitate intelligent behavior, but it cannot be equated with human intelligence.
- Pattern matching is often enhanced with AI planning that streamlines the pattern-matching process.
- Strong AI imbues machines with human qualities, including self-awareness and emotions, whereas weak AI enables machines to perform specific tasks.
- Strong AI remains relegated to the realm of science fiction.

2

The Rise of Machine Learning

In this chapter:

- Understanding what machine learning is all about
- Imitating neural networks
- Drilling down to the perceptron

The symbolic approach and artificial intelligence (AI) planning work great for applications that have a limited number of matching patterns, such as for a program that helps you complete your tax return. The IRS provides a limited number of forms and a collection of rules for reporting tax-relevant data. Combine the forms and instructions with the capability to crunch numbers and some heuristic reasoning, and you have a tax program that can step you through the process. With heuristic reasoning, introduced in the previous chapter, you can limit the number of patterns; for example, if you earned money from an employer, you complete a W-2 form. If you earned money as a sole proprietor, you complete Schedule C.

The limitation with this approach is that the database is difficult to manage, especially when rules and patterns change. For example, malware (viruses, spyware, computer worms, and so forth) evolves too quickly for anti-malware companies to manually update their databases. Likewise, digital personal assistants, such as Siri and Alexa, need to constantly adapt to unfamiliar requests from their owners.

To overcome these limitations, early AI researchers started to wonder whether computers could be programmed to learn new patterns. Their curiosity led to the birth of *machine learning* (ML)—the science of getting computers to do things they weren't specifically programmed to do.

ML got its start very shortly after the first AI conference. In 1959, AI researcher Arthur Samuel created a program that could play checkers. This program was different. It was designed to play against itself so it could learn how to improve. It learned new strategies from each game it played, and after a short period of time it began to consistently beat its own programmer.

A key advantage of ML is that it doesn't require an expert to create symbolic patterns and list all the possible responses to a question or statement. On its own, the machine creates and maintains the list, identifying patterns and adding them to its database.

Imagine ML applied to the Chinese room experiment. The computer would observe the passing of notes between itself and the person outside the room. After examining thousands of exchanges, the computer would identify a pattern of communication and add common words and phrases to its database. Now, it can use its collection of words and phrases to more quickly decipher the notes it receives and quickly assemble a response using these words and phrases instead of having to assemble a response from a collection of characters. It may even create its own dictionary based on these matching patterns, so that it has a complete response to certain notes it receives.

ML still qualifies as weak AI because the computer doesn't understand what's being said; it only matches symbols and identifies patterns. The big difference is that instead of having an expert provide the patterns, the computer identifies patterns in the data. Over time, the computer becomes "smarter."

ML has become one of the fastest growing areas in AI primarily because the cost of data storage and processing has dropped dramatically. We are currently in the era of data science and *big data*—extremely large data sets that can be computer analyzed to reveal patterns, trends, and associations. Organizations are collecting vast amounts of data. The big challenge is to figure out what to do with it. Answering that challenge is ML, which can identify patterns even when you really don't know what you're looking for. In a sense, ML enables computers to find out what's inside your data and let you know what it found.

ML moves past the limitations with symbolic systems. Instead of memorizing symbols, a computer system uses *machine learning algorithms* to create models of abstract concepts. It detects statistical patterns by using machine learning algorithms on massive amounts of data.

So a machine learning algorithm looks at the eight pictures of different dogs. Then it breaks down these pictures into individual dots or pixels. After that, it looks at these pixels to detect patterns. Maybe it sees a pattern for all these animals having hair. Maybe it sees a pattern for noses or ears. It could even see a pattern that humans are unable to perceive. Collectively, the patterns create what might be considered a statistical expression of "dogness" (Figure 2.1).

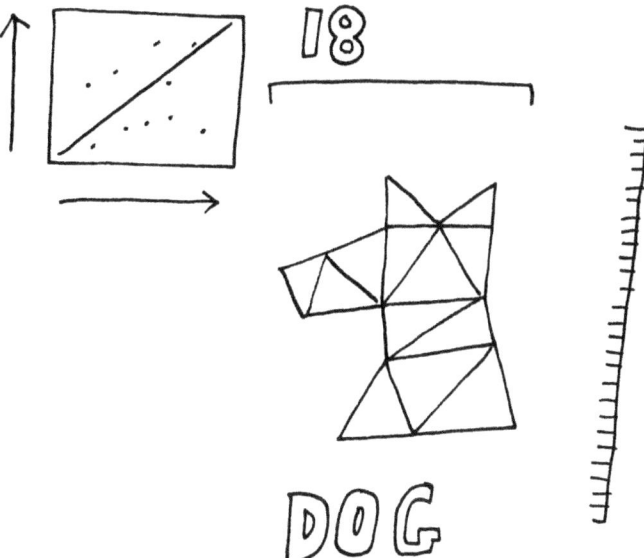

Figure 2.1 "Dogness"

Sometimes humans can help machines learn. We can feed the machine millions of pictures that we've already determined contained dogs, so the machine doesn't have to worry about excluding images of cats, horses, or airplanes. This is called *supervised learning*, and the data, consisting of the label "dog" and the millions of pictures of dogs, is called a *training set*. Using the training set, a human being is teaching the machine that all the patterns it identifies are characteristics of "dog."

Machines can also learn completely on their own. We just feed massive amounts of data into the machine and let it find its own patterns. This is called *unsupervised learning*.

Imagine a machine examining all the pictures of people on your smart phone. It might not know if someone was your husband, wife, boyfriend, or girlfriend. But it could create clusters of people that it sees are closest to you.

Practical Applications of Machine Learning

One of the best ways to understand ML is to look at its various applications in the business world (Figure 2.2):

Figure 2.2 Applications of machine learning

- **Data security:** In an attempt to avoid detection, people who produce malware constantly change the code, typically 2 to 10 percent, but with ML, security software can accommodate this small percentage in variation and accurately identify the newly created malware. It can also look for patterns in how data is accessed to identify possible security threats.
- **Investing:** ML enables computers to process vast amounts of financial data and use its findings to predict changes in the market and in prices of individual stocks and bonds. Computers can also execute trades at higher speeds and volumes than can traditional traders, enabling them to generate large profits for investors.
- **Online software development:** Online software developers can use ML to gather data about how users interact with their software and analyze that data to improve usability and come up with ideas for new features and new ways to monetize the software.
- **Healthcare:** With ML, doctors can use computers to do everything from diagnosing illnesses significantly earlier than they would otherwise be diagnosed to identifying variables that predict whether a patient will develop a specific illness.
- **Personalized marketing:** ML enables companies to personalize their marketing by analyzing a user's online behavior. For example, if you start searching for cars on the Web, you're likely to be inundated with car ads on various sites you visit. Netflix and Spotify use ML to recommend movies and music to users based on their viewing or listening history. Amazon provides recommendations based on your purchase history.
- **Fraud detection and prevention:** Credit card companies and other financial institutions can use ML to identify transaction patterns that are out of sync with a customer's purchase history and either suspend usage of the card or notify the cardholder of the suspicious activity.
- **Online searches:** Google and other online search sites use ML to rank items in their search results. If you search for a term, click a certain link and remain on that page for some time, Google assumes that the page provided what you needed, which may give a boost to that page in the rankings for when you or someone else searches for that same word or phrase.

- **Smart devices:** Smart devices collect data regarding their usage and personalize their operation based on those patterns. For example, a smart thermostat can learn your schedule and start cranking up the heat just before you come home from work and crank it down just before you go to sleep.

Artificial Neural Networks

ML has gotten a big boost recently because it works particularly well with *artificial neural networks* (often referred to simply as *neural networks*)—computer systems that are modeled after the neural structure of the human brain.

A biological brain is composed of billions of neurons that communicate with one another electrochemically across minute gaps called *synapses*. A single neuron can have up to 10,000 connections with other neurons. The human brain has about 100 billion neurons communicating with one another across well over 100 trillion synapses (up to 1,000 trillion synapses by some estimates).

These neurons increase the strength of their connections based on learning and practice. For example, when you're learning to juggle, your neurons strengthen existing connections and create new connections for developing that skill. That's why the more you practice the better you get; your brain builds new paths to improve your hand-eye coordination.

Artificial neural networks consist of interconnected nodes organized into layers: an input layer, hidden layers, and an output layer (Figure 2.3).

Figure 2.3 Neural networks consist of layers

All layers are connected through connections between nodes in the various layers.

Imagine the nodes as players in a marching band and each row as a layer. Assume that none of the players knows how to read music. Unlike a traditional marching band, in which all the players can see the band leader during practice, in this marching band, only the first layer of players can see the leader. The band leader gives the first layer of players a signal that's passed through the rows (layers), enabling all players to coordinate their movements and the playing of their instruments (Figure 2.4).

Figure 2.4 The signal is passed through the layers/rows

Initially, players would be bumping into one another and playing the wrong notes, but as they moved and played, they would choose a number that indicated their confidence level in the movement they made or note they played; for example, they might indicate that they're 90 percent confident that they played the right note or made the right move. If they were really off, they may signal a 10 percent confidence level. Over time, they would make adjustments based on signals from the layer in front of them to increase their confidence level, with the goal of achieving 100 percent confidence.

The idea behind these artificial neural networks is that the nodes will eventually make enough adjustments to produce the correct output, without receiving additional information at the input level. In the marching band example, even though nobody in the band knows how to read music, they eventually make the right moves and play the right notes through trial and error, learning from their mistakes.

A key challenge of this approach is that it can be very time-consuming. You have many different players with different instruments, each of whom is trying to match the sound and movement and communicate their confidence levels. To overcome this challenge, experts in artificial neural networks often try to tweak the network to make it more efficient. For example, they may give the drum section more weight because the drums set the rhythm of the music and movement.

Another key challenge is that the neural network is not *generalizable*. You have to clearly define a task at the beginning. So our neural network is tasked with producing music. We can't change our marching band's task to mowing lawns, baking cakes, or washing cars. The band specializes in performing a specific task. In neural networks this is usually called *defining an optimization function*.

Eventually, the band delivers a nicely choreographed and well-orchestrated performance to the output layer. When this occurs, the neural network creates and stores a model for future reference. The model can be as simple as a description of all the band member positions, their instruments and their movements, along with the confidence scores. After the neural network has the model, you can pass a million songs through it, and it can tell you with complete confidence whether that song matches the model.

As you can see, the real benefit of an artificial neural network is that it trains itself to understand the input and can then recognize that input when looking through massive amounts of data.

The Fall and Rise of the Perceptron

You may be wondering why ML took so long to catch on. After all, Arthur Samuel created his revolutionary checkers program in 1959. ML was poised to become the dominant form of AI. It had the wind at its back.

What happened is that ML took a backseat to other innovations, such as the symbolic approach. Not until the late 1980s and early 1990s did researchers start thinking again about ML.

The rise and fall and rise again of ML is both sad and interesting. It shows how few researchers were instrumental in building out the field.

In 1958 Cornell professor Frank Rosenblatt created an early version of an artificial neural network. Instead of using nodes and neurons, he used perceptrons and tied them together to create a complex form of machine intelligence.

Rosenblatt thought that these perceptrons were the most promising path to AI. He created a machine called the Mark 1 Perceptron. It tied together thousands of these perceptrons into a neural network. It had small cameras and was designed to learn how to tell the difference between two images. Unfortunately, it took thousands of tries, and even then the Mark I had a hard time distinguishing even basic images.

While Rosenblatt was working on his Mark I Perceptron, MIT professor Marvin Minsky was pushing hard for a symbolic approach. Minsky and Rosenblatt debated passionately about which was the best approach to AI. The debates were almost like family arguments. They had attended the same high school and had known each other for decades.

In 1969 Minsky coauthored a book called *Perceptrons: An Introduction to Computational Geometry*. In it he argued decisively against Rosenblatt's perceptrons approach to AI, proving that it failed to include some simple logical functions. Sadly, a few years after the book was published, Rosenblatt died in a boating accident. Without Rosenblatt to defend perceptrons, much of the funding for this approach dried up.

Minsky later dedicated the work to his one-time rival, but it was too late. Perceptrons and artificial neural networks languished for nearly a decade.

One reason that Rosenblatt's Mark 1 Perceptron fell short is that it did not include a hidden layer—a key component that enables artificial neural networks to solve more challenging problems.

Without a hidden layer, Rosenblatt's perceptron was limited to solving *linear* problems. There had to be a straight line from problem to solution. Using a straight line, a machine can classify two groups by drawing a straight line between the two groups; for example, dogs would be on one side of the line and cats would be on the other (Figure 2.5).

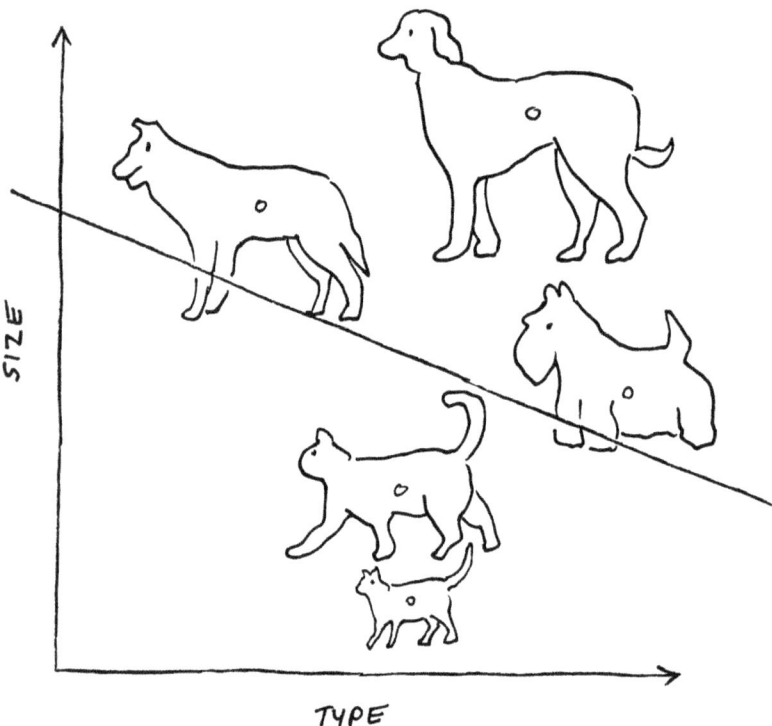

Figure 2.5 A linear problem

A hidden layer enables the network to work on nonlinear problems. So if you wanted to determine different breeds of dogs, you could have each layer break down the problem into different outputs. The first layer could look at the nose. The second layer could look at the eyes. Each of these layers could break down your dog into different probabilities that it belongs to a certain breed.

One of the main challenges with this multilayer neural network was that it was difficult to get each layer to teach what it learned to the next layer. In the mid-1980s Carnegie Mellon professor Geoff Hinton showed how multilayered neurons could be trained efficiently. He added in a new way to train each hidden layer so it could accumulate more knowledge as it passed through the network.

This addition enabled his artificial neural network to tackle much more complicated challenges. However, these early artificial neural networks continued to struggle; they were slow, having to review a problem several times before becoming "smart" enough to solve it.

Later, in the 1990s, Hinton started working in a new field called *deep learning* (Figure 2.6)—an approach that includes many more hidden layers between the input and output layers. The added layers provide the artificial neural network a greater capacity to learn. The pioneers of deep learning also developed new ways to facilitate learning, such as *backpropagation*, which enables the nodes to spread their knowledge more rapidly.

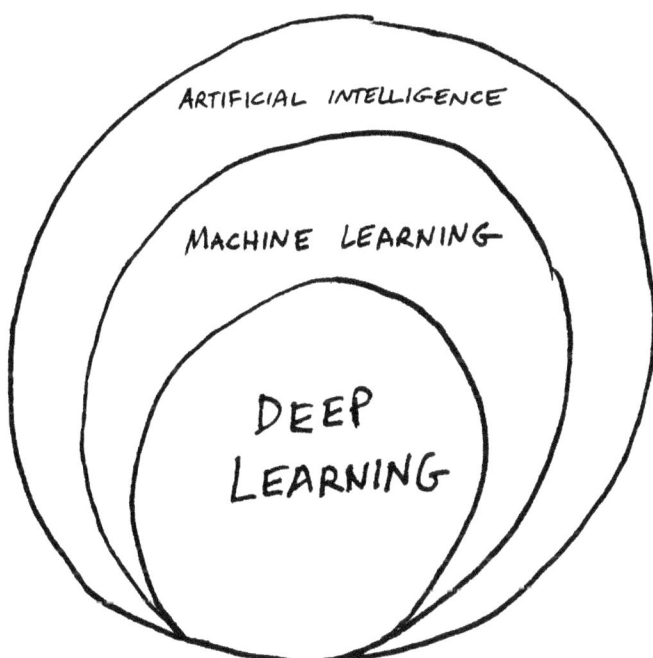

Figure 2.6 Deep learning

Deep learning networks also use *clustering* to help identify patterns. Clustering enables the network to create categories and then sort the new information into these categories. For example, suppose you wanted to use a deep learning network to distinguish cats from other animals. You could load a million photos of various animals into the network, and the network would cluster them into groups of photos that showed animals with similar characteristics. Then, each time you loaded a photo into the network, it would add the photo to the relevant group or discard it as not being a photo of an animal.

It can do this without actually knowing anything about cats. In fact, it won't even understand the label "cats" until a human provides this information. Instead, it will just group images with similar characteristics. There might be a grouping of pixels that looks like whiskers. Or even a grouping of pixels that looks like a tale. When the network sees these groupings, it will cluster them together. Then a human might come in and label this cluster as "cats."

Big Data Arrives

Fueling the rise of ML and deep learning is the availability of massive amounts of data, often referred to as *big data*. If you wanted to create an AI program to identify pictures of cats, you could access millions of cat images online. The same is true, or more true, of other types of data. Various organizations have access to vast amounts of data, including charge card transactions, user behaviors on websites, data from online games, published medical studies, satellite images, online maps, census reports, voter records, economic data, and machine-generated data (from machines equipped with sensors that report the status of their operation and any problems they detect).

This treasure trove of data has given ML a huge advantage over symbolic systems. Having a neural network chew on gigabytes of data and report on it is much easier and quicker than having an expert identify and input patterns and reasoning schemas to enable the computer to deliver accurate responses.

In some ways the evolution of ML is similar to how online search engines evolved. Early on, users would consult website directories such as Yahoo! to find what they were looking for—directories that were created and maintained by humans. Website owners would submit their sites to Yahoo! and suggest the categories in which to place them. Yahoo! personnel would then vet the sites and add them to the directory or deny the request. The process was time-consuming and labor-intensive, but it worked well when the Web had relatively few websites. When the thousands of websites proliferated into millions and then crossed the one billion threshold, the system broke down fairly quickly. Human beings couldn't work quickly enough to keep the Yahoo! directories current.

In the mid-1990s Yahoo! partnered with a smaller company called Google that had developed a search engine to locate and categorize web pages. Google's first search engine examined backlinks (pages that linked to a given page) to determine the relevance and authority of the given page and rank it accordingly in its search results. Since then, Google has developed additional algorithms to determine a page's rank (or relevance); for example, the more users who enter the same search phrase and click the same link, the higher the ranking that page receives. This approach is similar to the way neurons in an artificial neural network strengthen their connections.

The fact that Google is one of the companies most enthusiastic about AI is no coincidence. The entire business has been built on using machines to interpret massive amounts of data. Rosenblatt's perceptron could look through only a couple of grainy images. Now we have processors that are at least a million times faster sorting through massive amounts of data to find content that's most likely to be relevant to whatever a user searches for.

Deep learning architecture adds even more power, enabling machines to identify patterns in data that just a few decades ago would have been nearly imperceptible. With more layers in the neural network, it can perceive details that would go unnoticed by most humans. These deep learning artificial networks look at so much data and create so many new connections that it's not even clear how these programs discover the patterns.

A deep learning neural network is like a black box swirling together computation and data to determine what it means to be a cat. No human knows how the network arrives at its decision. Is it the whiskers? Is it the ears? Or is it something about all cats that we humans are unable to see? In a sense, the deep learning network creates its own model for what it means to be a cat, a model that as of right now humans can only copy or read, but not understand or interpret.

In 2012, Google's DeepMind project did just that. Developers fed 10 million random images from YouTube videos into a network that had more than 1 billion neural connections running on 16,000 processors. They didn't label any of the data. So the network didn't know what it meant to be a cat, a human, or a car. Instead, the network just looked through the images and came up with its own clusters. It found that many of the videos contained a very similar cluster. To the network this cluster looked like what is shown in Figure 2.7.

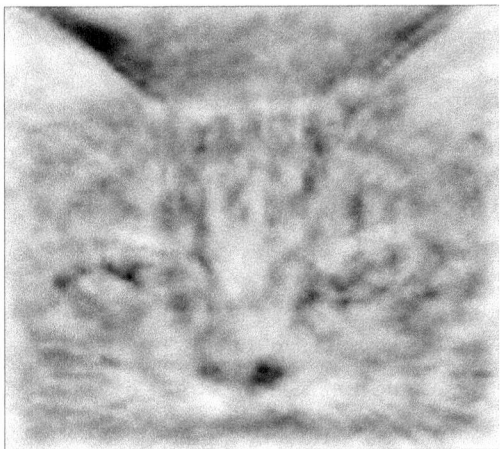

Figure 2.7 A "cat" from "Building high-level features using large-scale unsupervised learning"

Now, as a human you might recognize this as the face of a cat. To the neural network, this was just a common something from many of the videos. In a sense it invented its own interpretation of a cat.

A human might go through and tell the network that this is a cat, but this isn't necessary for the network to find cats in these videos. In fact, the network was able to identify a "cat" 74.8% of the time. In a nod to Alan Turing, the Cato Institute's Julian Sanchez called this the "Purring Test."

If you decide to start working with AI, accept the fact that your network might be sensing things that humans are unable to perceive. AI is not the same as human intelligence, and even though we may reach the same conclusions, we're definitely not going through the same process.

Chapter Takeaways

- *Machine learning* is the science of getting computers to perform tasks they weren't specifically programmed to do.
- A key benefit of ML is that it can be used to analyze vast amounts of data to identify patterns that people would never have thought to look for.
- The increasing availability of vast amounts of data is driving the development of ML.
- Artificial neural networks are designed to function like the human brain by connecting various nodes arranged in three (or more) layers: an input layer, a number of hidden layers, and an output layer.
- A *perceptron* is an artificial neuron that serves a similar function as a node in earlier artificial neural networks.
- *Deep learning* refers to an artificial neural network that contains numerous hidden layers.

3

Zeroing in on the Best Approach

In this chapter:

- Deciding whether an expert system or machine learning is best
- Choosing between supervised and unsupervised learning
- Using backpropagation of errors to facilitate a machine's ability to sort and classify
- Employing regression analysis to identify connections

Prior to starting your own artificial intelligence (AI) program, you need to make some choices, such as whether an expert system or machine learning (ML) is best for your particular use case. Although ML is certainly more advanced, an expert system is often best for certain applications. If you decide to go the ML route, you have additional considerations to make, such as whether to use supervised or unsupervised learning, whether to use backpropagation to fine-tune your system, and whether to use regression analysis to weigh the importance of different factors. This chapter explains these options, so you can make well-informed choices.

Expert System Versus Machine Learning

Prior to starting an AI project, the first choice you need to make is whether to use an expert system (a rules-based system) or ML. Basically the choice comes down to the amount of data, the variation in that data, and whether you have a clear set of steps for extracting a solution from that data. An expert system is best when you have a sequential problem and there are finite steps to find a solution. ML is best when you want to move beyond memorizing sequential steps, and you need to analyze large volumes of data to make predictions or to identify patterns that you may not even know would provide insight—that is, when your problem contains a certain level of uncertainty.

Think about it in terms of an automated phone system (Figure 3.1).

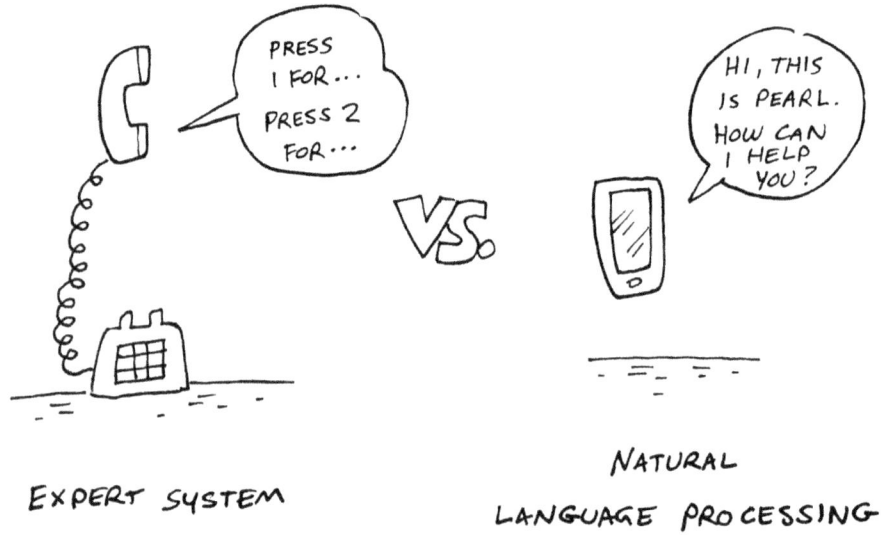

Figure 3.1 Automated phone systems driven by expert system or natural language processing

Older phone systems are sort of like expert systems; a message tells the caller to press 1 for sales, 2 for customer service, 3 for technical support, and 4 to speak to an operator. The system then routes the call to the proper department based on the number that the caller presses.

Newer, more advanced phone systems use natural language processing (NLP). When someone calls in, the message tells callers to say what they're calling about. A caller may say something like, "I'm having a problem with my Android smart phone," and the system routes the call to technical support. If, instead, the caller said something like, "I want to upgrade my smart phone," the system routes the call to sales.

The challenge with NLP is that what callers say and how they say it is unpredictable. An angry caller may say something like, "That smart phone I bought from you guys three days ago is a piece of junk." You can see that this is a more complex problem. The automated phone system would need accurate speech recognition and then be able to infer the meaning of that statement so that it could direct the caller to the right department.

With an expert system, you would have to manually input all the possible statements and questions, and the system would still run into trouble when a caller mumbled, spoke with an accent, or spoke in another language.

In this case, ML would be the better choice. With ML, the system would get smarter over time as it created its own patterns. If someone called in and said something like, "I hate my new smart phone and want to return it," and they were routed to sales and then transferred to customer service, the system would know that the next time someone called and mentioned the word "return," that call should be routed directly to customer service, not sales.

When you start an AI program, consider which approach is best for your specific use case. If you can draw a decision tree or flow chart to describe a specific task the computer must perform based on limited inputs, then an expert system is probably the best choice. It may be easier to set up and deploy, saving you time, money, and the headaches of dealing with more complex systems. If, however, you're dealing with massive amounts of data and a system that must adapt to changing inputs, then ML is probably the best choice.

Some AI experts mix these two approaches. They use an expert system to define some constraints and then use ML to experiment with different answers. So you have three choices: an expert system, ML, or a combination of the two.

Supervised Versus Unsupervised Learning

Like people, machines can learn through supervised or unsupervised learning. With supervised learning, a human *labels* the data. So the machine has an advantage of knowing the human definition of the data. The human trainer gives the machine a stack of cat pictures and tells the machine, "These are cats." With unsupervised learning, the machine figures out on its own how to cluster the data.

Consider the earlier example of the marching band neural network. Suppose you want the band to be able to classify whatever music it's presented, and the band is unfamiliar with the different genres. If you give the band music by Merle Haggard, you want the band to identify it as country music. If you give the band a Led Zeppelin album, it should recognize it as rock.

To train the band using supervised learning, you give it a random subset of data called a *training set*. In this case, you provide two training sets—one with several country music songs and the other with several rock songs. You also label each training set with the category of songs—country and rock. You then provide the band with additional songs in each category and instruct it to classify each song. If the band makes a mistake, you correct it. Over time, the band (the machine) learns how to classify new songs accurately in these two categories.

But let's say that not all music can be so easily categorized. Some old rock music sounds an awful lot like folk music. Some folk music sounds a lot like the blues. In this case, you may want to try unsupervised learning. With unsupervised learning you give the band a large variety of songs—classical, folk, rock, jazz, rap, reggae, blues, heavy metal, and so forth. Then you tell the band to categorize the music.

The band won't use terms like jazz, country, or classical. Instead, it groups similar music together and applies its own labels, but the labels and groupings are likely to differ from the ones that you're accustomed to. For example, the marching band may not distinguish between jazz and blues. It may also divide jazz music into two different categories, such as cool and classic.

Having your marching band create its own categories has advantages and disadvantages. The band may create categories that humans never imagined, and these categories may actually be much more accurate than existing categories. On the other hand, the marching band may create far too many categories or far too few for its system to be of use.

When starting your own AI project, think about how you'd like to categorize your data. If you already have well-defined categories that you want the machine to use to classify input, you probably want to stick with supervised learning. If you're unsure how to group and categorize the data or you want to look at the data in a new way, unsupervised learning is probably the better approach; it's likely to enable the computer to identify similarities and differences you would probably overlook.

Backpropagation of Errors

I have a vivid memory of being a kid splitting a small bag of jellybeans with my friend. We were good at sharing the bag. He would eat two, and then I would eat two. We worked together to empty the bag.

As we ate our way down, I noticed that my friend was ignoring the black jellybeans. So when we got close to the bottom the number of these beans increased. I asked him why he left the black candy beans.

He said he knew that those were my favorite, so he was saving them all for me. I didn't have any memory of eating a black jellybean, but since he said they were my favorite I was anxious to try them. Without thinking I drew out two black beans, popped them into my mouth, and began to chew. These little beans were one of the vilest things I'd ever tasted. They tasted like a mixture of soap, bug spray, and candles. I spit them out into the bag, ruining the rest of the jellybeans.

From that day forward I was deeply suspicious of any of the darker colored jellybeans. I figured I had made a calculation error by eating those two black jellybeans, so I set out to correct the error by staying closer to the other end of the color gradient.

My friends and family encouraged me to move further down the color gradient. I delved into more experimental colors like green, red, and even purple. Each time I achieved some success with a darker color, I would go further down the gradient.

I wasn't thinking about it at the time, but I was actually using a gradient descent to do a form of backpropagation. *Backpropagation* (backprop for short) is a popular way to optimize the *gradient descent* by adjusting the weights of the connections between neurons. These algorithms twist the dials of your artificial neural network to gradually produce more accurate outputs.

To understand gradient descent, imagine a color gradient that shows a shaded progression of colors from white to black (see Figure 3.2).

Figure 3.2 Gradient descent

In my jellybean example, I gradually moved along this gradient choosing darker and darker colors. I didn't move on to a darker color until I knew that the jellybean I had just eaten was safe. In other words, I made tiny adjustments along the color gradient and tasted the jellybeans as a form of feedback to tell me that I was on the right track.

Gradient descent and backpropagation enable adjustments like these in an artificial neural network. If an artificial neural network were learning to expand its menu of jellybeans, it would start out with white jellybeans and would move along the color gradient to sample darker and darker jellybeans. The network would test the flavor of each until it eventually tasted a black jellybean, at which point, the backprop algorithm would kick in and tell the neural network that it had gone too far on the color gradient. (Keep in mind that backprop is typically only used for supervised learning.)

These algorithms work by adjusting the weights of each connection. Each neuron in an artificial neural network has a weight (typically 0 through 1), which shows its strength to a previous or a succeeding neuron. The closer the weight is to the number 1, the stronger the connection. The closer the weight is to 0, the weaker the connection. A neural network adjusts the weights of these connections over time to match different patterns. A strong connection shows a clear match. A weaker connection shows only a possible match or no match at all (see Figure 3.3).

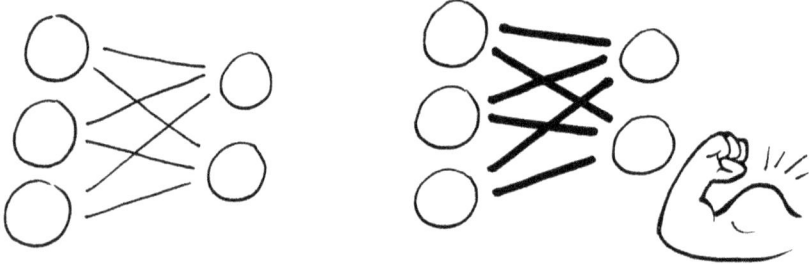

Figure 3.3 Weak and strong connections

With supervised learning, you need a way to let the neural network know when it has made a mistake—when it has failed to identify a match or has falsely identified a match. Suppose the neural network mistakes a purple jellybean for a black jellybean. The backprop algorithm tweaks the weight of the neural connections to reduce the possibility that the neural network will make this same mistake in the future.

Remember that my friends and family had to coax me into trying darker color jellybeans. The same is true with an artificial neural network. A human being must identify the white and black jellybeans and then help the network twist the dials of the gradient to expand its menu of acceptable jellybeans.

Regression Analysis

Classification isn't the only form of supervised ML. You can also have your artificial neural network use something called *regression analysis*, the purpose of which is to identify the relationship between a dependent variable and one or more independent variables.

To understand regression analysis, imagine those sausage-shaped balloons you see at children's parties. You squeeze one end, and the other end bulges. If you let it go, the balloon returns to normal. If you squeeze both ends, the center bulges. Release one end, and the bulge moves to the opposite end. Each squeeze is an independent variable. Each bulge is a dependent variable; it differs depending on where the balloon is squeezed.

Now think about what happens at your typical children's party. Some wacky balloon performer will twist together five or six of these balloons to create various balloon animals. The relationship between squeezing and bulging has become much more complex. If you squeeze the body, maybe the tail bulges. If you squeeze the head, maybe two legs bulge. Each change to the independent variable results in a change to one or more dependent variables. Sometimes that relationship is easy to predict, and other times it's extremely difficult.

I once worked for a credit card processing organization that was trying to look for warning signs of when a customer would have trouble paying their bill. They used a regression in their artificial neural network to try to find relationships between different variables. What they found is that many customers start to put essentials on their credit card just before they have trouble paying their bill. A customer who typically used her card only for large purchases, such as a television or a computer, would suddenly start using it to buy groceries and gas and pay her electric bill. The credit card company also found that people who had a lot of purchases under $5 were likely to have trouble paying their bill.

The dependent variable was whether the person would have enough money to pay the credit card bill. The independent variables were the items the customer purchased and the payment amounts. The artificial neural network identified a relationship between the dependent and independent variables that provided valuable insight to the credit card company.

The dependent variable in the case of classification is a label or category, such as cat, dog, apple, or jazz music. The dependent variable in regression is mostly a numerical value, such as income, height, weight, or population.

Even though the information you get from regression analysis differs from the information you get through backpropagation, the way you use your artificial neural network is similar. It still requires massive amounts of data to identify patterns. The network examines this data to identify patterns that a person may never have thought to look for. The difference is that backprop (with neural networks) is a classification algorithm. So you're using classification to predict a label or category. In regression, you find relationships between independent and dependent variables so the neural network can predict the behavior of a dependent variable.

When you're starting your own AI project, you need to consider whether the job requires sorting and connecting. If it requires sorting, backpropagation is the better choice. If it requires identifying connections, go with regression analysis.

Keep in mind, however, that whether you're using backpropagation or regression analysis, your artificial neural network can only show you the patterns. It doesn't necessarily provide the answers, and it doesn't offer explanations. For example, in the credit card example, the network pointed out that when customers started using their cards for purchases of $5 or less, they were likely to have trouble paying their credit card bill, but it didn't explain why. After the network identified the pattern, it was up to human beings to determine why.

Perhaps at some point these artificial neural networks will be able to create their own theories for why these patterns exist. For now, it's up to humans to find meaning in these connections.

Chapter Takeaways

- An expert system is best when you have consistent inputs and clear steps from input to output.
- Machine learning is best when you have large amounts of data in various forms and are unsure of what the output will be.
- With supervised learning, humans teach the machines; with unsupervised learning, the machines learn on their own.
- Gradient descent and backpropagation are algorithms used in supervised ML to fine-tune the way machines classify data.
- Regression analysis enables machines to identify the relationship between a dependent variable and one or more independent variables.
- Use backpropagation for classifying and labeling. Use regression analysis to identify connections.

4
Common AI Applications

In this chapter:

- Checking out a few applications of artificial intelligence
- Getting physical with intelligent robots
- Understanding spoken language with natural language processing
- Using AI to manage the Internet of Things (IoT)

The fact that machines analyze, classify, and sort massive amounts of data and hone their abilities through supervised and unsupervised learning is truly amazing, but even more impressive is when this advanced data crunching is applied to real-world tasks. For example, personal digital assistants such as Siri and Alexa are powerful data processors that spend most of their time and resources processing data, but at the end of the day nobody's interested in how well they do their homework. Users need these machines to understand what they're told and to respond in an intelligent manner.

In this chapter, you explore three important uses for artificial intelligence (AI) and machine learning (ML): robotics, natural language processing (NLP), and processing the massive amounts of data generated by the *Internet of Things (IoT)*—the interconnection, via the Internet, of digital devices embedded in everyday objects, such as cars and thermostats, that are capable of generating and exchanging data.

Intelligent Robots

One of the most practical and observable applications of AI is in the world of robotics—using machines to perform physical labor, such as packing boxes, assembling products, painting automobiles, and vacuuming floors.

Until recently, robotics has been limited to creating highly specialized machines. The automobile manufacturing plants where I grew up employed several specialized robots. They accomplished feats that even the strongest humans would find impossible. Some could easily lift a car up on the assembly line so people could install parts underneath. As impressive as they were, these robots were limited in what they could accomplish. They're great for performing repetitive tasks and even better for performing dangerous tasks, but they still require programmers to "tell" them what to do.

Combining robotics with AI produces machines that can adapt to changing environments and learn how to perform additional tasks. For example, many robotic vacuum cleaners now use a form of symbolic AI to map different rooms and determine the most effective paths to take to vacuum the entire floor. When they're losing their charge, they can return to home base and dock with the charging station. They are careful to avoid stairs and other obstacles, so you don't return home to your robo-vac's shattered remains.

A more complex example is the self-driving car. The newest vehicles employ an artificial neural network and are outfitted with a host of complex sensors that feed data into the network. The neural network looks for patterns for successful driving. Early versions of self-driving cars had steering wheels and accelerator and brake pedals and required a human in the driver's seat who could override the neural network. This approach provided a form of supervised learning in which the driver would correct the neural network when it made a mistake. Recently, GM introduced a self-driving car without a steering wheel or other manual controls.

With any new robotics project, you must first consider the type AI that's most applicable. You basically have three options, as illustrated in Figure 4.1.

- **Expert system:** You tell the robot what to do and how to do it by programming it.
- **Supervised learning:** You teach the robot what to do, correcting it when it makes a mistake.
- **Unsupervised learning:** You provide the data and algorithms, and the machine learns how to perform the task.

CHAPTER 4 • COMMON AI APPLICATIONS   47

Figure 4.1 Three AI options

For example, suppose you want to create a robot that fills prescriptions. It needs to be able to read and decipher a prescription, fill a bottle with the correct medication in the right amount, label the bottle, and hand it to the customer. Assuming you have the medications arranged in fixed locations, the task is fairly straightforward. You can give the robot a specific set of instructions, and it can carry out the task. You certainly don't want to use unsupervised learning; you don't want the robot learning from its mistakes—mistakes that could cause harm to customers.

With a self-driving car, on the other hand, the car needs massive amounts of data to move from point A to point B. This data can come from an assortment of sensors, including cameras, radar, SONAR, GPS, and LIDAR. It can figure out how to navigate from a point of departure to a destination as many people already do—by following directions from a program like Google Maps. However, it must also be able to read and interpret street signs, classify nearby objects, adjust to driving conditions, and much more. Nobody could program into a self-driving car all the possible variables the car may encounter, so it must be able to learn, either by having a driver teach it (supervised learning) or by learning on its own (unsupervised learning).

Say you wanted to create a robot that distributes prescription medication for senior citizens in a retirement community. You wouldn't necessarily want to use the same technology they use for autonomous vehicles.

Google famously said that they think of their self-driving cars not as a robotics problem but as a big data problem. Getting a car to turn left or right is relatively easy when compared to the challenge of enabling a car to understand *when* to turn left or right. When choosing a type of AI to use for a robotics project, consider the role that data will play in the robot's operation. If you're looking at a massive amount of data and a huge number of variables, you'll probably need to employ ML.

Natural Language Processing

As human beings, we're always trying to do a better job communicating, so it's little surprise that we want our machines to do the same. In many ways machines do a much better job communicating with each other than we humans do. Getting two machines to communicate is fairly easy, as demonstrated billions of times a day across the Internet. You may experience packet loss from time to time, but data typically transfers without a hitch. Human beings, on the other hand, are always struggling to reach a greater understanding. If you can get someone to totally understand 10 percent of what you're saying, you're a master communicator.

The main challenge is that we can't communicate with machines in the same way they communicate with one another. Thankfully, we are not like Neo in the *Matrix*; we don't have a port in the back of our heads that connects us directly to the network. For machines and humans to communicate, the machine must do a better job of existing in our world.

To enable machines to converse with humans, AI programs use natural language processing (NLP). If you've met Siri, Alexa, or Cortana or used speech-to-text on your smart phone, you've already experienced NLP. As you speak, the computer identifies the words and phrases and appears to understand what you said.

NLP makes the interaction much more human. For example, if you need a waffle recipe, you might Google "best waffle recipe," but with NLP, you could say something like, "I'm cooking breakfast. Can you give me a good recipe for those big fluffy waffles like the ones they serve at the Breakfast Nook?" Creating an expert system that could anticipate this question, figure out what the person wanted, and deliver one or more recipes for great Belgian waffles would be impossible.

An artificial neural network, however, could handle the job. It might pick out a few key words, such as *breakfast*, *recipe*, and *waffles*, and give you a recipe for waffles. Or it might focus on *Breakfast Nook* and rattle off a list of local restaurants. Or it might key in on *recipe* and *big fluffy waffle* and figure out that you wanted a recipe for Belgian waffles. It might even ask for clarification and respond with a question like, "Would you like me to search for a Belgian waffle recipe?"

If the neural network delivered the wrong answer, the person could simply say, "No, I need a recipe for Belgian waffles," and the neural network would learn that the next time the two of you had a similar conversation, it should retrieve a recipe for Belgian waffles, not a list of local restaurants.

Many organizations interested in AI also offer free communication services, and they use machine language to analyze conversations. They aren't interested so much in analyzing what you say, but how you say it. Google has access to anonymized versions of your email and voicemail. Apple offers iMessage. Microsoft has Skype. These services give their AI programs a treasure trove of different types of human communications. They can use ML to identify patterns and draw conclusions about how humans use their natural language.

Natural language processing isn't just about understanding the words; it's also about understanding the context and meaning. A few years ago one of the top Google searches was, "What is love?" At the time, when you plugged that question into Google, you would get a long list of results. Most of them were about pairing rituals and the importance of feeling connected. This was the kind of response you'd expect from a network that's just matching keywords across a database.

NLP enables machines to better understand the larger world. Now if you ask Siri or Alexa "What is love?", it understands that you're probably more interested in romantic notions of love, so you're likely to get a range of more poetic and philosophical answers. And as you converse about love with these artificial neural networks, they'll begin to learn more about what you really want to know.

The Internet of Things

The *Internet of Things* (IoT) refers to the large and growing collection of everyday objects that connect to the Internet and to one another (Figure 4.2). These devices include smart thermostats that learn your daily habits and adjust automatically to keep you comfortable, smart watches that can track your daily activity and let you know when you're meeting your fitness goals, and smart refrigerators that can order groceries when supplies are running low. Some devices can even monitor your health and let you know when you need to see your doctor.

Figure 4.2 IoT Devices

Certain devices can also communicate with one other. For example, your smart watch can tell your smart locks to unlock the doors when you approach your home or turn on music when you enter your living room.

As you can imagine, these smart devices generate massive amounts of data that can be very valuable. As a result, many IoT companies invest heavily in AI programs. With AI, organizations can analyze this data to identify patterns that enable the organizations to react quickly to problems or to take advantage of emerging opportunities. An IoT car coupled with AI could monitor the car's operation and identify patterns that indicate when the car needs to be taken in for service. You can now purchase an electrocardiogram (EKG) sensor that is nearly as accurate as the ones in your doctor's office. These devices can check your heart's electrical activity.

These IoT devices are inexpensive enough that many companies are embedding them into smart phone cases and watches. Using AI, these companies can identify patterns in the data using unsupervised ML on a neural network. The network can review the EKG data of thousands or even millions of different participants to find patterns that might accurately predict if someone has an impending health issue.

With these sensors, AI may not yet be able to discover breakthrough preventive measures or cures for serious illnesses, but it can identify patterns that provide doctors with additional insights to help them come up with preventive measures and cures. These devices can also notify you when your data matches an alarming pattern, so you know to check in with your doctor before your health condition becomes more serious.

Remember that neural networks operate in a black box. No one except maybe the network really knows how the machine identifies patterns. We can create intelligent machines, but we still don't completely understand how they "think."

Chapter Takeaways

- Machine learning can be applied to robotics, natural language processing, and the Internet of Things to reap a host of practical benefits.
- Intelligent robots can adapt to changing conditions and learn how to perform additional tasks.
- Machines can learn to communicate with people more effectively by identifying and analyzing vocabulary and speech patterns.
- Through ML, IoT devices can communicate more effectively with one another and provide massive amounts of data that other machines can use to identify patterns.
- Although ML can identify patterns that provide insight into potential problems, human intelligence is still required to come up with answers and solutions.

5
Putting AI to Work on Big Data

In this chapter:

- Getting up to speed on big data
- Differentiating machine learning from data mining
- Understanding the role of data science
- Distinguishing machine learning from data science

As mentioned in Chapter 2, the explosive growth of data and its availability have driven the development of artificial intelligence (AI). Without massive amounts of data, digital personal assistants such as Alexa and Siri wouldn't be able to understand what people are saying or develop reasonable responses. The more information you feed an artificial neural network, the faster it learns and the more capable it becomes.

Prior to starting an AI program, you need to consider the role that data will play in that program and how you'll be using that data; for example, you must decide whether you simply want to analyze data to gain insight or you need a machine to analyze the data for you and make predictions. To make these decisions, you need to understand a few key concepts, including big data, data science, and data mining.

This chapter sheds some light on the role that data plays in AI programs and helps you make informed decisions about how to apply AI to make the most of the massive volumes of data you currently have access to and the growing volumes of data you'll have access to in the future.

Understanding the Concept of Big Data

Big data has come to be used to describe huge data sets that can be analyzed by computers to reveal patterns, trends, and associations. But if you go back to the original report in which that term was coined, you'll see that the authors weren't thinking of "big data" as a term. They used it to describe a problem, as in "We have a BIG data problem," not as in "We have a BIG-DATA problem."

The problem is that we are having trouble storing and processing the massive amount of data being generated. Soon after a company upgrades its on-premises data warehouse, it's likely to outgrow that warehouse. The warehouse can't keep up with the volume and variety of data flowing into it, or it doesn't have sufficient processing power to generate reports from that data. Many companies now run their reports at the end of the day so the report will be done the next morning or afternoon. At other companies, where numerous employees are querying the data at the same time, they must wait hours for results, and if the system crashes or freezes due to its lack of processing capacity, they have to start over. Many of these businesses (such as a stock exchange) rely on real-time reporting to remain competitive.

The problem is growing. According to one estimate, within the next decade there will be more than 150 billion networked sensors in the world, each of which will be generating data 24/7 365 days a year. And just imagine all the data that humans generate in a single day on Facebook, Twitter, Google, online shopping sites, online gaming sites, and more.

The takeaway here is that big data is both a problem and an opportunity. It's a problem in that you need to determine whether you need to work with huge data sets or have more modest needs. Perhaps you merely need to use smaller data sets to monitor and analyze website usage or gauge the effectiveness of your marketing campaigns. However, if you need to analyze huge data sets (for example, to find a cure for the common cold), you need to plan for storage and processing. But big data is also an opportunity. Without it, AI wouldn't have the data it needs to identify patterns from and make predictions on that data.

Teaming Up with a Data Scientist

If you're developing an AI program that requires big data, you would be wise to team up with or at least consult with a data scientist. A *data scientist* is trained in various disciplines, including programming, data management and statistics, for the purpose of knowing how to collect, analyze, and interpret data, typically to assist a business in its decision-making.

Data scientists may work with or without the assistance of machine learning (ML). For example, a data scientist may ask questions you never thought of asking to help you develop a clearer picture of what you're trying to extract from the data—perhaps an answer to a question, a solution to a problem or insight into the possible contributing factors of a system failure. The data scientist could then use or recommend tools to gather, analyze and interpret the data to achieve that goal. Or, the data scientist may discover that you really don't know what you're looking for in that data and help you develop a ML system to identify patterns that may provide insight you never would have thought to seek.

In short, a data scientist can help you size up your data and analytical needs and provide solutions to get the most out of your data.

Machine Learning and Data Mining: What's the Difference?

When you're working with data (regardless of the size of your data sets), you're likely to encounter a great deal of terminology. Two terms that are often confused are data mining and machine learning (Figure 5.1).

Figure 5.1 Data mining versus machine learning

- *Data mining* is any way of extracting useful information or insights from data. (Note that you're not mining data; you're mining information and insights from that data.)
- *Machine learning* (ML) is the science of getting computers to do things they weren't specifically programmed to do.

Data mining may use ML to extract useful information or insights from data, but it doesn't necessarily do so.

Another key difference between ML and data mining is the technology they use. With ML, you start with training a model and then use one of the ML frameworks, typically written in Python, R, or some other computer language. Data mining typically uses a much broader set of tools, including visualization and business intelligence tools, many of which merely extract, sort, summarize, and present data in similar though more sophisticated ways than a spreadsheet application can do.

Making the Leap from Data Mining to Machine Learning

The leap from data mining to ML isn't as challenging as it may seem at first. If you're already working with big data and extracting insights from that data, you already have the expertise to manage that data. You can find plenty of software that enables you to create reports and visualizations using your data. ML is just another tool for extracting meaning from data.

Chances are good that you already have a data management team and those on the team are accustomed to working with large data sets. They're probably familiar with downloading frameworks in Python to manipulate these data sets. To employ ML, they just need to think about the data in a different way. Instead of directly mining the data for insights, they'll train the machine or neural network to find patterns on its own.

I have worked for a few companies that struggled for years with large big-data projects. They thought that the leap to ML would be just as difficult as the leap to big data. The reality is that it was a much smaller step. The teams already knew Python and R, and they were familiar with working with large data sets.

The big challenge is getting the teams to think differently about the data. They needed to create training sets and readjust the weights of the neurons (nodes) on their artificial neural network. This was different from the direct interaction with the data they had become accustomed to with their big-data tools.

A word of caution: If your organization is working with big data, keep in mind that just because you have a shiny new hammer doesn't mean that everything is a nail. Organizations that have big data tend to be seduced by the promises of ML, but ML isn't always the best choice. Smaller AI projects may work better with a symbolic approach. Don't assume that because you have the data, ML is always the best place to start.

Taking the Right Approach

When you're planning a project that involves data, perhaps the best approach is to ignore the terminology and the differences between data science, data mining, and ML. Focus instead on the question you're trying to answer or the problem you're trying to solve, and team up with or consult with a data scientist to determine the best approach. Here are some general guidelines:

- If you need to extract insight from data and you have a clear idea of the insight you hope to gain, such as the number of people visiting your website over a specific period of time, a database or data warehouse coupled with basic business intelligence software is probably sufficient.

- If you're working with big data and haven't the foggiest notion of how to answer a question or solve a particular problem (or you don't even have a question or problem in mind), then you probably need to employ some type of ML (supervised or unsupervised). With unsupervised learning, you can throw all your data into the machine and see what it comes up with.

Think of it this way: Imagine you manage a hospital and you need to identify patterns in successfully treated patients. You could approach this challenge from several different angles (Figure 5.2).

Figure 5.2 Data science team versus machine learning

One option would be to assemble your own data science team and figure out the types of data you needed to analyze. For example, one member of the team may ask, "Which doctors on staff have the greatest success rates?" or "Which patient follow-up programs resulted in the least number of return visits to the doctor?" Then the data science team would choose relevant data sets, analyze the data, produce reports, and discuss their findings. The reports could lead to more questions requiring additional analysis. The whole process would be a tight loop of human interaction.

Another approach would be to use unsupervised ML on an artificial neural network. You throw all the data into the artificial neural network hoping that it will identify useful patterns. With patterns in hand, it's up to you and your team to determine the relevance of those patterns and find out the cause behind the relevant patterns.

Each of these approaches has its own advantages and disadvantages. The data science team would probably come to know much more about the data behind their insights. They would get an intuitive feel for the data and start to ask more interesting questions. ML with an artificial neural network is more likely to identify unexpected patterns; it views the data in a different way than humans typically do. This approach can also find noninterpretable patterns, which may make sense to the machine but not to the humans.

The big downside to using an artificial neural network is that it can't explain why certain patterns exist. For example, the artificial neural network may show that one type of antibiotic used at the hospital had a higher success rate than other antibiotics for treating certain infections, but it doesn't explain why. The reason could be that it worked better, but maybe it just had fewer side effects, so patients were more likely to stay on it.

Another possibility is that the machine outputs its results, but anyone (person) examining the results is unable to interpret their meaning. In other words, the results make sense to the machine, but not to people. So, we may reverse engineer and try to understand why the network worked that way. However, because the "rules" are noninterpretable, we may not know *why* the network produced the results it did.

The data science team would likely have a much better feel for the data. They would've asked questions and used human learning and understanding to find key insights. Instead of looking at infinite possibilities, they would narrow the scope of their inquiries to likely patterns, such as the doctors, medicines, or procedures that had the highest success rates.

Chapter Takeaways

- "Big data" refers to huge data sets that can be analyzed by computers to reveal patterns, trends, and associations.
- Big data presents big opportunities and big problems—opportunities in providing knowledge and insight and problems in data storage, management, and processing.
- Consider teaming up with a data scientist, who can size up your data and analytical needs and suggest the best approach for extracting knowledge and insight from that data.
- *Data mining* is any way of extracting useful information or insights from data.
- *Machine learning* is the science of getting computers to do things they weren't specifically programmed to do.

- The leap to using machine learning to analyze data is much easier than the leap to collecting and managing big data.
- Machine learning on a neural network is the best option when you're working with big data and haven't the foggiest notion of how to answer a question or solve a particular problem (or you don't even have a question or problem in mind).
- Using standard business intelligence software is best when you have a fairly clear idea of the insight you hope to gain.

6

Weighing Your Options

In this chapter:

- Matching the technology to the task
- Deciding whether you even need AI
- Determining whether machine learning or an expert system is the right approach

Artificial intelligence (AI) has been around since the early 1950s. Interest in it has waxed and waned over the years due to fluctuating cycles of overhype followed by periods of disappointment and disinterest, commonly referred to as AI winters. Currently, machine learning (ML) and artificial neural networks are experiencing a long, hot summer. Interest and activity around deep learning with large data sets seems to be at its highest level ever.

Yet, not everyone thinks that data and pattern matching are the surest paths to AI, and few people in the field have realistic expectations that machines will ultimately become conscious beings seeking to conquer the world. In fact, most people in the field see the current improvements in AI as advances in weak AI—machines are just getting better at performing very narrow tasks. They can drive a car, adjust the thermostat, and order groceries when we're running out of supplies. They can even pour through medical data to identify underlying mechanisms for diseases and help to identify effective medications and treatment plans. However, their effectiveness depends largely on what human beings feed into them.

As a human, your role is to decide the best approach for performing a given task, and the best approach isn't necessarily AI or ML. In fact, less sophisticated options may offer better solutions. Here are a few guidelines for choosing the right approach:

- Just because you have lots of data and need to find patterns in that data doesn't mean you need AI. Sometimes all you need is a spreadsheet program with charting capabilities. An example might be Excel or business intelligence software that enables you to query that data and present it in a meaningful way, such as via a table or chart.
- AI is the capability of a machine to imitate intelligent human behavior. Depending on the task you need the machine to perform, you may be able to "train" it simply by writing a program that tells it what to do—by creating an expert system. You don't necessarily need to use ML.
- ML is best when you need to classify objects, group objects, or predict future outcomes. If one of those is not the activity you need the machine to engage in, then ML is not the best fit. A machine doesn't just identify patterns. It tries to make sense from those patterns to classify, cluster, or predict. For example, you could feed the machine data on various companies listed on a stock exchange, and the machine could identify patterns that tell you when the company's shares are likely to increase or decrease in value.
- Neural networks work best for nonlinear problems—problems that can't be solved simply by drawing a line through the data. For example, facial, character, and speech recognition, along with natural language processing, are all nonlinear problems. You can't just solve these problems with a few carefully crafted "if-then" statements. You can use neural networks to *classify* with supervised learning or *cluster* with unsupervised learning. The key thing to keep in mind is that neural networks require a massive amount of data and a good deal of training. So you're looking at a big investment, but that investment might pay huge dividends.

Finally, don't assume that because some of the largest companies are using ML to perform a task that it's the best approach for your company or for a particular problem. For example, if you wanted to create a machine that would take customer orders at a fast food restaurant, ML would be very useful in natural language processing (NLP) to understand the customers, but you wouldn't need it to identify patterns in people's orders. All you would need to do is create a menu of items and options (such as ketchup, mustard, and pickles) that the machine could match with whatever the customer ordered and a list of prices so the machine could calculate the bill. You'd use ML to help interpret what customers said but an expert system to record and process the order.

In general, when you're starting in an AI project, ask the following question: Does the task require sequential reasoning, or does it just need detailed pattern matching? For sequential reasoning and problems that can be easily described, you should stick with a symbolic approach. These could be challenges like building software for preparing tax returns, analyzing loan applications and deciding to reject or approve an application, or checking medical prescriptions for errors. These are all challenges that can probably be broken down into if-then decisions, actions, and symbols.

For problems that cannot be easily described or for patterns that are difficult to see, opt for ML. These are some of the common challenges where you have neural networks find patterns or relationships in massive amounts of data.

The main thing you want to watch out for is that you apply the right approach to the right problem. If you use deep learning for an AI program that helps with tax preparation, then you might run into some difficult challenges. For one, most of the decision-making will be done in a black box. You won't necessarily know the machine's reasoning when it makes decisions about your tax returns.

Also, a system like this would be difficult to update. When you have the machine create its own models and algorithms, it's difficult for a human being to go into the system to make changes.

The more you think about the strengths and weaknesses of these different approaches to AI, the more likely you'll find an approach that works well. Don't assume that the current trends in AI will give you the most powerful approach or even the most valuable.

As of right now, weak AI is a powerful but narrow tool. The more time you spend figuring out what you want from this tool, the happier you will be with the result.

Chapter Takeaways

- Working with big data doesn't necessarily mean you need machine learning. You may need only standard database tools and a spreadsheet or more sophisticated business intelligence software.
- Use machine learning with an artificial neural network when you need a program to use inductive reasoning to draw conclusions or make predictions based on a large volume of data.
- Use an expert system to program machines to perform tasks normally attributed to humans.

Part II
Machine Learning

7 What Is Machine Learning?..67

8 Different Ways a Machine Learns 83

9 Popular Machine Learning Algorithms 95

10 Applying Machine Learning Algorithms 115

11 Words of Advice..125

7

What Is Machine Learning?

In this chapter

- What it means to learn
- Using data to teach machines
- Putting machine learning to practical use
- Surveying different types of machine learning

Machine learning (ML) has been around for a long time. You can tell because the term itself is a little old-fashioned. You don't often hear computers referred to as *machines*. The term *machine learning* got its start in 1959 when computer pioneer Arthur Samuel wondered if computers could learn their behavior instead of explicitly being programmed to do specific tasks. This was a big change from how most computer scientists viewed computers: a computer needed to be told exactly what to do.

Even today most of what computers do is a result of programmers writing instructions. Most programs tell the computer exactly what to do. That's why programmers need to be explicit when creating software for something like a banking application. As a programmer, you might create a task that says something like this: If a customer tries to withdraw money that exceeds their balance, then cancel the transaction. That's an explicit instruction: If you see this, then you do this.

In ML you're doing an entirely different type of programming. Here you're not creating explicit tasks. Instead, you're giving the computer the data and tools it needs to study and solve a problem without being told what to do. Then you're enabling the computer to remember what it learns so it can adapt and evolve (Figure 7.1).

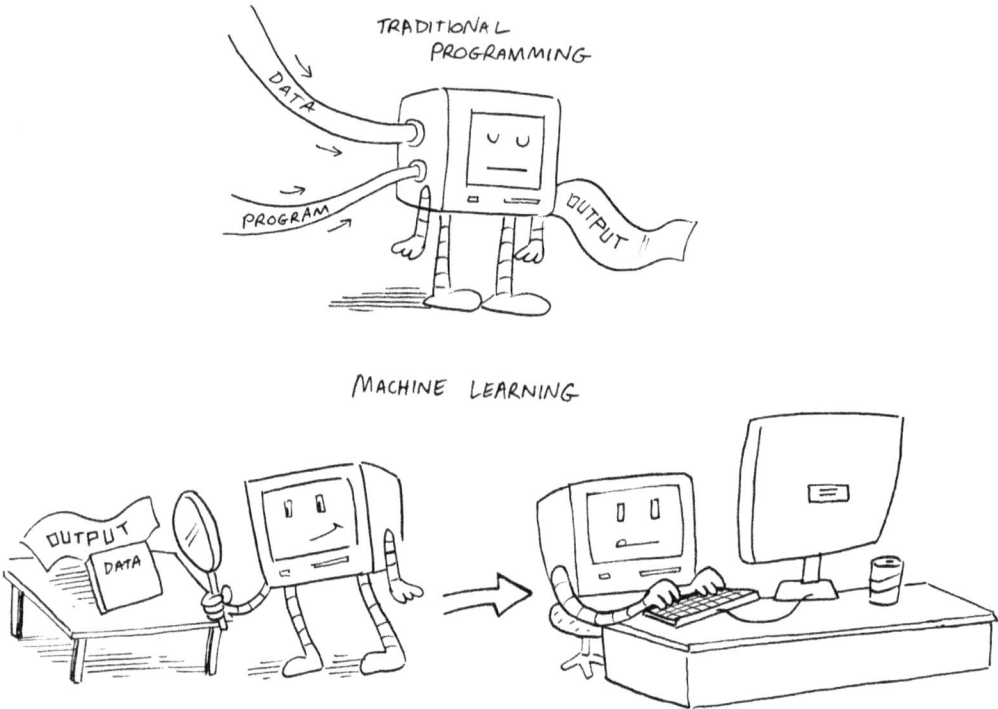

Figure 7.1 Traditional programming versus machine learning

If you think about it, that's not much different from how humans learn to solve problems. Several years ago, my wife and I purchased a new computer desk at IKEA. We did our best to wedge the box into the back of our car for the drive home. As soon as we opened the box and I saw all the parts, I realized that we had made a mistake. Assembly would be more involved than I had anticipated. But I couldn't tell my wife we had to go back, so I had some *human* learning to do.

I took a cursory glance at the instructions, mostly to remind myself what the final product should look like. I arranged the main parts on the floor, so I had some idea of their relative positions, and then I ripped open the package with all the hardware in it and started matching the dowels and screws and other hardware with holes in the parts where they needed to go. Reluctantly, I checked the instructions for confirmation, and my son was nearby to correct me when I made a mistake.

The kit had some weird connectors that I hadn't encountered before, but once I figured out how one of them worked (through trial and error), I created a rule in my mind that enabled me to easily install the other connectors. The more I learned, the less I had to consult the instructions or seek guidance from my son.

This human learning was part of a larger process. As I encountered challenges and overcame them, I created rules for meeting those challenges. If the rule I created didn't work for a certain part or connector, I took that feedback and modified the rule. As I developed rules and modified them, I stored what I learned in memory (Figure 7.2).

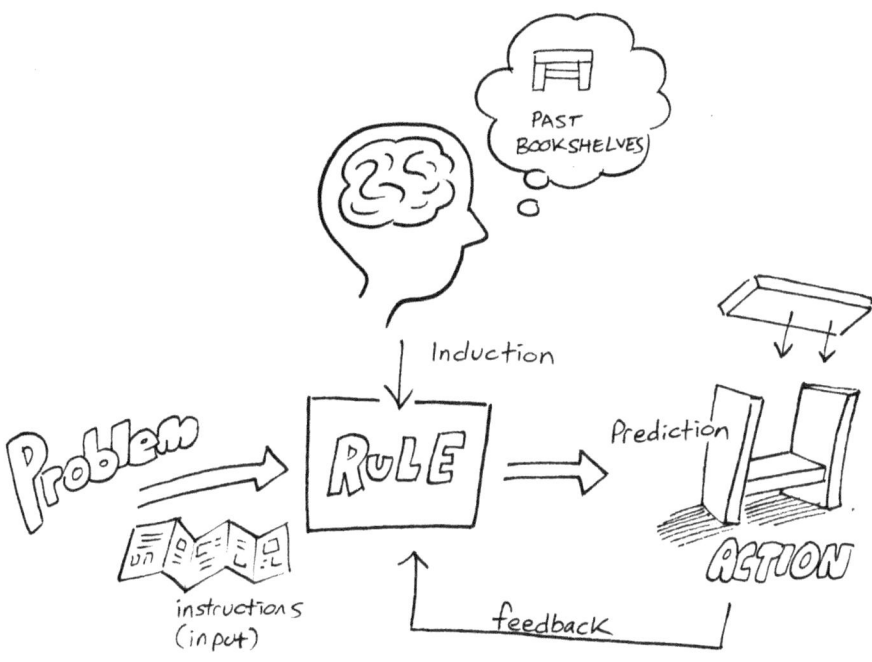

Figure 7.2 Human learning

After completing the project, I probably could've assembled a new computer desk of the same make and model in half the time, and I could use what I learned on similar assembly projects.

ML involves a similar approach (Figure 7.3). A person provides the machine with data and an algorithm to look at that data in some way. An *algorithm* is a set of rules for solving a problem in a fixed number of steps. With ML, algorithms include rules that the machine uses to form a model, test the model against examples, and then fine-tune the model, so the machine can use it to accurately interpret data that's fed to it in the future. The model that the machine creates may be very complex and may or may not be something that a human being can completely understand.

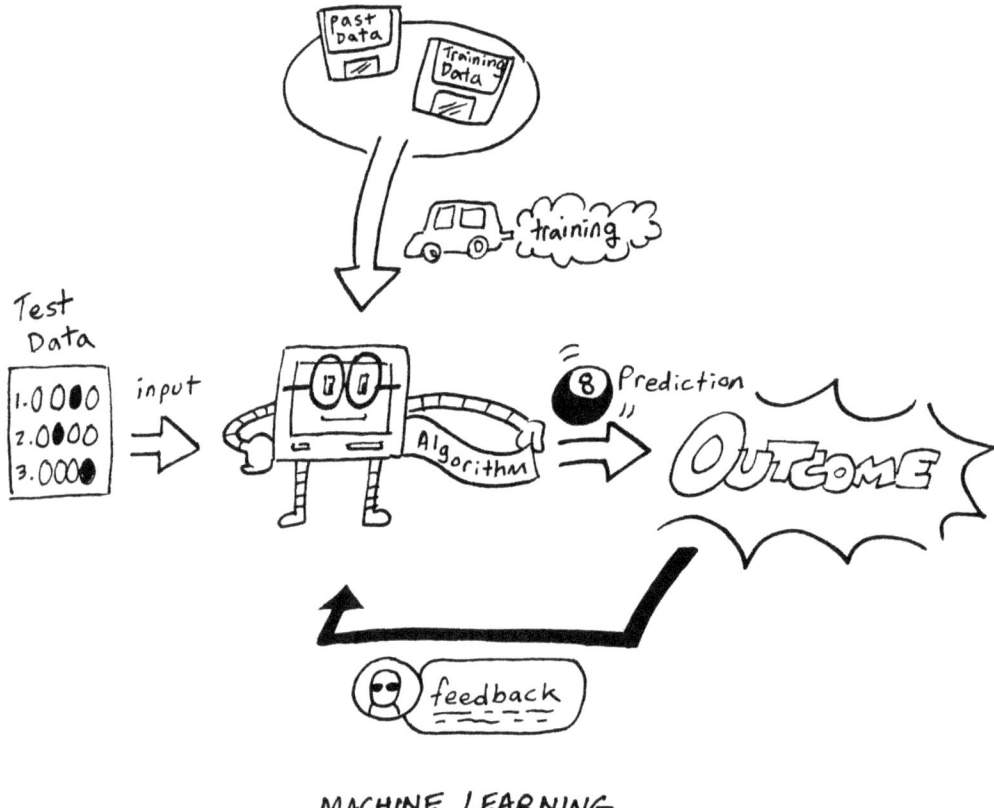

Figure 7.3 Machine learning

Like a person, a machine can learn from experience (environment or data input), from trial and error (mistakes), and from people (training and correction). When I was assembling our computer desk, I referenced the instructions, installed a part, and learned from that how to install other parts. As I made mistakes, I (or my son) provided a correction, and I learned from that. In the same way, a machine might start with a small data set, chart the data, and draw a line to describe the data, creating a model. When fed more data, the machine would chart it and perhaps readjust the line to create a more accurate model. It might go through that exercise several times to fine-tune the model. It could then store that model and use it to predict where future points on its chart would be likely to appear.

The machine and I both developed new knowledge and expertise. I learned how to assemble a bookcase, and the machine learned how to make accurate predictions.

How a Machine Learns

ML involves six primary components:

- **Learner:** The machine.
- **Data:** Input for training and testing the machine and for using the machine to interpret after training.
- **Algorithm:** A mathematical formula that receives and analyzes input data to predict outputs within an acceptable range.
- **Parameters:** Conditions that affect the way the algorithm works. Think of parameters as dials the machine can turn to control the operation of the algorithm.
- **Hyperparameters:** These are parameters that can't be learned from the data and are left to a human practitioner. This is usually choosing the right ML algorithm, coming up with a tuning metric (like k in k-means clustering), or setting the number of hidden layers in a deep neural network.
- **Model:** An algorithm with parameters that tells the machine how to process and interpret input data.

Figure 7.4 summarizes how ML works:

1. You add hyperparameters, so here you'd decide on an ML algorithm.
2. You feed the machine data, typically input-output pairs, to train it. Think of input-output pairs as questions and answers. During training, you feed the machine both the questions and the answers.

3. Using the algorithm, the machine performs calculations on the inputs, adjusting the model parameters, as necessary, to produce the outputs associated with those inputs.
4. As it processes the training data, the machine creates a model that consists of the algorithm and parameters that most accurately calculate outputs based on the given inputs.
5. When you feed the machine inputs with unknown outputs, the machine can now calculate (predict the outputs).

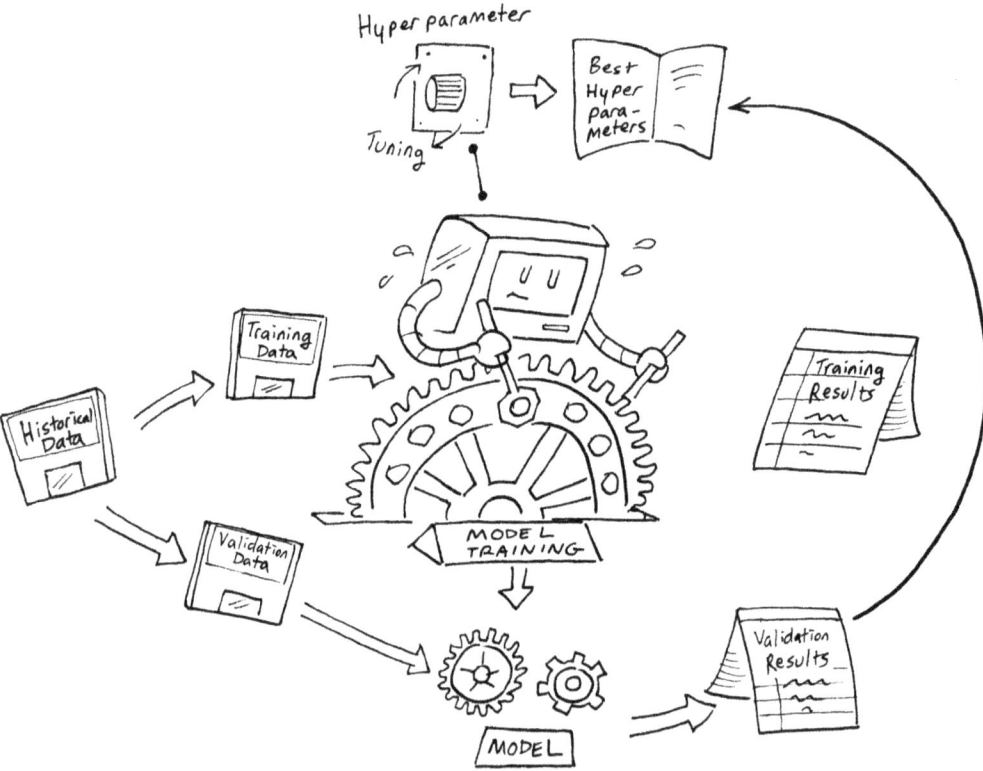

Figure 7.4 More machine learning

Here's a simple example. Suppose you have the following input-output pairs showing a direct correlation between the size of houses and their prices:

1,000 square feet = $150,000

1,500 square feet = $275,000

2,000 square feet = $300,000

2,500 square feet = $425,000

If you were to graph these values (Figure 7.5), you'd get a straight line, and this line could be described using the linear equation (algorithm) y = mx + b, where x is square footage (input), y is price (output), m is the slope of the line, and b is the point at which the line crosses the y-axis. In this algorithm, m and b are the parameters. Given the inputs and outputs, the slope of the line (m) is 1, and the line crosses the y-axis at 0 (zero). So the machine's initial model would be y = 1x + 0.

Figure 7.5 A graph of the first three value pairs

Figure 7.6 adds the fourth data pair.

Now suppose the machine were fed an input-output pair of 3,000 square feet = $475,000. If you were to plot that point on the graph, you would see that it is not on the line, so the machine's model is not 100% accurate.

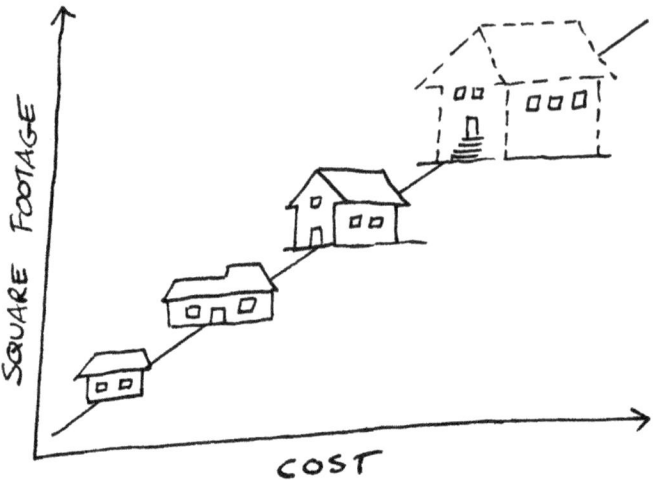

Figure 7.6 A graph with a predicted value pair

To fix the model, the machine can adjust one or both parameters. It can change the slope of the line (m) or the y-intercept (b) or change both. That's how the machine "learns."

Working with Data

Much of computer science is still about writing instructions that tell computers how to respond to various inputs. You could write a simple program called "Time" that, whenever a user runs the program, it checks the computer's clock for the time and displays it on the screen. The input is the command, and the output is a predetermined response.

Traditional programming is great when you can link inputs directly to outputs, but it's useless when the input can vary and the machine must interpret it or when you don't have a precise output in mind—when you want the machine to figure it out. In these cases you need a more flexible approach to programming. You need ML.

Imagine creating a program to detect spam. These email messages typically contain unsolicited advertisements or even malware. You could easily create a filter that identifies spam by searching the subject line of incoming email messages for commonly used words in spam, such as Viagra, lottery, or weight loss. Your email program would automatically delete these messages or redirect them to a Spam folder. Your filter would certainly screen out a lot of spam messages, but it would be easy to spoof. For example, a spammer could use zero (0) instead of the letter o in lottery. The filter could also lead to false positives, identifying legitimate email as spam; for example, if your friend sent you an email message about a great new weight loss program, it might be moved to the Spam folder.

With ML, you can create a much more precise spam screener that identifies common patterns in spam messages that were identified in massive volumes of email data. The spam screener might look at where the email message originated, entries in the Subject and From lines, the number or type of images included in the messages, email messages you responded to in the past, and so on to determine more precisely which incoming messages are spam and which are legitimate.

You use three types of data in supervised ML (Figure 7.7):

- **Training data:** The machine uses training data, along with an algorithm, to develop a *model*—a pattern that the machine can use to extract insight or make predictions based on future input. In the spam example, training data may include a set of email messages known to be spam and a set of messages known to be legitimate.

- **Test data:** After the machine learns a model, test data is used to assess the performance of that model. The test data doesn't contain any of the training data. In the spam example, test data would be a collection of email messages, —some spam and some legitimate—to see whether the machine could accurately distinguish them.

- **Validation data:** Sometimes a portion of training data may be set aside and used to fine-tune and adjust the parameters of your ML model. This is called the *validation data*. In the spam example, validation data is some of email messages that were part of the original data set. You'll set aside this email to test whether the model is correctly identifying spam messages as "spam."

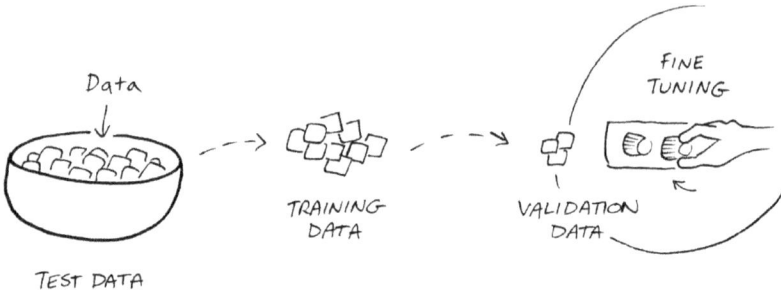

Figure 7.7 Three types of data in supervised learning

With traditional programming, you might create a program that says something like this: If the email contains any of these words, send it to the Spam folder; otherwise, send it to the Inbox (Figure 7.8). If any of those words change, you must rewrite the program. With ML, on the other hand, the machine identifies and learns the characteristics of spam and creates a model for identifying spam. If those characteristics happen to change or the user overrides the machine to indicate that an email flagged as spam is legitimate, the machine simply adjusts its model. In other words, traditional programs can't learn, but machines that engage in ML can.

Figure 7.8 Machine learning spam detection

Keep in mind that ML may still require human involvement, for better or worse. The programmer supplies the algorithm and the data. The machine decides what's spam and what's not. One of the drawbacks of ML is that humans select the data, and if there is any sort of bias in selecting that data, that bias is passed along to the machine. Likewise, if the person selects the wrong algorithm, the machine won't be able to make the proper distinctions. If traditional programming and ML have one thing in common, it's GIGO—garbage in, garbage out.

Applying Machine Learning

ML is already in widespread use in many industries. It's used for anti-lock braking, autopilot in airplanes, search engines, product recommendations, maps and driving directions, spam screeners, language translation, personal digital assistants, weather maps, and more. Any organization that has a lot of data and is looking for better ways to understand and use that data can benefit from this technology.

Several companies have used ML to build some of the most lucrative businesses on a getting-to-know-you-better platform. Google, Facebook, Apple, LinkedIn, and Twitter are all using ML to make sure you have access to relevant data. Some companies are even pushing the envelope of privacy by analyzing your search history or personal or professional connections. By learning more about you they can personalize their service for you. That's why your Facebook newsfeed is completely unique to you. It's also why two people Googling the same search term may get completely different results.

Any time you're on a website and you see something like *recommended for you*, you're probably benefiting from ML. Amazon may examine your previous purchases and then use ML to recommend other products you might like. Netflix tries to figure out your taste in movies to suggest other shows you might enjoy. YouTube tracks what you watch and recommends related videos. Each of these online services uses ML to try to turn you into a long-term customer or user.

Other organizations are using ML for automatic translation. YouTube might use it to transcribe video and generate captions. Some sites use a similar ML technology to translate captions into different languages. Through natural language processing (NLP), powered by ML, some services translate captions into a synthesized voice that sounds similar to a human being.

With ML, computers tap the power of AI to process massive data sets and extract valuable information from that data. They can find connections in the data that humans could never detect on their own and may never think to look for. Sometimes we can understand how these intelligent computers made the connection, and other times we cannot.

One of the most interesting aspects of ML is that it doesn't replicate human learning; it's a completely different way to find connections, make decisions, and gain greater understanding. So if you're planning to use ML in your organization, you have to start thinking about how machines learn, so you can start to collect data that will help the machine learn to perform the task you need it to perform.

ML didn't start to really gather steam until companies had large data sets, and that's not a coincidence; data is the fuel that drives ML. That's why some of the first companies that benefited from ML were the ones that had access to massive data sets. Data plays a crucial role in what the machine learns, how well it learns, and how fast it learns. Usually, the more data you have, and the better that data is, the sooner the machine will start delivering useful insights.

So before you start your ML project, you should think about your data. Is it high quality? Do you have enough for the computer to learn something new (Figure 7.9)? Is the data set broad enough to accurately represent whatever you're asking the machine to examine? The broader the view, the more likely it is to find something interesting. You don't want your program looking through a keyhole. If you plan to use this technology, think about some strategies for collecting diverse, high-quality data sets.

Figure 7.9 The machine learns more with more data

Different Types of Learning

Many people think of ML as a different name for something that's been around awhile. Some people have the misconception that ML is synonymous with statistics or is just a new way to talk about data science. To avoid these misconceptions, when you think about ML, focus on the term *learning*. ML certainly uses statistics, and both statistics and ML are components of data science, but ML is not the same as either of those other fields. *Learning* makes ML unique.

The key to understanding ML is to focus on what it means to learn. What are the different strategies that people use to learn something new? How can you take the strategies and apply them to machines? When you focus on learning, you'll see that ML is a much different approach to solving problems.

Imagine you want to learn how to play chess. You could do this in several different ways. You could hire a chess tutor, who would introduce you to the different chess pieces and how they move across the board. You could practice by playing against the tutor, who would supervise your moves and recommend different strategies. As you increased your mastery of the game, you could play it without supervision and perhaps even begin to develop your own strategies (Figure 7.10).

Figure 7.10 Supervised versus unsupervised learning

Another option would be to visit public parks and watch people play the game. You could awkwardly stand over their shoulders and observe how they move pieces across the board. If you were to do this long enough, you'd probably understand the game. You might not know the names of the chess pieces, but you could understand the moves and strategies from your hours of observations.

You might even try a combination of these two approaches. A chess tutor would show you the basic rules, and then you'd observe other people playing. You'd have a high-level overview of the game and the names of the chess pieces, but you'd rely on your own observations to learn new strategies and improve your game.

These three strategies are similar to how machines often learn:

- **Supervised learning:** Here you act like a tutor for the machine. You provide guidelines for the machine to follow, along with some training data, and you let the machine know when it made a mistake.
- **Unsupervised learning:** You feed the machine a set of data, and it discovers patterns in that data on its own and figures out its own rules and strategies for interpreting the data.
- **Semi-supervised learning:** This approach combines supervised and unsupervised learning. You train the machine just a little bit so it gets a high-level overview, and then the machine develops its own rules and strategies based on its examination of the data.

Each approach has strengths and weaknesses. For supervised learning you need a knowledgeable trainer. In the chess example, you'd need a chess master or someone else who knows the game and can teach it. However, although this approach is great for a 1,500-year-old game like chess, you may have trouble finding someone to train a machine to work on a groundbreaking project.

With unsupervised learning you need access to a lot of data. In the case of chess, you can watch people play at a park or community center, study games that have been played in the past, or get a computer program that shows famous games being played onscreen. You'd want to watch good players, not novices. The challenge with unsupervised ML is that you need to make sure you're feeding the machine good data. Remember, garbage in, garbage out.

With semi-supervised learning you get a double dose of challenges. You need to find a qualified trainer, and you need to feed good data into the machine. If you fall short in either of those endeavors, you're likely to be disappointed by the machine's performance.

You may be in a position to decide which approach works best, but often you just have to do the best you can with what's available. If you can't find a tutor, you need more and better data. If you don't have great data and a sufficient volume of it, you have to find an exceptional trainer. You can do semi-supervised learning only if you have access to both.

For a more in-depth discussion of the various ways machines learn, turn to the next chapter.

Chapter Takeaways

- With traditional computer programming, you write instructions that tell the computer (machine) exactly what to do and how to do it.
- With machine learning, you give the machine one or more algorithms (sets of rules) for learning how to interpret data. You then feed the machine training data. Using the algorithm and training data, the machine creates a model for interpreting that data. When given additional data, the machine can adjust its model, thus "learning" to accurately interpret data that's fed to it in the future.
- Traditional programming is great when you can link inputs directly to outputs, but it's useless when you want the machine to figure it out.
- A machine uses training data to develop a model for extracting insight from data or making predictions based on future input. It uses test data to validate the model and fine-tune it.
- ML is already at work delivering benefits to you in the form of more personalized services, better product recommendations, interactive maps and driving directions, personal digital assistants, anti-spam utilities, and much more.
- Machines learn in a variety of ways, including supervised, unsupervised, and semi-supervised learning.
- Data is the fuel that powers ML.

8

Different Ways a Machine Learns

In this chapter:

- Teaching machines with supervised learning
- Letting machines learn on their own with unsupervised learning
- Giving machines some direction with semi-supervised learning
- Using rewards to reinforce machine learning

People learn in all sorts of ways—through reading, listening, observing, sensing, feeling, playing, interacting, comparing, experiencing, reasoning, teaching, trial and error, and so on. And that just scratches the surface. Scientists are still trying to figure out how the brain works and identify the many ways the brain functions to learn new things.

The same is true about machines. They learn in different ways and combinations of ways. Although experts in artificial intelligence (AI) have developed several ways to enable machines to learn, they're still working on developing new ways and understanding how to combine different techniques. This chapter explores a few of the more common methods.

Supervised Machine Learning

When you know enough about your data, you can help your machine connect the dots through supervised learning. In *supervised learning* you show the machine the connection between a known outcome and the variables that affect that outcome; for example, the amount of time it takes you to drive home from work varies depending on weather conditions, traffic conditions, and the time of day. In machine learning

(ML), the amount of time it takes you to drive home is referred to as the *dependent variable*, and the conditions that affect it are referred to as *independent variables* (Figure 8.1).

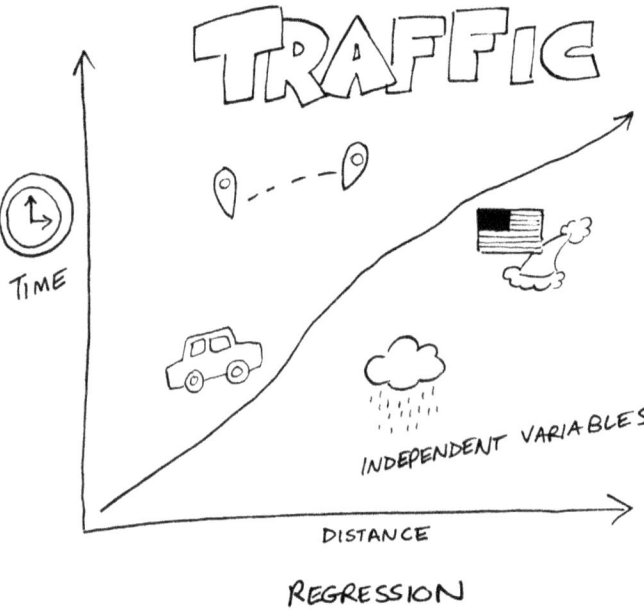

Figure 8.1 Independent and dependent variables

You can create a table or spreadsheet of this data with a column for each variable—drive time, weather conditions, traffic conditions, and time of day—and then enter data based on your drive to work over the past month. In ML, such a table is called *labeled data* because all the data is identified by name. This table and the data it contains serve as your *training data*. You feed this into the machine, and it identifies patterns; for example, if traffic is heavy, then your drive home may take an average of 30 minutes longer than when traffic is light. The computer may also find a connection between the time you left work and the time it takes you to drive home.

The machine (computer) examines all the data and creates a model that can predict your drive time based on any combination of conditions—whether traffic is light, heavy, or normal; whether it's raining, sunny, or clear; and the time you left work. The model may be able to predict, based on the conditions you enter, what your drive time will be within 10 to 15 minutes of your actual drive time. That's pretty good, but you want a more precise answer.

Now you can feed test data into the machine. The test data was not shown to the machine while it learned from the training data. This test data represents a scenario that may not have been observed earlier. Ideally, we would want to exhaust all the possible combinations of independent variables to predict a dependent variable with certainty. However, as the number of independent variables increases and if these variables are numeric, there are infinite possible values these variables can take. Therefore, it is impossible to collect and utilize all the combinations of the training data. Without looking at the actual drive times, the machine uses the model it created to make its predictions. Internally, the model may work in different ways to predict the dependent variable of a test sample. It may simply fit the rules it learned during training or try to linearly combine different independent variables, or it might combine them in mathematically complex and noninterpretable ways. The machine may also compare its predictions to the actual drive times. If its predictions aren't very accurate, a practitioner might try to adjust the hyperparameters (try a different algorithm) and the machine tries again. The process may be repeated several times until the model generates predictions that are much closer to the actual drive times.

Supervised learning isn't much different from how you might learn something new, such as driving a car (Figure 8.2).

To learn to drive, you might start out in a small parking lot with an instructor who teaches you the basics, such as accelerating, braking, stopping, turning, and backing up. When you're comfortable with the basics, you may expand your territory, heading out into the neighborhood, where you encounter traffic lights, stop signs, and speed limit signs and are required to hone your skills. When you're confident on side streets, you may head out on the open road, where you need to navigate the highway and its entrance and exit ramps. You don't master driving all at once. You make gradual adjustments over time to the model you've built in your mind.

The key to supervised learning is that you know enough about the data—the independent variables (input) and the dependent variable (output)—to train the machine. You may have some idea of how the independent variables affect the dependent variables, but you don't know exactly what the impact will be or how combinations of independent variables will influence the dependent variable. That's the machine's job. It creates the model. As you feed more data into the machine, it adjusts the model to more accurately align with the data.

Figure 8.2 A training set and a test set

Unsupervised Machine Learning

Unsupervised machine learning is like humans learning through observation and trial and error. It is, perhaps, the most natural way people learn. It's how most infants learn to crawl, walk, talk, and clap their hands. As they watch and listen, their developing brains identify patterns, make inferences, and develop new neural networks to capture what they learned and use their newly acquired knowledge to perform those activities. When they're learning how to crawl, walk, talk, and clap their hands, they usually do not even know what to call these skills.

Unlike supervised learning, in which you feed the machine labeled data—dependent and independent variables—with machine learning, you feed it algorithms and unlabeled data and let the machine interpret it. The unlabeled data means that you have one or more independent variables but no dependent variable. Just as parents can't predict what their children will say when they start talking, you can't predict what the machine will come up with, what it's output will be.

Think of unsupervised learning this way: Every Halloween for the past few years, my son has gone trick-or-treating.

At the end of the night, he comes home with a bag full of hundreds of different little pieces of candy (Figure 8.3). The first thing he wants to do is sort the candy based on what he likes the most. In machine learning this would be called a multi-class classification problem.

Figure 8.3 A trick-or-treat multiclassification problem

Prior to knowing how to sort his candy, he could have learned how to do it through supervised or unsupervised learning. With supervised learning, I could have taught him the basics by creating a separate stack for chocolates, chocolates with nuts, fruit chews, hard candies, mints, gums, suckers, and so on. I could have shown him some of the key characteristics of each labeled data set. Mints are almost always small, and they smell like toothpaste. Fruit chews are squishy. Gum usually comes in a rectangular package. Suckers have sticks. I could create a training set by sorting a small portion of the candy into groups, he could try sorting the rest into these groups, and I could correct him when he made a mistake.

The other option would be to use unsupervised learning (Figure 8.4). We dump the candy onto the table, and I tell him to sort the candy into groups, placing similar candy into each group. With this approach, I would have no idea of how he would group these candies. He could sort them by color, shape, size, hardness, smell, packaging, whatever. He might even come up with categories I never would have imagined. My son has grandparents who live in a different country. Every year they send my son a large bag of local candy from different shops and friends. One year my son created a grouping he called "perfume candy" for candies made from roses and orange blossoms.

Figure 8.4 Unsupervised learning

With unsupervised machine learning, you provide the data and algorithms and let the machine figure out how to interpret the data. Pharmaceutical companies use this approach to try to repurpose medications for use in treating other illnesses. They may feed the chemical composition of an existing medication into a machine along with the chemical composition of thousands of other medications. The machine makes the comparisons and spits out a list of medications with similar chemical compositions. The company can then examine the illnesses that those other medications are used to treat, which may shed light on whether their medication might be useful in treating those other conditions, with or without some modification. Most of the unsupervised algorithms work on the notion of *similarity*. Depending on the chosen similarity, different objects may be grouped in different ways. However, the objects within one group must be more similar to each other based on that *similarity* than objects in the other group.

The key to success with unsupervised machine learning is access to massive amounts of data. The more data you have, the easier it is for the machine to observe and identify patterns that might lead to a worthwhile grouping.

Semi-Supervised Machine Learning

Semi-supervised learning is a crossover approach with the advantages of both supervised and unsupervised machine learning. With semi-supervised learning, you give the machine some initial direction and then let it work out the details. In essence, in a semi-supervised learning scenario, you have some labeled data and lots of unlabeled data.

Imagine you want to create a machine learning program that transcribes voicemail into text. You couldn't use supervised learning exclusively because it would be too labor intensive to label all the words and their corresponding sounds. You could never create a training set that was large enough to translate all the possible spoken words and variations on how people say them. Nor could you use unsupervised learning exclusively because the machine wouldn't be able to identify patterns in such disparate data—text and audio.

One possible solution would be to use semi-supervised learning. You would start with a small training set of *labeled* data—common words and phrases along with their audio equivalents, as you would do with supervised learning. Then you would feed your training set to the machine to provide it with some guidance on how to spot patterns in the *unlabeled* data. Basically, the machine uses knowledge it gained from the labeled data to interpret the unlabeled data.

Using the labeled data, the program could use a form of inductive reasoning to try and expand its own vocabulary. If the training data contained the word "photo" and the sound "photo," the machine could possibly use inductive reasoning to connect the words "photograph," "photographer," "photocopy," or even "photon torpedo" with their corresponding spoken versions (Figure 8.5).

Figure 8.5 Semi-supervised learning

Each time the machine makes a new connection, it improves the model and adds the translation to memory.

But inductive reasoning is not the only form of reasoning machines can use to learn. A machine can also use *transductive reasoning* to narrow the possible matches by thinking about what it already knows about the data. For example, voicemails typically contain information about people, places, or things. They're likely to include dates, times, and callback numbers. A typical voicemail message might be something like, "Hi Jeff. I was just calling to confirm our meeting next Tuesday. Give me a call if there's a change." This is much different from a random sampling of audio that you might get from listening to people chatting in a restaurant. So transductive reasoning tries to improve the model by making better guesses about what's in the unlabeled data.

CHAPTER 8 • DIFFERENT WAYS A MACHINE LEARNS   91

Semi-supervised learning is not that common, but it works well in certain applications. It often works well when the data set is too large to be practical for supervised learning and when it isn't extremely difficult for the machine to create useful groups. You may see semi-supervised learning used for classifying web pages into different categories or grouping different pictures of insects.

The key to remember is that semi-supervised learning makes sense only when either of the other two approaches would have difficulty solving the problem. You should also keep in mind that inductive and transductive reasoning can lead to greater errors and mislabeled data. So try to think of them as the best solution for a problem and not necessarily the best place to start with your machine learning algorithms.

Reinforcement Learning

One type of machine learning that has gotten a lot of attention over the past few years is *reinforcement learning*—a technique that involves rewarding the machine for its performance.

When I was younger, most people who played video games played one game in particular—*Pong* (short for ping-pong). You and your opponent (a person or the computer) each had a paddle, in the form of a vertical line, on either side of the "net." You'd turn a dial to move your paddle up or down on the screen to hit the ball back to your opponent (Figure 8.6).

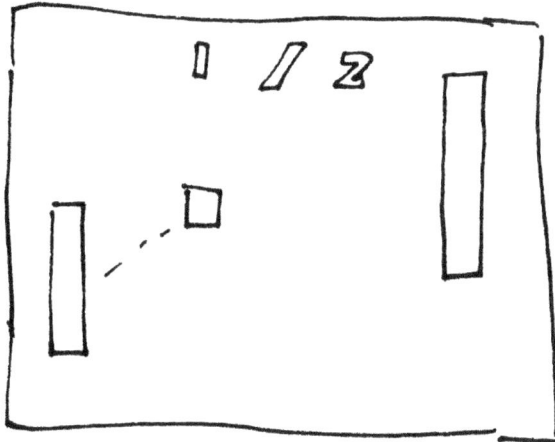

Figure 8.6 Pong

In 2013 Google's DeepMind project experimented with Pong and other Atari games to see if they could teach a computer how to play this game. For Pong, they set up a reward system, rewarding the computer every time it hit the ball and every time its opponent missed. Then it allowed the computer to play against itself and try to gather as many rewards as possible. Quickly, the computer started to master the game and consistently beat human players.

The Google team used something called Q-learning with some of the more complicated games that needed more sophisticated rewards. In Q-learning, an application of reinforcement learning, you have a set of environments or states typically represented by the letter S, possible actions that can respond to the states represented by the letter A, and quality of performance represented by the letter Q.

Suppose you have an Atari game like *Space Invaders* that requires you to blast aliens with your laser cannon as they descend from the sky. Blasting aliens is more complex than moving a paddle up and down; you must aim and then shoot a moving target. To help the computer learn how to play, you might have S represent the number of aliens descending and the speed of descent and A represent actions the computer takes to shoot aliens out of the sky, thus improving Q, which represents the score of the game. Each time the computer successfully shoots down an alien, it's rewarded with an increase in Q. Q-learning is iterative—learning through repetition and reward until it develops an effective strategy.

In 2015 Google's DeepMind project made the news when its AlphaGo program first beat a human player in the game called *Go*. The accomplishment was considered one of the big scientific breakthroughs of the year. AlphaGo had learned how to play the game through unsupervised learning—observing how great players have played the game.

In October 2017, Google introduced a newer version of AlphaGo called AlphaGo Zero that relied primarily on Q-learning to figure out how to play the game. This newer version learned without any observation of human-created data. It simply went through the game and tried different actions as a way to change the state in ways that would raise Q. In a sense, it learned the game entirely on its own. After only 70 hours of learning, AlphaGo Zero beat AlphaGo in the last 100 of the games they played.

Reinforcement learning, specifically Q-learning, enables machines to quickly grow beyond our understanding. It can help you skip the steps required for collecting data and then feeding the machine training data and test data. The machine essentially creates its own data as it engages in iterative trial and error.

Chapter Takeaways

- Use supervised learning when you have a general idea of the relationship between independent variables (input) and the dependent variable (output).
- Use unsupervised learning when you have massive amounts of data and you're unsure about how that data is related; you want the machine to identify relationships.
- Use semi-supervised learning when you have a small amount of labeled data and a large amount of unlabeled data that you need the machine to make sense of.
- Use reinforcement learning when you want the machine to learn a complex task on its own, and it can improve its performance on that task through iteration.

9

Popular Machine Learning Algorithms

In this chapter:

- Recognizing the two classifications of problems that machine learning is good at solving
- Understanding common machine learning algorithms
- Choosing the right algorithms for your machine learning program

In the HBO show *Silicon Valley*, one of the characters uses machine learning (ML) to solve a real-world problem. He uses a smart phone to take a picture of the food in front of him, and then the application tells him whether or not it's a hot dog. He aptly named his application "Not Hotdog." He created the application by giving the machine a small training set of hot dog pictures and then feeding it millions of different food pictures from online sources.

Even though this application was intended to be funny, it's still a really good example of a typical ML problem. For this problem, the developer used supervised learning to do a form of *binary classification*, which means two classes—in this case hot dog and not hot dog.

Even though you can use supervised ML to solve a variety of problems, problems generally fall into the following two categories:

- **Classification:** In classification problems, the machine tries to figure out in which group a new input belongs. Classification problems are further subdivided into binary and multiclass classification. With binary classification, the machine has only two classes, such as hot dog and not hot dog. With multi-class classification, the machine has more than two classes, such as whether a picture contains a car, building, dog, house, doghouse, and so on.

- **Regression:** In regression problems, the machine tries to come up with an approximation based on the data input. For example, you may have an ML program that predicts stock prices. Here, the answer to the question isn't a specific class or category; it's a value in a continuous range of values.

Another way to look at the difference between classification and regression is that with classification the output requires a class label, whereas with regression the output is an approximation or likelihood.

On the other side, unsupervised learning is generally used for clustering.

- **Clustering:** In clustering problems, the machine segregates data with similar traits and moves them into clusters. So you're dividing up your data so that it's grouped based on similarity. The machine decides what goes in or out and often creates clusters that might otherwise be imperceptible to humans.

Figure 9.1 summarizes the types of ML and types of algorithms used in them.

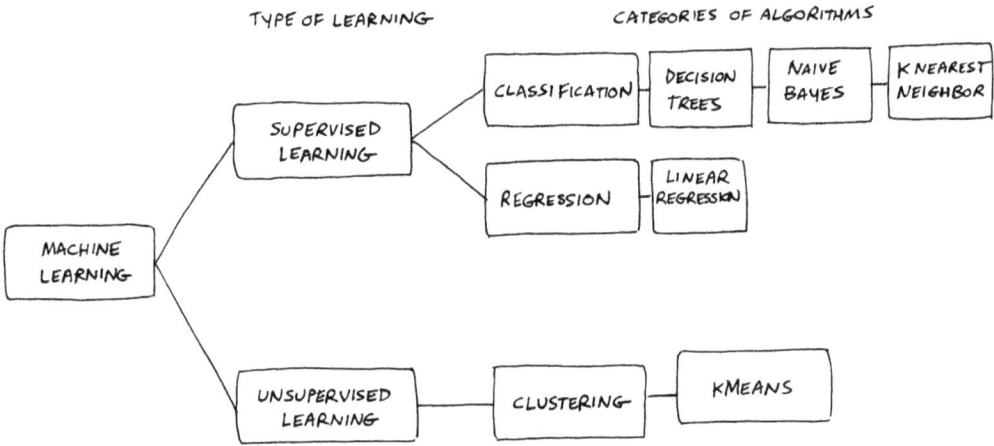

Figure 9.1 Types of machine learning and their respective categories of algorithms

Every ML problem is solved by one or more algorithms. As defined in the previous chapter, an *algorithm* is a set of rules for solving a problem in a fixed number of steps. Common machine learning algorithms include decision trees, *k*-nearest neighbor, *k*-mean clustering, regression analysis, and naïve Bayes, all of which I cover in greater detail later in this chapter. Regardless of the type of problem you're trying to solve, you'll use one or more of these algorithms. The challenge is deciding which ones to use.

Let's start with binary classification, one of the most common ML challenges. With binary classification you have only two possible outcomes (Figure 9.2). Is the hotel room going to be booked next week or not? Will the stock market go up this afternoon or not? Does this picture contain a hot dog or not? Each of these questions has two and only two answers; either this or that. Sometimes the answer is a simple yes or no. To solve a binary classification problem, you typically use decision trees or naïve Bayes.

Figure 9.2 Binary classification

Nearly all binary classification uses supervised learning. You supply training data that defines the two classes, and then you feed the machine test data to enable it to test and fine-tune the model it uses to sort new data input into one class or the other.

With multiclass classification, you have three or more classes, up to an unlimited number (Figure 9.3). For example, you may have an ML program that looks at an image of a food item and classifies it based on several predefined categories, such as meal, drink, or dessert. You would use various statistical algorithms to assign inputs to classes. The most common algorithms for this type of challenge are *k*-nearest neighbor (kNN), naïve Bayes, and decision trees.

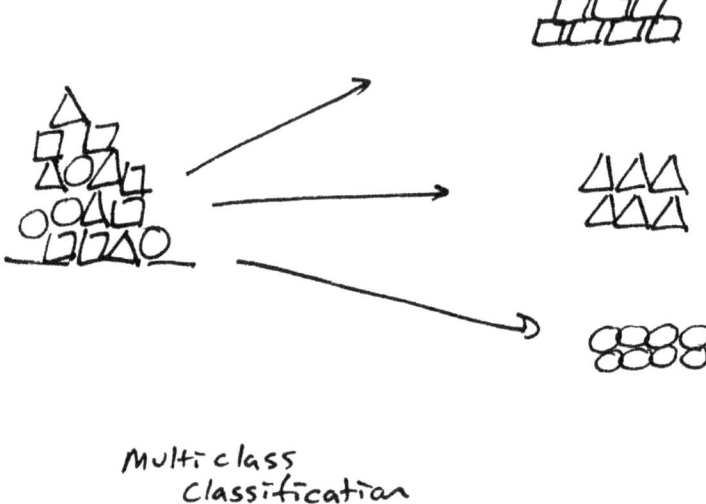

Figure 9.3 Multiclass classification

With regression, you're looking for a value along a continuous range of values (Figure 9.4). For example, although you may use binary classification to predict whether a room in a hotel will be booked or not, the hotel manager may use regression to predict the number of rooms that will be booked on a given day. You have no predefined outcomes or classes. Instead, the answer will be a value in a continuous range of possibilities. You can use statistics to predict the number of rooms that will be booked.

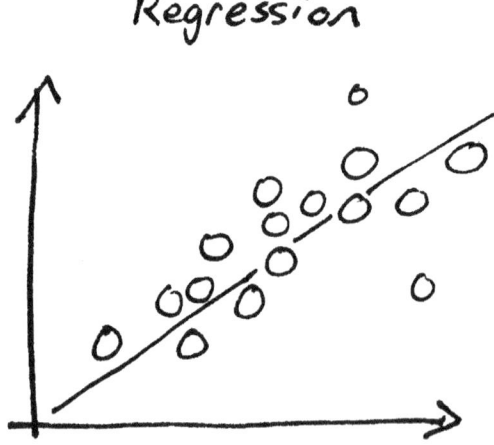

Figure 9.4 A regression with a clear trendline

Like binary classification, regression typically uses a form of supervised learning. With regression, training may come in the form of a trend line on a linear regression diagram. To create such a diagram, the machine plots points on a chart that represent historical data (your training data), such as the number of rooms booked over the past month. The machine then draws a straight line through those points that approximates the average. The linear regression diagram becomes the machine's model. After the machine has its model in place, as you feed it additional data, it fine-tunes the model to make more accurate predictions.

Now that you know the different categories of problems that ML solves, the next step is to review the algorithms that enable machines to solve these problems.

Decision Trees

A *decision tree* is a flow chart for choosing a course of action or drawing a conclusion. It's often used for supervised learning binary classification problems. You can find plenty of graphics programs online for creating decision trees.

With a decision tree, you specify a number of predictors that determine a given outcome. For example, suppose you wanted to create a decision tree to predict whether someone will go to the beach.

The next step would be to create training data based on Joe's choices in the past. You could create a four-column table with the columns labeled Sky, Humidity, Wind, and Joe Goes to the Beach (Figure 9.5). You'd enter data in all four columns—predictors in the first three columns and outcomes in the Joe Goes to the Beach column. You can probably see a correlation in the data just by glancing at it; if the day is sunny, with low humidity and little wind, yes, Joe goes to the beach. If the day is humid and it's raining, regardless of the wind, no, Joe doesn't go to the beach.

You don't need a decision tree to spot the patterns (especially in a small problem domain), but for the sake of this example, let's go ahead and create one (Figure 9.6). To create your decision tree, you might start with Sky, which branches off into three possible conditions: sunny, rainy, or overcast. Each of these then branches off into two conditions: high humidity or low humidity. And each of these then branches off into weak or strong wind. Making a decision is then a simple matter of following the branches of the tree. If the day is sunny, you follow that branch to the next decision point—whether it's a weekday or a weekend. If it's a weekend, then you follow that branch to the next decision point—whether the wind is strong or weak. And at the end of each path is your outcome—yes or no.

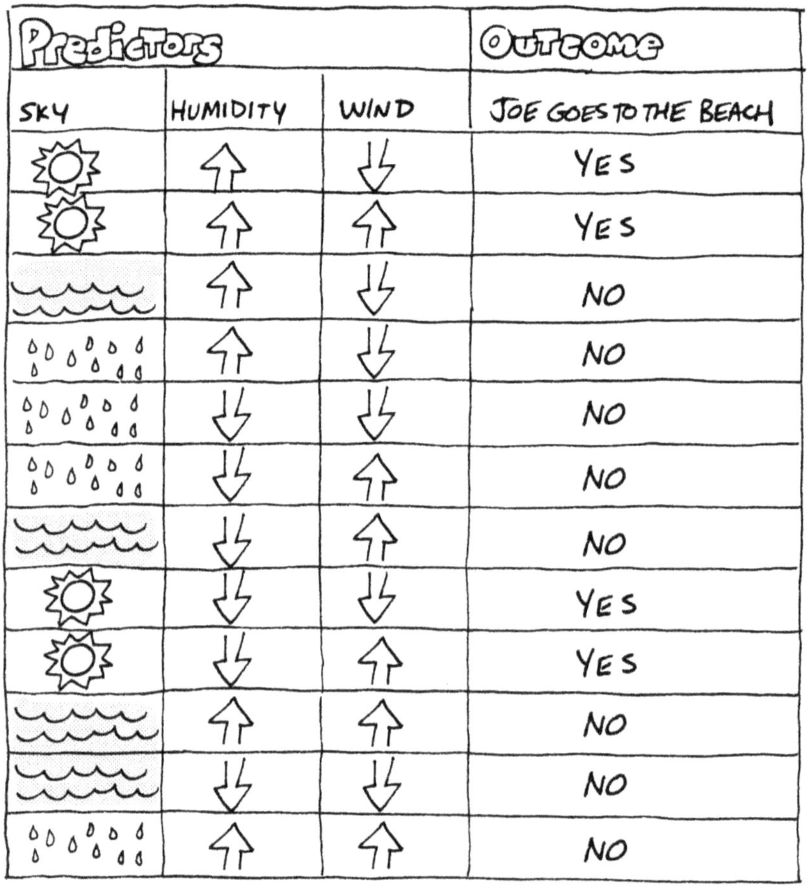

Predictors			Outcome
SKY	HUMIDITY	WIND	JOE GOES TO THE BEACH
☀ (sunny)	↑	↓	YES
☀ (sunny)	↑	↑	YES
～ (cloudy)	↑	↓	NO
💧 (rainy)	↑	↓	NO
💧 (rainy)	↓	↓	NO
💧 (rainy)	↓	↑	NO
～ (cloudy)	↓	↑	NO
☀ (sunny)	↓	↓	YES
☀ (sunny)	↓	↑	YES
～ (cloudy)	↑	↑	NO
～ (cloudy)	↓	↓	NO
💧 (rainy)	↑	↑	NO

Figure 9.5 A four-column table of predictors and outcome

To reduce the complexity of the tree, you can prune some of the branches. For example, if Joe goes to the beach only when the sky is overcast or sunny, you don't need to branch off from rainy to weekend/weekday or strong/weak wind, because Joe already made his decision at this point—no, he won't go to the beach when it's raining.

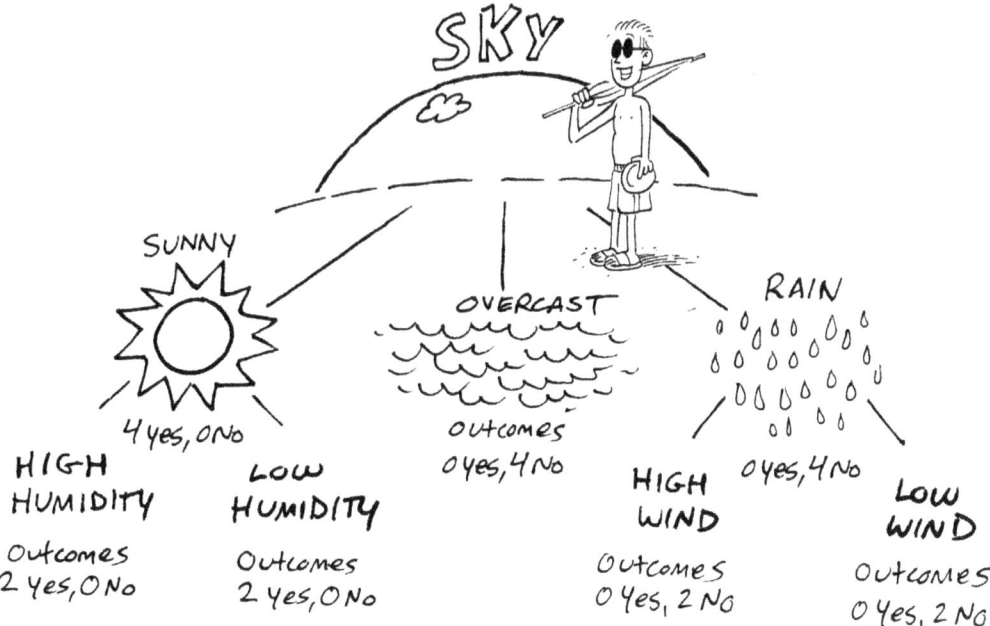

Figure 9.6 Decision tree

When you create a decision tree, you want to have a clear path to a yes or no outcome. If you have trouble getting there, your tree may have too much *entropy*—it's too messy and takes too long to get to a yes or no answer. You can also prune the tree if you see a predictor that doesn't help; for example, if Joe goes to the beach regardless of whether it's windy, then you want to eliminate or replace that predictor.

k-Nearest Neighbor

The *k*-nearest neighbor (*k*NN) algorithm classifies data based on similarities, making it useful for multiclass classification. With *k*-nearest neighbor, you're essentially charting points on a graph that represent known things with certain characteristics. Then you plot a point on the same graph for some new unknown thing and categorize that thing based on the category of its nearest neighbors. The *k* represents the number of nearest neighbors. *k* = 1 means only 1 nearest neighbor. *k* = 2 means two nearest neighbors. The higher the *k* value, the broader the category or class.

Think of it this way: When I was younger I used to work for an animal shelter in downtown Chicago. One of the most difficult jobs was trying to classify the breed of each new dog (Figure 9.7). There are hundreds of different dog breeds, and dogs aren't particular about their partners, so most dogs were a mix of several breeds.

Figure 9.7 A new dog

Every time we got a new dog we would compare it to known breeds. We would consider several characteristics, including the shape of the head, the color, the size and shape of the ears, the body shape and size, how the dog held its tail, and so on. To classify the dog as a certain breed, we were using the equivalent of *k*-nearest neighbor. We wanted to figure out which breed or two breeds the dog was most similar to.

We usually couldn't figure out whether one of a dog's parents was a Boston terrier or a French poodle; we were simply trying to find the closest possible match. We were trying to minimize the distance between the unknown dog and the known breeds. The lesser the difference, the closer the match, the nearest the neighbor.

Minimizing the distance is a key function of *k*-nearest neighbor. The closer the match, the more accurate will be the machine's predictions. The most common way to find the nearest neighbor is through the use of Euclidean distance, which is essentially the shortest distance between two points.

Imagine having millions of dogs to classify based on their breed. To start, you might choose two key characteristics that serve as predictors, say weight and hair length. Suppose you chart your data on a graph with an x- and a y-axis. You chart hair length along the y-axis and weight along the x-axis. You create a training data set based on 1,000 dogs whose breeds you know and chart them based on their weight and hair length. A new dog comes in. You measure its hair length and weigh it and plot a point on your chart for the new dog. Although the point isn't likely to be right on top of one of the existing points, it's close to several neighboring points.

Let's say that for this data set we use $k = 5$. This means that you draw a circle around the points you plotted for your unknown dog and its five closest neighbors (Figure 9.8).

Figure 9.8 Your unknown dog and its five closest neighbors

Now look at the five closest neighbors (Figure 9.9). You can see that three of them are shepherds and two of them are huskies. So you can be somewhat confident to classify your unknown dog as a husky-shepherd mix. If the task is to give one class for the test object, we may have to count the votes obtained for each class of these nearest neighbors and choose the class with the largest number of votes. In this example, the dog may be classified as a shepherd.

Figure 9.9 The five closest neighbors

k-nearest neighbor is a common and powerful ML algorithm because it can do much more than identify a dog's breed. In fact, it's commonly used in finance to find the best stocks and even predict future performance. The downside is that this takes a lot of computation power, so if you're using *k*NN on large data sets, the machine may take a while to deliver its output.

k-Means Clustering

Another common ML algorithm is *k*-means clustering, which is commonly confused with *k*-nearest neighbor (*k*NN). However, whereas *k*-nearest neighbor is a supervised ML algorithm, *k*-means clustering is an unsupervised ML algorithm. Another difference is that the *k* in *k*-nearest neighbor represents the number of nearest neighbors used to classify the unknown item, whereas the *k* in *k*-means clustering represents the number of groups you want the machine to create.

Let's return to the animal shelter in Chicago. The shelter had a large social room where all the dogs could get together and play for an hour each day. The dogs were like people; they had their group of friends that they liked to hang out with. Each time they had a social hour they would self-organize into these different social groups.

Now imagine that the shelter is closing, and all the dogs are going to be distributed into three different shelters across the city. The organizers of the animal shelter meet and decide to cluster the dogs into three social groups based on the dogs' social affiliations. So, $k = 3$.

They pass this information along to the machine that uses *k*-means clustering. To start, the machine puts a different color collar (red, yellow, and blue) on three randomly selected dogs (Figure 9.10). Each collar represents a potential cluster based on the dog's social group. These are the centroid dogs. The dogs enter the social room and join their usual three groups. The machine places the same color collar on the dogs that are closest to each centroid dog.

Figure 9.10 Different collar colors

As you can imagine, because these centroid dogs were selected randomly, chances are pretty good that the machine's clusters aren't accurate. Maybe all three centroid dogs were in the same social group, which would make the machine's clustering useless. Fortunately, the machine hasn't completed its task. It tries over and over again (Figure 9.11), placing the colored collars on different dogs and measuring distances. It might try using one collar at a time.

Figure 9.11 Iterations

At the end of each iteration, the ML algorithm checks the variance between each dog and the centroid. It can use statistics to tell whether the mean distance between the dogs is too high to be a useful cluster. There may be an additional step of reassigning the centroid dog after every iteration to represent a social group more consistently. After it has identified the three centroid dogs, it's pretty straightforward to assign any new dogs to each cluster. If a new dog enters the social room, you can tell which group it joins just by measuring the distance from the centroid dogs.

Keep in mind that the dogs themselves did not cluster into three groups. They may have divided up into five or six different social groups. But with only three shelters available, the ML algorithm must do its best to create clusters that best represent the dog's social grouping. Also note that K-means clustering, in this example, works only because the dogs form social groups. If the dogs jumped from group to group, clustering wouldn't work because there would be a *high overlap of data*.

Another challenge with *k*-means clustering is that it can be highly sensitive to *outliers*—data points that are far distant from the norm. So if a dog is not really interested in hanging out with any of the other dogs, it will still be clustered into one of the three groups.

Now, organizing dogs into three clusters so they can be sent to three different shelters is probably not a problem you'll run into every day. But *k*-means clustering is actually one of the most commonly used ML algorithms.

One of the more interesting applications is when large retailers use clustering to decide whom to invite to their loyalty programs or when to offer promotions. They might create three clusters that they call loyal customers, somewhat loyal customers, and lowest-price shoppers (Figure 9.12). Then they could create strategies to try to elevate somewhat loyal customers to loyal customers. Or they could just invite their loyal customers to participate in their loyalty program.

Other companies use clustering to decide where to place new stores. So if you were selling athletic footwear, you might look for places that have the highest concentration of active runners.

Note that *k*-means clustering and *k*-nearest neighbor are both instance-based learning (lazy learning) algorithms. You pump all your data into them, and they find the answer in one big instance.

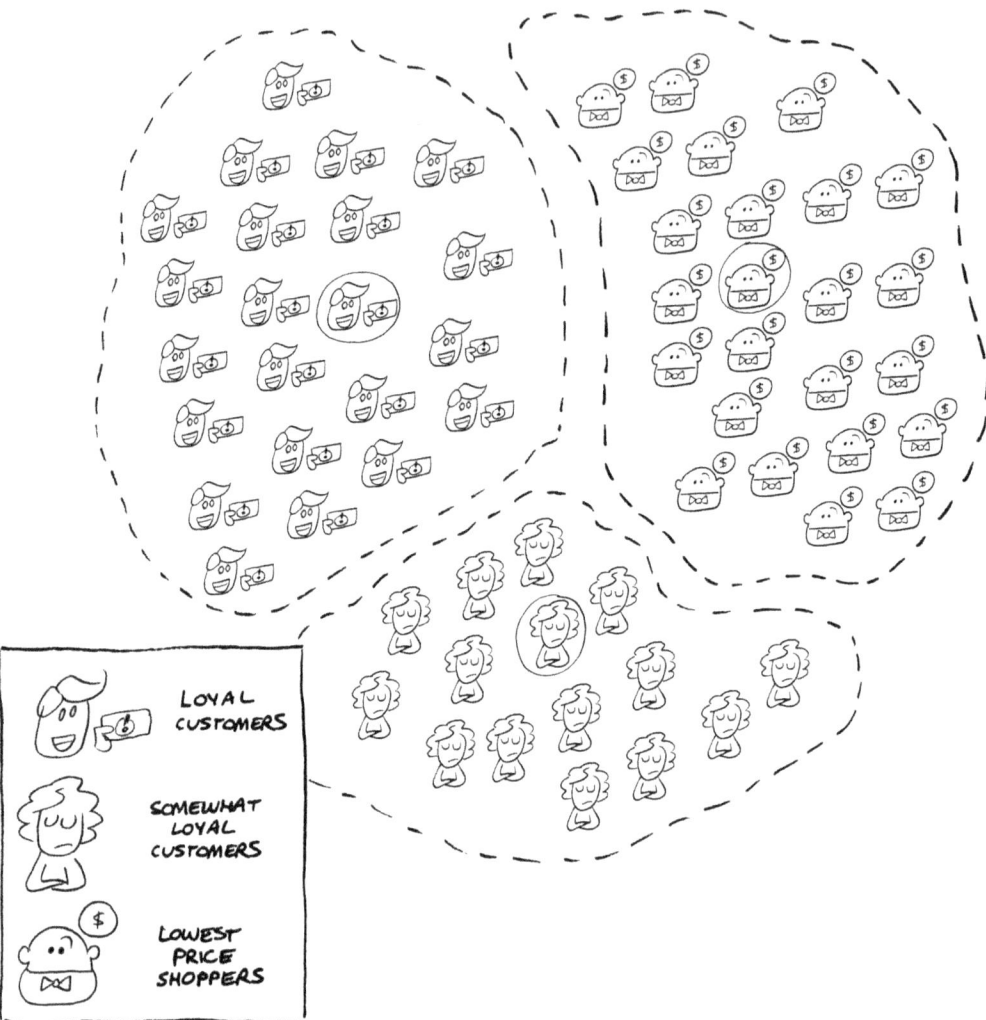

Figure 9.12 Customer clusters

Regression Analysis

Regression analysis looks at the relationship between predictors and outcomes to make predictions of future outcomes. (Predictors are also referred to as *input variables*, *independent variables*, or even *regressors*.) With ML, you feed the machine training data that contains a small collection of predictors and their associated known outcomes, and the machine develops a model that describes the relationship between predictors and outcomes.

After the machine develops its model, you feed test data into the machine, and it uses its model to try to predict the outcomes based on the new predictors you presented it. The machine tries repeatedly to predict the outcomes, all the while fine-tuning its model until it arrives at the most accurate predictions. This approach is a type of supervised learning.

After the machine has a model that's fairly good at making predictions, whenever you feed the machine a predictor, it can tell you the likely outcome.

Linear regression is one of the most common types of ML regression algorithms. With linear regression you want to create a straight line that shows the relationship between predictors and outcomes. Ideally, you want to see all your different data points closely gathered around a straight line, but not necessarily touching the line or on the line.

Let's look at how this might work. Suppose you're an owner of an ice cream shop. Over the past year you've collected sales data. You then purchase weather data from your local weather station. Using the data, you create a scatterplot chart with an x- and a y-axis. Along the x-axis you list daily sales, and along the y-axis, you add a temperature scale from 60°F to 110°F. You plot data points on the chart such that each point represents the high temperature of the day and the total sales on that day. You draw a straight line through that collection of points that approximates the pattern those points form (Figure 9.13). Such a line is often referred to as a *trendline*.

You can see a clear trendline in this scatterplot diagram. The higher the temperature, the greater the ice cream sales. You can also see a few outliers—data points that are far away from the trendline. This could be due to a local festival or because someone had scheduled a birthday gathering at the shop that day. Having several outliers makes it much more difficult to predict ice cream sales.

This example has many outliers, so you can use linear regression to try to predict your daily sales. So let's look at a point in the scatterplot. Suppose the weather forecast predicts a high temperature of about 95°F all week. You can look at the trendline to find the corresponding ice cream sales and see that you can expect to sell around $3,500.

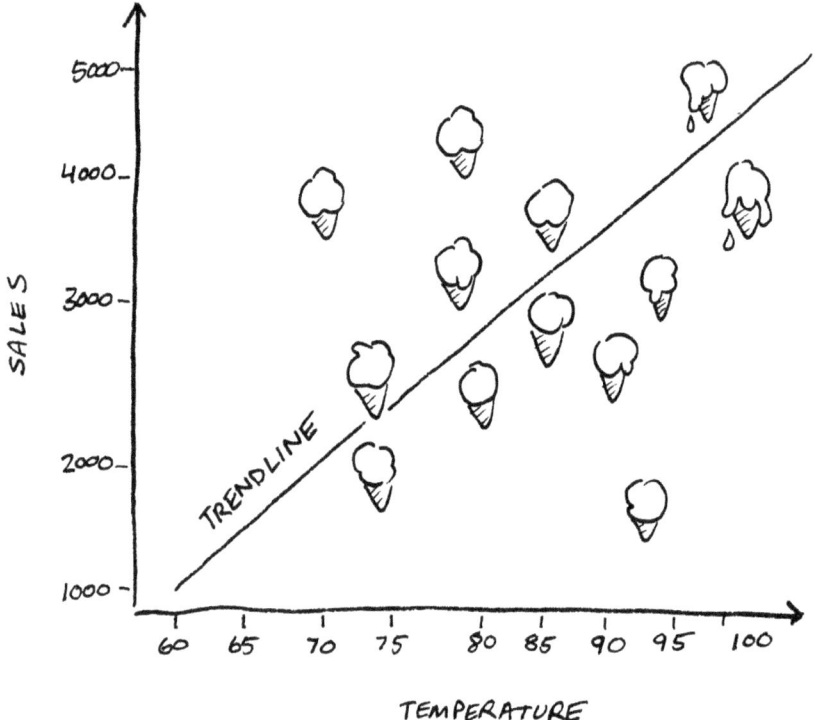

Figure 9.13 Ice cream sales follow a trendline

If you're thinking about using regression, keep in mind that the more data you have, the more accurate the trendline and the more precise your predictions will be.

One interesting thing about linear regression is that there's some debate about whether it's actually ML because the machine is not actually learning anything new about the data. It's just using the data to create a standard statistical model. It's less about learning and more about predicting.

Either way, regression is a popular way to try to accurately predict future outcomes or behaviors. The key is to find the right predictors and to look for some type of linear connection with the outcome.

Näive Bayes

Näive Bayes is considerably different from the ML algorithms covered so far. Instead of trying to find patterns among predictors, näive Bayes uses conditional probability to determine the likelihood of something belonging to a certain class based on each predictor independent of the others. It's called naïve because it naïvely assumes that the predictors aren't related. Even though it takes a different approach from the algorithms presented earlier in this chapter, naïve Bayes is used primarily for binary or multiclass classification problems.

Let's return to the animal shelter in Chicago. Imagine that we want to classify all the dogs in the shelter based on their different breeds. Remember that there are hundreds of different dog breeds and that most dogs in the shelter are mixed breeds.

With a naïve Bayes ML algorithm, you might create three classes of dog breeds: terrier, hound, and sport dogs (Figure 9.14).

Figure 9.14 Classes of dog breeds

Each class has three predictors—hair length, height, and weight. Height and weight are closely related because a tall dog is likely to be heavier than a short dog. However, naïve Bayes considers each of these predictors independently. That's why it's called naïve.

Once you have the classes and predictors, the naïve Bayes ML algorithm starts to do something called *class predictor probability*. For each predictor, it determines the probability of a dog belonging to a certain class. For example, the algorithm first checks the dog's hair length and determines that there's a 30% chance the dog is a terrier, a 50% chance it's a hound, and a 20% chance it's a sport dog. Then it checks the dog's height and determines that there's a 40% chance the dog is a terrier, a 20% chance it's a hound, and a 40% chance it's a sport dog. Finally, it checks the dog's weight and figures that there's a 30% chance that the dog is a terrier, a 25% chance that it's a hound, and a 45% chance that it's a sport dog.

So now you have this table with the class predictor probability for this unclassified dog. If you look at the table, you can tell that the dog is probably a sport dog, but let's not be that naïve. With most classification problems, some predictors may have more predictive value than others, so you can assign relative weights to the predictors. For example, you may assign a weight of 3 for hair and 2 for height and weight.

For the weighted multiplication function, take each predictor, multiply it by the weight you assigned to that predictor, and then total the numbers: Likelihood of class = Sum (Predictor × Weight). For the unclassified dog in the example, we'd have three equations:

Likelihood of terrier = (.30 × 3) + (.40 × 2) + (.30 × 2) = 2.3
Likelihood of hound = (.50 × 3) + (.20 × 2) + (.25 × 2) = 2.4
Likelihood of sport dog = (.50 × 3) + (.70 × 2) + (.85 × 2) = 2.3

When you add up the weighted predictors for hair length, height, and weight, you can see that this unclassified dog is most likely a hound. It's less likely that it's a terrier or a sport dog.

The preceding formulation works well when all three classes are equally likely. That is, you expect to observe the terrier, hound, and sport dog with 33.33% chance (or 0.33 probability). This is called *prior probability*, which is our belief in observing a class of objects before we observe them. The goal of naïve Bayes classifier is to find the *posterior probability*, which is the probability of a particular class given the observations. Mathematically, it is proportional to the multiplication of prior probability of the class and likelihood that a test sample belongs to a class. In our example, we can ask about the posterior probability of a dog being a terrier, given a test sample. We calculate the posterior probability for each class, given a test sample, and the one with maximum value is assigned the class. If the posterior probabilities are equally likely, only computing likelihood is sufficient because probabilities do not change order if they're multiplied by constant values.

However, there is no reason that prior probabilities for different classes should be equally likely. For example, the sport dog is more commonly in a particular geographic region, where this study is being conducted. Therefore, there's a greater chance of picking up a sport dog than other breeds. The prior probabilities of the terrier, hound, and sport dog may be, say 0.25, 0.25, and 0.5. You then have to multiply those numbers with their likelihood to get the proportional posterior probabilities and classify the objects accordingly.

Chapter Takeaways

- Machine learning is good at solving two types of problems: classification and regression.
- With classification problems, the output requires a class label, whereas with regression problems, the output is an approximation or likelihood.
- A *decision tree* is a flow chart for choosing a course of action or drawing a conclusion.
- *k-nearest neighbor* is an algorithm that classifies data based on similarities, making it useful for multiclass classification.
- *k-means clustering* is an algorithm that groups data points into any number of clusters you specify as the *k* value.
- *Regression analysis* looks at the relationship between predictors and outcomes to make predictions of future outcomes.
- *Näive Bayes* uses conditional probability to determine the likelihood of something belonging to a certain class based on each predictor independent of the others.

10

Applying Machine Learning Algorithms

In this chapter:

- Understanding the bias-variance trade-off
- Building a model that fits your data
- Understanding the concepts of underfitting and overfitting
- Choosing the right algorithm(s) for the job

In the movie *All the President's Men,* the top informant of the Watergate scandal, code-named Deep Throat, met with *Washington Post* reporter Bob Woodward in a dark parking garage and told him to "follow the money." Only by following the money could the reporter find the truth. I'm reminded of the phrase when I think about machine learning (ML) algorithms. Except instead of following the money you must "follow the data" (Figure 10.1).

Unfortunately, that's easier said than done. In fact, one of the biggest challenges in ML is figuring out whether the model the machine created has bias or variance as it relates to the data. The question is whether the model the machine created is a good fit for the data.

Bias is an error that results when a model is too simple for the complexity of the data. *Variance* is an error that results when a model is too complex for the simplicity of the data. If the model has a high bias, predictions based on that model will be consistently wrong. If the model has high variance, predictions will be inconsistent. Creating a model that produces accurate results is a trade-off commonly referred to as the *bias-variance trade-off* or *bias-variance dilemma*. A model will always have some bias and some variance; you just want them to balance.

Figure 10.1 Machine learning's version of "follow the money"

Here's an example of bias and variance in action: A few months ago I went with my wife and son to visit his summer camp. Over the course of a long weekend the camp's staff tries to give the parents a taste of the camper's experience. On the very first morning, our guide took us to the archery range to show us how to shoot a bow and arrow.

The instructor gave each one of us a bow and five arrows. He showed us how to shoot the target and let loose his five arrows, which landed in the center of the target. His aim was a very good example of low bias and low variance. All five of his arrows landed tightly in the center of the bull's-eye.

My wife was the second person to try (Figure 10.2). She shot her five arrows, each of which struck the target with a satisfying thwack, and although only one arrow hit the bull's-eye, the other four landed fairly close. Her aim was a good example of low bias and high variance; all the arrows hit the target (low bias), but they were scattered (high variance).

Figure 10.2 My wife had never shot an arrow before but seemed to have a knack for it.

I was the third archer. I had gone to summer camp myself, so I knew a little bit about how to shoot a bow and arrow. Unfortunately, I wasn't wearing my glasses, so I couldn't really see the target. I shot my five arrows, but my aim had a high bias and low variance. All my arrows were concentrated in the upper-right corner of the target. I'd shot the arrows consistently, but I was consistently off-target.

My son was last. He had a difficult time pulling back on the bow. A couple of his arrows hit the corner of the target, one hit a tree behind the target, and two stuck in the dirt just in front of the target. His aim was an example of high bias and high variance. He inconsistently overshot or undershot the mark.

Figure 10.3 summarizes the combinations of bias and variability.

In ML, you encounter the same challenge. You can choose an algorithm and data and feed it to the machine, and the machine's classifications or predictions can consistently hit the target with little variability, like the archery instructor; be right on track but a little off, like my wife's aim; be consistently off track, like my aim; or be consistently off track and all over the place like my son's aim. However, with some adjustments, we could all improve our aim. My son's aim would require the most adjustment, my aim would require less, and my wife's aim would require very little.

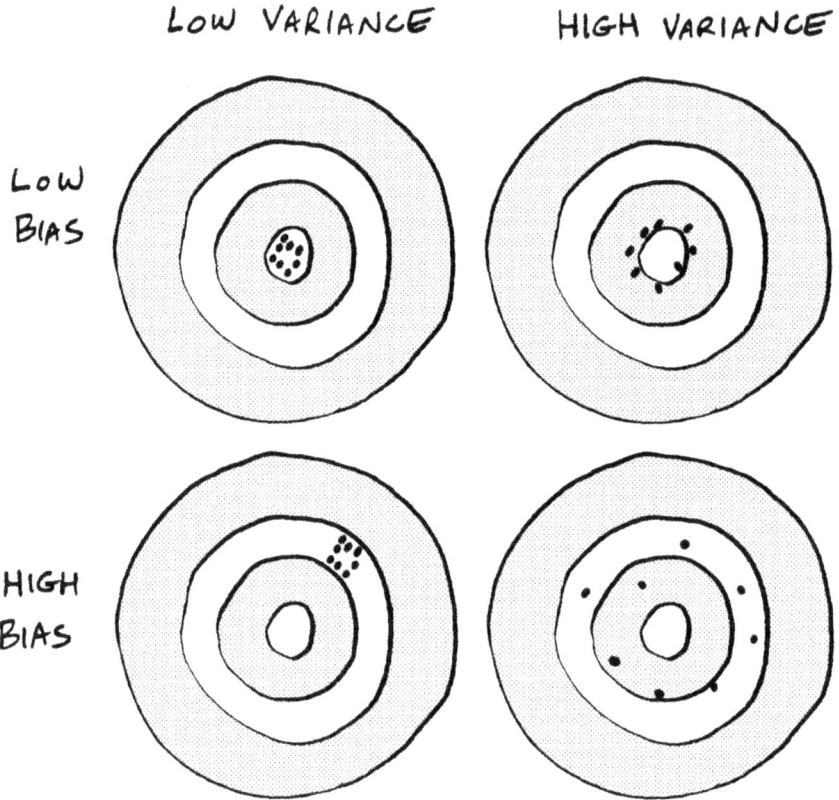

Figure 10.3 Bias and variance

Bias and variance are ways of measuring the difference between the prediction and the actual outcome. Data and algorithms are like dials you can turn to reduce bias and variance, thus improving the accuracy of the predictions. You use different techniques based on whether you have too much bias or too much variance. In the case of our archery analogy, all I needed to do was adjust my aim a little down and to the left. My wife just needed a little more practice to refine her aim. My son needed both training and practice. In the same way, when you're preparing a machine to learn, you need to provide it with the right algorithms and a sufficient amount of quality data. If the machine's predictions or classifications don't hit the target consistently, you need to adjust the dials to reduce bias or variance.

Fitting the Model to Your Data

In ML, making better predictions is a matter of *fitting the model to the data*. The machine needs to develop a model that consistently and accurately predicts outcomes based on the data you feed it. Fitting the model to the data is just as it sounds. The machine isn't pulling a suit off the rack. It tailors the model by making adjustments.

ML algorithms are the tools you use to create your model, but these algorithms aren't off-the-rack suits. You need to tailor the hyperparameters for your specific use. For example, in the previous chapter's discussion of the naïve Bayes algorithm, I explained how to give different weights to the predictors. This fine-tuning of hyperparameters is a big part of what data scientists do. They run experiments on small data sets, analyze the results, and tweak the hyperparameters to get more accurate results.

Poor performance of a model can often be attributed to underfitting or overfitting. With *underfitting*, a simple model enables the machine to learn faster but lacks precision. Underfitting results in high bias. With *overfitting*, the model tries too hard to account for all the data and thus is overly sensitive to small variations in the training data. Overfitting results in high variance.

Let's look at underfitting and overfitting in a real-world example. Imagine you work for a website like Zillow that estimates home values based on the values of comparable homes. To do this you create four main predictors: square footage, location, number of bathrooms, and number of bedrooms. You can use supervised learning and regression to create trend lines to predict the value.

Unfortunately, the model the machine creates isn't very accurate at estimating prices. You look at the data and notice that it has a lot of variance (noise). Houses in the same neighborhood with the same square footage and the same number of bathrooms and bedrooms have very different prices. To help the machine fine tune its model, you add complexity. Maybe you create new predictors such as nice view, modern kitchen, and walkable neighborhood. As you add predictors, the machine makes the model more flexible, but also more complex and difficult to manage. The machine will have more difficulty identifying relationships between all the predictors. By adding predictors, you run the risk of overfitting the machine's model to the data.

To avoid overfitting, you decide to try a different approach. To keep things simple, you create a basic regression chart that shows the relationship between the location of a house, its square footage, and its price. Your chart shows that big houses in nice areas are more expensive. This model benefits from being intuitive. You would think that a big house in a nice area is more expensive than a small house in a rundown neighborhood. It would also be easy to visualize.

Unfortunately, this model isn't very flexible. A big house could be poorly maintained. It might have a lousy floor plan or be built on a floodplain. These factors would affect the home's value, but they wouldn't be considered in the model. In a sense, the model would have a low variance but a high bias. This model would suffer from underfitting. Because it's not accounting for enough data, it's likely to make inaccurate predictions.

To avoid underfitting and overfitting, you want to capture more signal and less noise. *Signal* is the collective term used to describe predictors that drive accurate predictions and classifications. Noise is irrelevant data or randomness in a data set that reduces the accuracy of predictions or classifications.

Choosing Algorithms

Your choice of algorithm depends on what you want the algorithm to do:

- **Decision:** If you want the machine to make a decision, choose the best course of action, or draw a conclusion based on the evidence provided, a decision tree algorithm is probably the best choice.
- **Classification and Clustering:** If you want the machine to classify, categorize, or group, you'll want to consider a classification algorithm, such as k-nearest neighbor, k-means clustering (for grouping), and naïve Bayes.
- **Prediction/Estimation:** If you want the machine to predict a value in a continuous range of values, a regression algorithm is best.

When choosing an algorithm, you can try a more empirical (experimental) approach. After narrowing your choice to two or more algorithms, you can train and test the machine using each of them with the data you have and see which algorithm delivers the most accurate results. For example, if you're looking at a classification problem, you can run your training data on k-nearest neighbor and naïve Bayes and then run your test data through each of them to see which one is best able to accurately predict which class a particular unclassified entity belongs to.

Ensemble Modeling

You can also try *ensemble modeling*. The ensemble modeling can be done in different ways. One option is to combine the outcomes of two or more algorithms. Another option is to create different data samples, feed each data sample to an ML algorithm, and then combine the two outputs to make a final decision. There are three approaches to ensemble modeling:

- **Bagging:** You create two or more data sets, such as by taking two random samples (Figure 10.4). Then you feed each data set to a classifier algorithm, say a decision tree algorithm. The result is that the machine creates two different decision trees based on variants of the same data. Given a test sample, these decision trees may give different outputs. The machine can then combine those outputs to make a final decision. A common way to combine these outputs is by *majority voting*, or taking the average of different decisions. The bagging approach on decision tree will result in reduction of variance, which in turn can improve the overall performance compared to using a single tree.
- **Boosting:** In boosting, an ML classifier focuses on the data objects that are difficult to classify correctly and gives them high weights or importance (Figure 10.5). The process runs iteratively and learns different classifiers by reweighting the data such that the newer classifiers focus more on the data objects that previous ones misclassified. Boosting also results in reduction of variance, but it can be sensitive to outliers.
- **Stacking:** You use two or more different ML algorithms (or different versions of an algorithm) and combine their outcomes using another meta-learner to improve the classification performance (Figure 10.6). The team that won the Netflix prize used a form of stacking called *feature-weighted linear stacking*. They created several different predictive models and then stacked them on top of each other. So you could stack k-nearest neighbor on top of naïve Bayes. Each one might add just .01% more accuracy, but over time a small increase in

accuracy can result in significant improvement. Some winners of this ML competition stacked 30 algorithms or more.

Figure 10.4 Bagging

Figure 10.5 Boosting

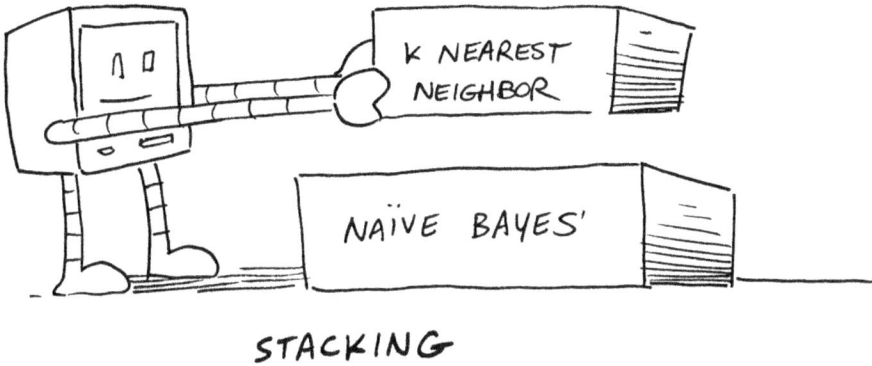

Figure 10.6 Stacking

Think of each ML algorithm as a tool. You can experiment to find the best one or combine tools to improve accuracy.

Deciding on a Machine Learning Approach

Another decision you need to make is the ML style you want to use. To make this decision, you need to follow the data:

- **Supervised:** If your data is clearly and consistently labeled, supervised learning is best. You feed the machine predictors and outcomes, and it identifies the relationship between the two.
- **Unsupervised:** If you have massive amounts of unlabeled data, unsupervised learning may be your only choice. You feed whatever data you have in whatever form it's in, and the machine figures out how it's related. Then it's up to you to determine why the machine categorized or grouped items as it did.
- **Semi-supervised:** If you have some labeled data and a lot of unlabeled data, semi-supervised learning is the right approach.

Chapter Takeaways

- *Bias* is an error that results when the model is too simple for the complexity of the data; underfitting a model increases its bias.
- *Variance* is an error that results when the model is too complex for the simplicity of the data; overfitting a model increases its variance.
- By fitting a model to the data, the machine creates a healthy balance between bias and variance, which results in more accurate predictions or classifications.
- To enable a machine to fit a model to the data, you must choose the right algorithm(s).
- A decision-tree algorithm is great for when you need the machine to make a decision, choose the best course of action, or draw a conclusion based on the evidence provided.
- A classification algorithm is best when you need the machine to classify, categorize, or group items based on their characteristics.
- A regression algorithm is best for having a machine predict a value in a continuous range of values.
- You can use two or more algorithms via ensemble modeling to enable a machine to create a more accurate model.

11

Words of Advice

In this chapter:

- Embracing and encouraging an exploratory mindset
- Recognizing the importance of keeping your training and test data separate
- Managing expectations
- Knowing your tools—algorithms

Machine learning (ML) poses plenty of technical and organizational challenges. You need to ask the right questions, gather quality data, pick the right algorithm(s), adjust your algorithm(s), and often find the meaning in whatever outcome the machine delivers.

In this chapter, I offer a few tips that will help you and your organization overcome these challenges and start your ML program on the right path.

Start Asking Questions

Organizations often want to start reaping the benefits of ML, but they have little to no idea of what they want to accomplish. They don't have specific problems they want it to solve, questions they want it to answer, or insights they hope to gain. They launch an ML initiative and hire people with the requisite technical expertise, who then spend their time playing with the technology because nobody in the organization can tell them how to apply it. Nobody has taken the time to connect the organization's business needs to the ML technology.

To avoid this common mistake, the first step you should take is to educate everyone in the organization about ML and encourage them to start asking questions. Instruct them to look for problems they need to solve, questions they need to answer, or insights that would be helpful for improving the organization or for doing their jobs. Create a list of problems, questions, and desired insights; prioritize the items on the list; and then consider which technology would be the most effective for addressing each item. Keep in mind that the best technology isn't necessarily ML.

I once worked for an organization that wanted to make a large investment in ML. They hired a half a dozen ML experts from a local university. This team immediately got to work setting up the technology infrastructure they needed to work with large data sets. Once that was all set up they started to ask people, "What questions do you need answered?" "What problems do you need to solve?" "What insights gained would help drive business?"

The newly hired ML experts were fresh out of graduate school, so they were used to running small data experiments and learning from the results. What the organization lacked was leadership that was experienced in asking good questions and identifying problems and potential opportunities. When they did ask a question, it was something like, "What type of promotions do our customers like?" Yet that was something that could be solved with traditional database tools.

The members of the ML team felt as though they had built a Formula One race car and were being forced to show everyone how to parallel park it.

Of course, questions, problems, and desired insights vary depending on the organization, but here are a few sample questions to get you thinking:

- What have we learned?
- Is what we're doing working?
- Are we collecting the right data?
- What does the data tell us about our customer?
- What data do we need to make more accurate predictions?

Don't Mix Training Data with Test Data

A key to improving the performance and accuracy of a model is to never mix training data with test data. As explained in Chapter 7, "What Is Machine Learning?", training data is a data set that helps the machine figure out the relationships between inputs and outputs. Test data is a data set that gauges the machine's ability to make accurate predictions of outcomes based on unknown inputs. If, after training the machine, you add your training data into your test data, you won't have a clear picture of how well the machine performed on the test. It would be like giving students a sheet of paper with some of the test questions and their correct answers just before they take the test. The test results wouldn't accurately represent what they had learned or where they were struggling.

It's tempting to mix training data with test data, especially if you have only a small amount of test data. You might think you'll get better results if your test data set were larger, so you add the training data to it. Resist the temptation. Keep your training data and test data separate. When you run your test, you want the machine to look at unfamiliar data.

Don't Overstate a Model's Accuracy

After training a machine, many people get caught up in a wave of enthusiasm because they finally taught a machine how to do something useful. Now they want to announce their accomplishment to the world, or at least to their organization. They schedule a presentation and, using the test data, they demonstrate the power and precision of their new ML model.

Big mistake!

Prior to running a large test data set through a model, you don't have any idea of how powerful or precise the model will be. If you announce success prior to testing, you may dazzle the crowd, but you're setting them up for disappointment. Later, if they use the model and it misses the mark, you'll suffer the consequences.

You can avoid the potential embarrassment by running a new model on test data first, so the machine can adjust the model, if necessary, to improve its accuracy. You may need to go through several rounds of testing and adjustment. If you just can't wait to reveal your machine's amazing new model, at least demonstrate it using test data. If the model is off the mark, your managers and the rest of the organization will have a realistic view of its accuracy.

Know Your Algorithms

If data is the fuel that drives ML, algorithms are the engine. To create high-performance models, you need to choose the right engine. In this book, I cover only a few algorithms and classes of algorithms, and not in great depth. To achieve success in ML, you must become more familiar with different ML algorithms, so you can choose the right algorithm(s) for the job.

Keep in mind that you may need to use two or more different algorithms to produce the results you want. For example, if you're looking at a classification problem, you can use a decision tree or *k*-nearest neighbor. You can even stack them to try to improve the accuracy of the classifications. You may prefer one algorithm over another, and that's okay. Some algorithms may seem more intuitive than others. Algorithms can be like old songs that bring back pleasant memories.

Although it's good practice to become familiar with a broad range of algorithms, you don't need to use the latest, greatest algorithms. Sometimes you can get more work done with your favorite tool than with the newest tool.

Chapter Takeaways

- Before you launch a machine learning initiative, identify questions you want to answer, problems you need to solve, or insights you'd like to gain.
- Don't mix training data with test data; doing so reduces the validity of predictions and classifications.
- Avoid overstating a model's accuracy. Test the model with a large data set prior to unveiling it to your organization.
- Become familiar with algorithms; they are the engines that drive ML. Data is the fuel.

Part III
Artificial Neural Networks

12 What Are Artificial Neural Networks? 131

13 Artificial Neural Networks in Action 143

14 Letting Your Network Learn 155

15 Using Neural Networks to Classify or Cluster 169

16 Key Challenges 175

12

What Are Artificial Neural Networks?

In this chapter:

- Grasping the basics of artificial neural networks
- Taking a close look at an individual neuron—the perceptron
- Enabling machines to make decisions
- Getting a machine to identify complex patterns

In a sense, an *artificial neural network* is inspired by the human brain. The keyword here is *inspired*, the same way a paper airplane is *inspired* by a supersonic jet. Whereas the brain is composed of physical entities called *neurons*, an artificial neural network is composed of *nodes*. Each node accepts and combines weighted input, adds bias (an adjustment), and performs a function on the result to produce an output. That output can then be transferred to other nodes for additional processing.

Artificial neural networks enhance a machine's ability to learn by layering nodes similarly to how neurons are layered in the human brain, so that each node can connect with many other nodes in the network. In an artificial neural network, nodes are arranged in three layers: input, hidden, and output (Figure 12.1). Signals pass through the network from the input layer, through the hidden layer, to the output layer. The hidden layer, which may comprise one or numerous layers, does the heavy lifting—it performs the complex calculations. It's called *hidden* because you don't see it doing its job. All you see are the data you feed into the machine at the input layer and the results the machine delivers at the output layer.

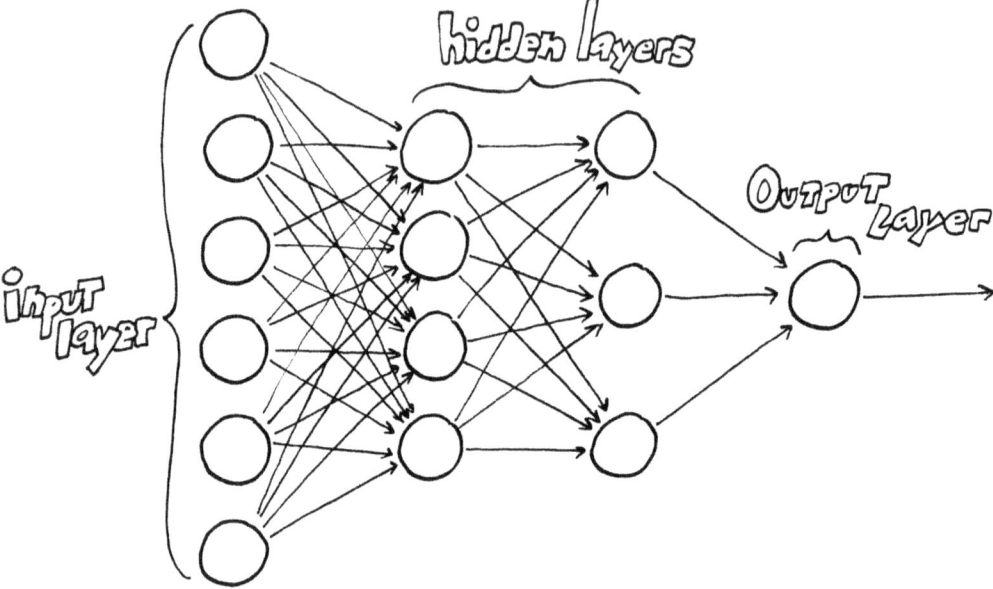

Figure 12.1 A neural network is made up of input, hidden, and output layers

The connections between nodes are weighted to establish their relative strengths. With weighted connections, a node receiving input from two or more nodes can determine which inputs to pay more attention to. It can accept or reject an input or use their weighted average when performing its function.

After receiving and aggregating the weighted input, the neuron can add *bias*—a positive or negative value added to the sum of the inputs that can increase or decrease the value of the output.

Weighted connections and bias enable an artificial neural network to learn. Just as your brain's neurons strengthen connections as you learn, the nodes in a neural network adjust the strength of their connections to improve the network's ability to produce accurate output. For example, if you're using supervised learning to train an artificial neural network, you may feed known inputs into it (labels and the objects those labels refer to), so it can identify the relationship between those labels and objects. This relationship is learned by minimizing the difference between the actual and the predicted labels, which is also called *error*. When a training sample is fed to a neural network, it calculates the outputs (classifying the objects) to the best of its ability. If its outputs are off target, the error is fed back through the neural network, so the nodes can adjust the strength of their connections (the weights) and the bias and try again. This feedback and adjustment process occurs over and over, between and within the nodes, until the artificial neural network generates sufficiently accurate outputs.

Why the Brain Analogy?

There's a good reason why computer scientists were inspired by biological neurons. The human brain is extremely efficient at classification. Using your brain, you can quickly distinguish different handwriting styles, ethnic foods, and species of animals. You probably have no trouble understanding the words you hear even if someone has a strong accent or tends to mumble.

In a sense you're so good at finding these patterns that it's hard to imagine how a machine could possibly do it. What's simple and second nature to you is extremely difficult for even the most advanced computer systems. The advantage that machines have is that they can process massive volumes of data in a fraction of the time. Artificial neural networks are about taking what we do easily and upsizing it to harness the scalability of modern computers. With this power, a machine can classify images on a massive scale, translate languages, and even transcribe audio files into text files quickly and fairly accurately.

Just Another Amazing Algorithm

An artificial neural network is just another machine learning (ML) algorithm. (See Chapter 9, "Popular Machine Learning Algorithms," for descriptions of commonly used ML algorithms.) As with other ML algorithms, an artificial neural network is most effective with large data sets. The more quality data it has, the more accurately it can predict outputs. And like other ML algorithms, the machine can learn through any of the following approaches:

- **Supervised learning:** You use a small training data set to show the machine the relationship between labels and objects, you feed the machine a larger and unfamiliar collection of objects to assess its accuracy at classifying the objects, and then you tweak the model to improve its accuracy.

- **Unsupervised learning:** You feed large data sets of unlabeled data into the machine to have the machine identify patterns in the data that you can then examine to extract insights.
- **Semi-supervised learning:** You feed the machine both labeled and unlabeled data, relying on the machine to identify patterns in the different data types, and then use that data to make classifications or predictions.
- **Reinforcement learning:** You give the machine a task to perform and then reward improvements in performance.

Having a machine learn to perform complex tasks faster and more accurately than humans has the potential to significantly improve productivity while enabling an organization to focus on strategy and operations. With ML on artificial neural networks, you can analyze massive volumes of data from social media to develop new product ideas. Doctors can use a computer to analyze x-rays and identify patterns that indicate early signs of certain types of cancer. You can analyze data from customer communications and identify patterns that point to product defects or shortcomings in customer service. The potential applications are endless. Modern neural networks even can exceed our skills at performing characteristically human tasks, such as translation, transcription, and even driving a car.

When you're working with artificial neural networks, keep the following key points in mind:

- You need massive amounts of high-quality data to take full advantage of artificial neural networks. If you don't deliver the data, the machine won't be able to fine-tune the connections between its nodes. It won't learn anything.
- Take a more empirical approach with artificial neural networks than with other ML algorithms. Run several small experiments and make adjustments to improve results. Modern neural networks give you plenty of opportunity to change your configurations.

Later in this chapter you'll see just how many dials can be turned and numbers can be changed to optimize the performance of neural networks. Who or what turns these dials? You can make adjustments, but it's usually the machine turning the dials (with weights and bias). You can try various functions and different statistical methods. Sometimes you may be making adjustments without really knowing how they'll affect performance. You can just try various adjustments to see what works best. Likewise, the machine makes adjustments, weakening or strengthening the connections between nodes, using trial and error as guidance.

This empirical (experimental) approach makes neural networks an exciting area in ML. Experts and teams are constantly experimenting with different techniques, publishing their results, and encouraging others to experiment. You can try these techniques on your own artificial neural networks or use them as inspiration to create your own amazing algorithms.

Getting to Know the Perceptron

Artificial neural networks got their start in the 1950s when Professor Frank Rosenblatt developed the first *perceptron*—essentially a single node (a building block) in an artificial neural network. The perceptron acts like a tiny machine for making decisions. It takes several inputs, multiplies them with their corresponding weights, totals them, and performs a mathematical function on the result to produce an output (Figure 12.2).

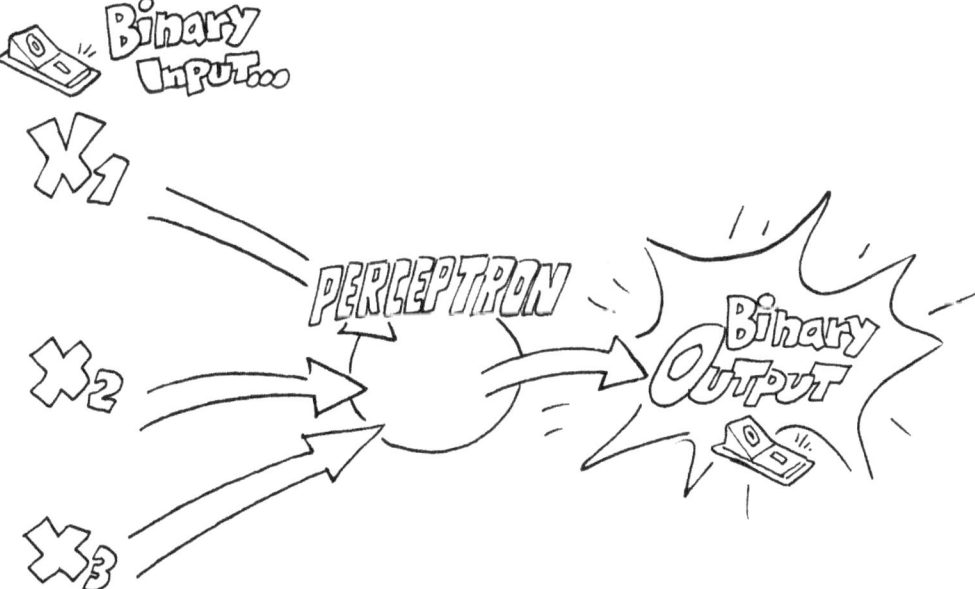

Figure 12.2 A perceptron

Imagine a perceptron as a small circle. Entering that circle are three inputs, each shown as an arrow. Let's call our inputs x1, x2, and x3. Out of that perceptron you have one output, again shown as an arrow. Because all arrows are pointing in the same direction, this is a *feedforward* perceptron.

So let's use this perceptron to make a decision. I love tacos and typically consider three factors to determine whether I'm going to eat a taco at a certain restaurant. My three inputs are as follows:

x1 is whether the restaurant is clean.

x2 is whether there is a Spanish version of the menu, because a Spanish version of the menu usually indicates that the restaurant serves traditional food.

x3 is whether there is a sombrero on the wall because in my years of travel I've found that a sombrero on the wall usually means it's a bad Mexican restaurant.

Now I'll assign binary values to each of these inputs. While binary values are usually 0 and 1, they can be something else, such as 1 and −1. I'll use 1 and −1, so when I multiply input values by the weight of each connection, I won't get 0. Here are the values I'll use:

x1 = 1 if the restaurant is clean and x1 = −1 if it's dirty.

x2 = 1 if the restaurant has a Spanish version of the menu and x2 = −1 if it doesn't.

x3 = −1 if the restaurant has a sombrero hanging on the wall and x3 = 1 if it has no sombrero on the wall.

Now suppose my perceptron weighs all those factors equally and performs a simple addition/subtraction function. It adds 1 (one) if the restaurant is clean and subtracts 1 if it isn't, adds 1 if the restaurant has a Spanish version of the menu and subtracts 1 if it doesn't, and adds 1 if no sombrero is hanging on the wall and subtracts 1 if a sombrero is hanging on the wall. It performs this function, and if the total meets a specified threshold, I'll eat at the restaurant. If it doesn't meet that threshold, I won't eat there. I determine that the threshold must be 2 or higher.

I come to a restaurant and discover that it's dirty, has a Spanish version of the menu, and no sombrero on the wall. I feed my inputs into the perceptron: x1 = −1, x2 = 1, and x3 = 1. My perceptron totals the binary values: −1 + 1 + 1 = 1. It then compares that total to my threshold of 2, and because that value doesn't meet the threshold, my perceptron produces an output of 0, telling me not to eat at this restaurant.

Unfortunately, this perceptron is too simple to be of much use because it would tell me to eat at a particular restaurant only if it meets all three of the conditions that are important to me. It also has no way to learn. All it does is perform its addition function and spit out the recommendation—thumbs up or thumbs down.

To improve this perceptron, let's assign relative weights to the inputs. I like a clean restaurant, so I give that connection a weight of 3. I really like more traditional Mexican food, so if there's a Spanish menu I give it a weight of 6. A sombrero on the wall is a minor annoyance, so I give that a weight of 2. Again, I set my threshold at 2.

To account for the weighted inputs, the perceptron multiplies each input value by its weight before making its decision. Now suppose I arrive at a dirty restaurant with a sombrero on the wall that has a Spanish version of the menu: x1 = −1, x2 = 1, and x3 = −1. The perceptron multiplies these values by their respective weights and totals the results. The equation would look like this:

$$(-1 \times 3) + (1 \times 6) + (-1 \times 2) = 1$$

If I come to a restaurant that's clean, has no Spanish menu, and has no sombrero on the wall, the equation would look like this:

$$(1 \times 3) + (-1 \times 6) + (1 \times 2) = -1$$

With this function and these weights, I would eat at a restaurant only if it had a Spanish version of the menu and was either clean or had no sombrero on the wall or both; for example:

$$(1 \times 3) + (1 \times 6) + (-1 \times 2) = 7$$

The good news is that the perceptron can learn, by adjusting the weights, as I feed it more data. Suppose I feed it data that shows I've eaten at Mexican restaurants in the past that don't have a Spanish version of the menu. It can look at that data and adjust the weights to make the model more accurate. It may decide to lower the weight of having a Spanish version of a menu to 4 and increase the weight of cleanliness to 4, in which case I might eat at a restaurant that's clean, has no Spanish menu, and no sombrero on the wall:

$$(1 \times 4) + (-1 \times 4) + (1 \times 2) = 2$$

The perceptron could also add bias to increase or decrease the output as a way of improving the accuracy of the output.

Keep in mind that these examples are oversimplified. The key points to remember are that a perceptron performs a function on multiple inputs to produce a single output and that a perceptron can learn by adjusting the weights of its inputs and by adding bias.

An artificial neural network may contain hundreds or thousands of these perceptrons, each of which accepts input and performs a function on that input to produce output. The perceptrons in the input layer accept the input you feed into the machine, produce outputs, and pass them to perceptrons in the hidden layer. Those perceptrons pass their outputs to other perceptrons until the collective outputs are passed along to the output layer. The output layer delivers the results.

Note that a perceptron or individual neuron in an artificial neural network is often referred to as a *single-layer perceptron*. Artificial neural networks with hidden layers are often referred to as *multilayer perceptrons*.

Squeezing Down a Sigmoid Neuron

The perceptron I used to make my restaurant decision has a binary input of 1 or −1—a thumbs up or thumbs down. All inputs and all outputs are thumbs up or thumbs down, nothing in between. That perceptron is likely to err in two ways: it could steer me clear of a lot of good restaurants, and it could have me eating at some really bad restaurants.

What I'd really like is a sliding scale that gives me some indication of the relative quality of the restaurant—ideally a number between 1 and 0. The closer I am to 1, the more confident the network is in the quality of the restaurant. If it's close to 0, I should probably go somewhere else. For this purpose, I might try to use something different—a *sigmoid neuron* (Figure 12.3).

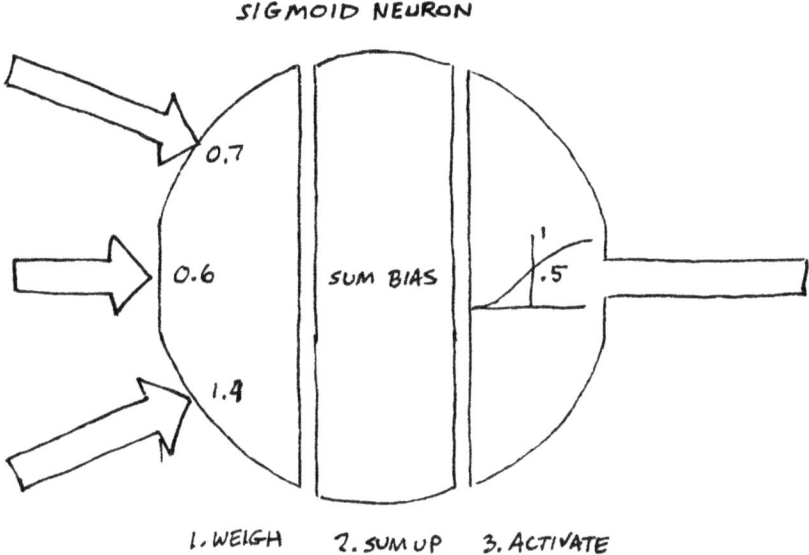

Figure 12.3 A sigmoid neuron

A sigmoid neuron can handle more variation in values than the binary choice you get with a perceptron. In fact, you can put any number you want in a sigmoid neuron and then use a sigmoid function to squeeze that number into something between 0 and 1. It's called a *sigmoid function* because the function's output forms an S-shaped curve when plotted on a graph. This makes a lot of sense because an S is almost like a line that's been squeezed into a smaller space (Figure 12.4). That's exactly what we're going to do with this number.

Like the perceptron we looked at in the previous section, sigmoid neurons use weighted inputs. The key difference is that the sigmoid function provides infinitely more variation in values than you get with a simple binary 0 or 1.

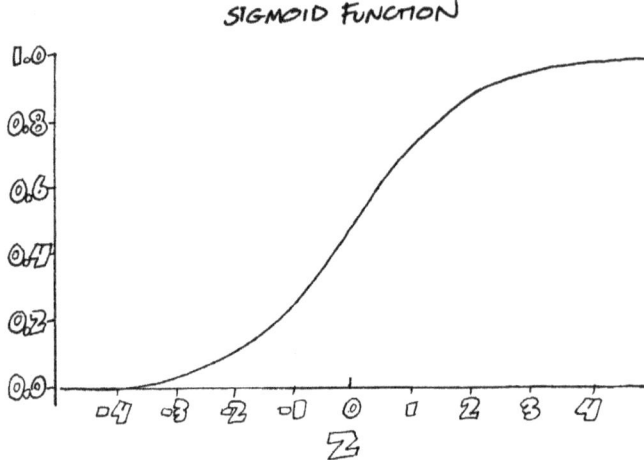

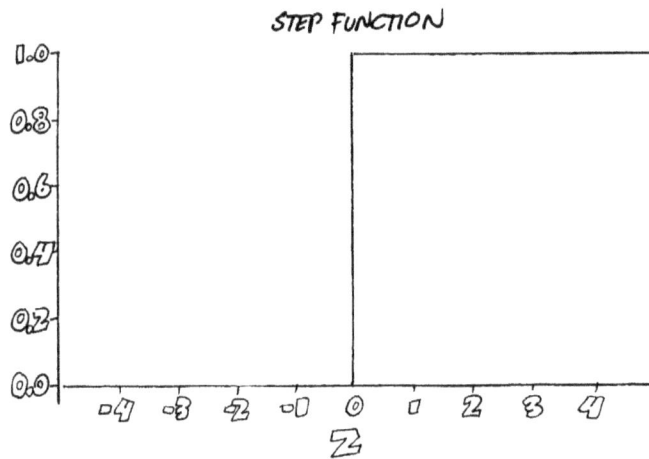

Figure 12.4 A smoothed-out version of a step function

So let's return to our taco neural network. We'll use the same criteria for the input layer:

 x1 is whether the restaurant is clean.

 x2 is whether there is a Spanish version of the menu.

 x3 is whether there is a sombrero on the wall.

In our perceptron, we could use only a 0 or –1 for each of these input values. In our sigmoid neuron, we can use any number between 1 and 0. Maybe the restaurant is 0.5 clean. Maybe the menu contains 0.3 of Spanish. And perhaps there's a sombrero on the restaurant's sign but not on the wall, which rates a score of 0.2.

You can use the same weights you used for the perceptron in the previous section. Cleanliness gets a weight of 3, Spanish menu gets 6, and sombrero gets 2.

Now multiply each input value by its weight and total the results:

$$(0.5 \times 3) + (0.3 \times 6) + (0.2 \times 2) = (\text{sigmoid squeeze } (3.7))$$

This output is a more precise approximation of the restaurant's quality because the inputs provide a more precise evaluation of each factor. As with a perceptron, a sigmoid neuron can learn by checking the accuracy of its predictions against actual outcomes and then adjusting the input weights accordingly.

Adding Bias

Setting a certain threshold enables perceptrons and sigmoid neurons to behave in a way similar to biological neurons, which can either fire or not fire. In binary notation, this can be represented as 0 for not fire and 1 for fire. A perceptron fires only if the result of its function meets the specified threshold.

If you find that a perceptron isn't firing when it should, you can add *bias* to its function to move the threshold. Bias simply moves the line that defines the threshold without changing that line's shape or orientation. Bias is just another number that works with input values and weights to encourage neurons to fire or remain silent.

So, let's say that we're using our taco neural network and you find that it's far too conservative in its recommendations on whether to eat at a certain restaurant. You're missing too many good meals because your network is saying the restaurants are not clean enough or don't have enough Spanish on the menu. So, you decide to add a bias to the connection between the input and the function. For example, if you add a bias of +5, that value is added to the sum of the inputs before being passed to the function for processing.

Bias can also be negative. For example, if the neuron is recommending too many restaurants where you would never choose to eat, you can add a negative bias to move the threshold in the opposite direction.

In Chapter 10, "Applying Machine Learning Algorithms," I presented an example based on an experience I had on the archery range at my son's camp. When I shot some arrows, they landed in a cluster at the upper right of the target, but far from the bull's-eye. I explained that this was an example of low variance and high bias. To make my aim more accurate, I would need to add a negative bias, so my arrows would land lower and more to the left.

The key point to remember is that bias gives you another dial to turn to fine-tune outputs. It's another tool that artificial neural networks use to learn.

Chapter Takeaways

- An *artificial neural network* is a much less sophisticated computerized version of the human brain. It is a type of machine learning algorithm.
- An artificial neural network has three layers: input, hidden, and output. The hidden layer is where all the complex calculations take place.
- Connections between nodes in an artificial neural network are weighted. The machine learns by adjusting the weights until it produces sufficiently accurate results.
- A perceptron is a single node in an artificial neural network, and it's often referred to as a single-layer perceptron. A multilayer perceptron is an artificial neural network with multiple nodes.
- Whereas a perceptron is a binary system supporting only two input and output values (typically zero and one), a sigmoid neuron can use any number between 0 and 1.
- Bias gives neurons a way to adjust their outputs, which is another way artificial neural networks learn.

13

Artificial Neural Networks in Action

In this chapter:

- Leveraging the power of data
- Putting hidden layers to work
- Going behind the scenes with activation functions
- Tweaking inputs with relative weights
- Tweaking a neuron's output with bias

You've seen that machine learning (ML) is an extremely robust form of pattern matching. You can use ML algorithms to find complex relationships or even classify data based on patterns that defy human perception. Neural networks take this to the next level. Here you can use thousands or even millions of artificial neurons to analyze data and identify subtle patterns.

Let's look at a fairly common ML classification problem. Imagine you want to create a neural network that could identify a dog's breed in a photo. You would feed a photo of a dalmatian into the input layer, and the machine would output the dog's breed—dalmatian. How does an artificial neural network accomplish such a feat?

Feeding Data into the Network

Think about an image the way an artificial neural network would see it—a collection of different bits of data. You can break down an image into pixels, each pixel being a tiny colored dot. Your smartphone's camera supports thousands of pixels (megapixels). The more pixels, the bigger and sharper the image (Figure 13.1).

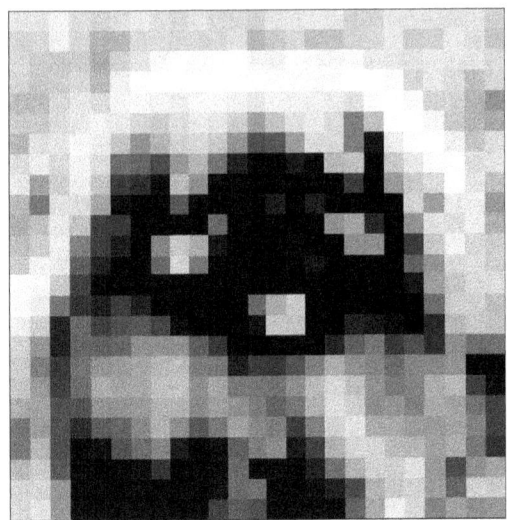

Figure 13.1 A small image has fewer pixels and presents a lower quality image

Imagine a photo of a dog as a collection of pixels. To keep things simple, assume that the machine converts the image to grayscale. Suppose your image is 25 pixels tall and 25 pixels wide. This tiny image is composed of 625 pixels (25 × 25 = 625). Because it's a grayscale image, some of the pixels may be totally white, others totally black, and most somewhere in between. In any given photo, the number of colors or shades of gray varies (Figure 13.2); for example, an 8-bit pixel can be white, black, or 256 shades between white and black. A 16-bit pixel supports 65,536 shades of gray.

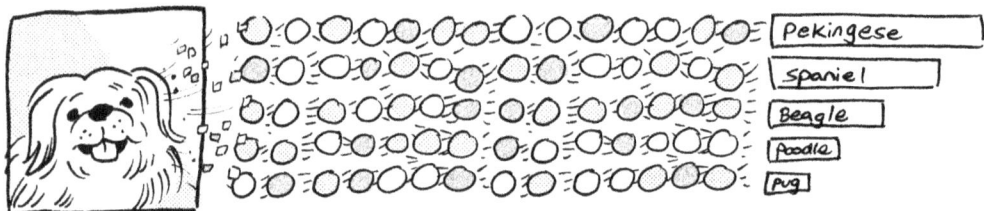

Figure 13.2 White, black, and shades of gray

Imagine using these 625 pixels to create an artificial neural network. Each pixel represents an individual neuron (node). We assign a value from 1 to 0 to each node based on its shade of gray—0 is black, and 1 is white, so medium gray is 0.5. Assuming we're using an 8-bit pixel, shades of gray are in increments of about 0.0039; that is, each shade starting from 0.0 (black) is about 0.0039 lighter than the previous shade. (These are *sigmoid neurons* because each can output a range of values between 0 and 1, not just 0 and 0 or 1 and −1.)

The input layer of the neural network contains 625 nodes that correspond to the 625 pixels. To keep things simple, we limit our model to ten breeds, so we have 10 nodes at the output layer—one for each breed. In between are two hidden layers that perform the functions used to identify the dog's breed. Again, to keep things simple, we use two hidden layers of 20 neurons each.

At the output level, we use 0 and 1 to identify the probability of a given breed, with 0 representing no match, 1 representing a definite match, and all numbers in between representing the probability of a match. For example, one output node may show a 0.95 or 95% probability that the photo is of a German shepherd, and another output node may show a 5% probability that the photo is of a dachshund.

Although you handle the inputs and read the outputs, the machine does most of the work in between—in the hidden layers. Each neuron in the hidden layer totals its inputs, adds bias, performs a function on the result, and passes its output to one or more neurons in the next layer. We assign random values between 0 and 1 to the connections between the neurons. These random values represent the relative strengths of the connections (the weights). We also assign random values for the bias within the neurons. The machine learns by adjusting these weights and biases as it goes through training and through multiple iterations of testing. In fact, the artificial neural network never ceases to learn. It continues to improve with each photo it's fed.

What Goes on in the Hidden Layers

At the input layer, each neuron has a number between 0 and 1 that represents its shade of gray. Zero is black, 1 is white, and between 0 and 1 are different shades of gray. When you feed a photo into the artificial neural network, the shades of gray on the photo are converted into values that are passed from the input layer to the first hidden layer.

Each input neuron connects to each neuron in the first hidden layer. With our dog-breed artificial neural network, the input layer contains 625 neurons, corresponding to the 625 pixels in the image. Each hidden layer has 20 neurons. Each of the 625 neurons in the input layer connects to each of the 20 neurons in the first hidden layer. That means 12,500 connections link the input layer to the first hidden layer (Figure 13.3).

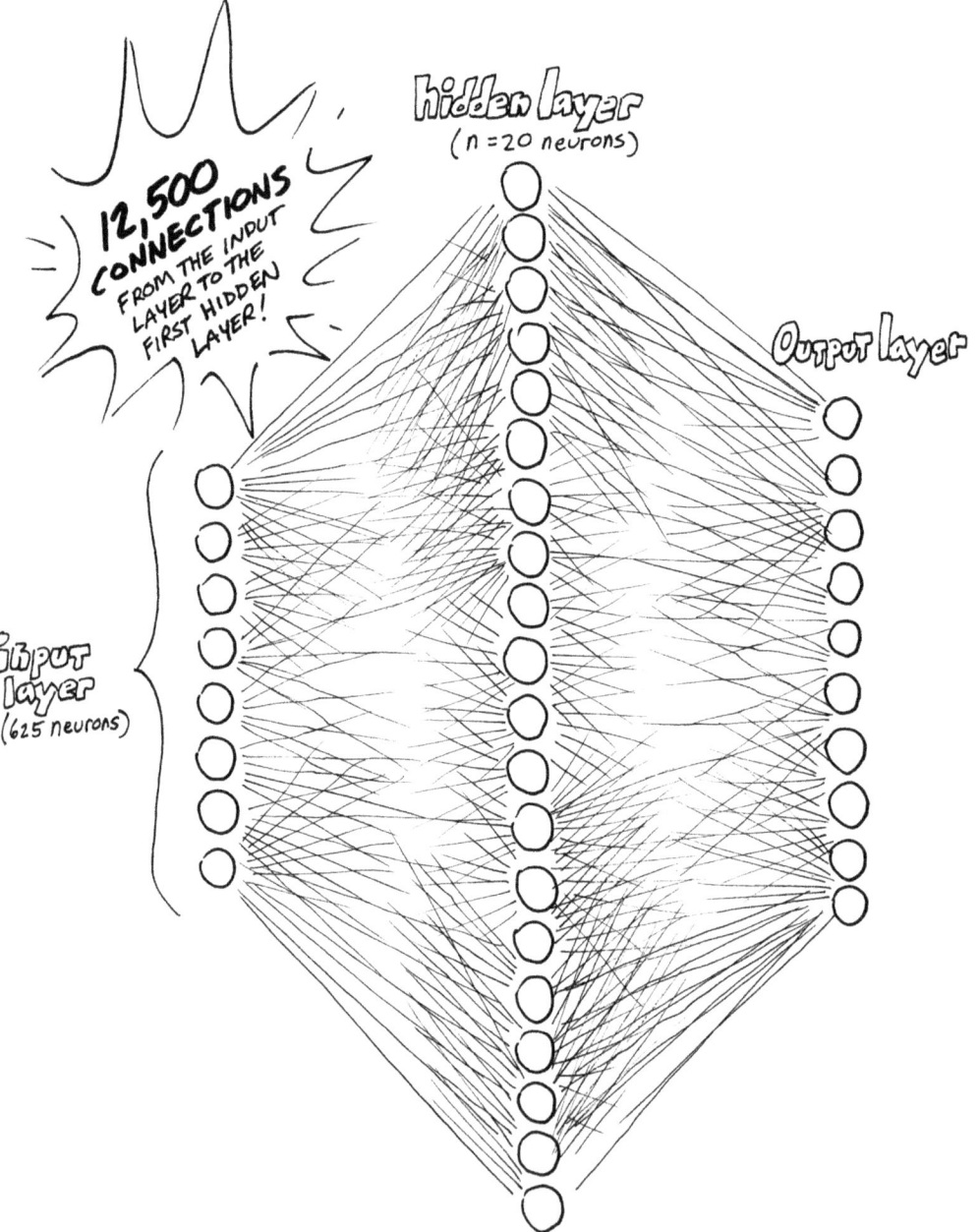

Figure 13.3 12,500 connections

These 12,500 connections are crucial because each connection can be dialed up or down to make the connections stronger or weaker. For example, neurons that correspond to pixels near the periphery of the image, which are less likely to be part of the dog, may have strong connections to a neuron that tries to figure out what the background is and very weak connections to the other 19 neurons.

One of those remaining 19 hidden neurons may be tasked with finding patterns that identify the eyes; another, the ears; another, the shape; another, the size; another, fur length; and so on (Figure 13.4). Each neuron in the first hidden layer can dial up or down its connections with the 625 input neurons feeding into it to determine what it needs to focus on in the image, just as you might focus on different parts of an image (Figure 13.5).

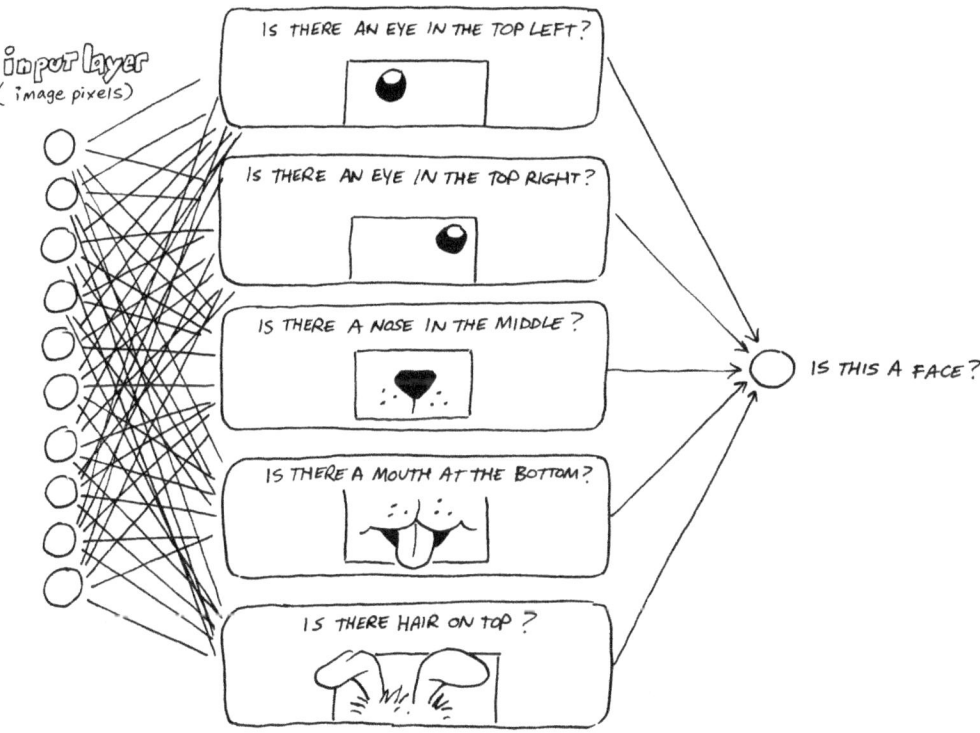

Figure 13.4 The hidden neurons may be tasked with finding facial features

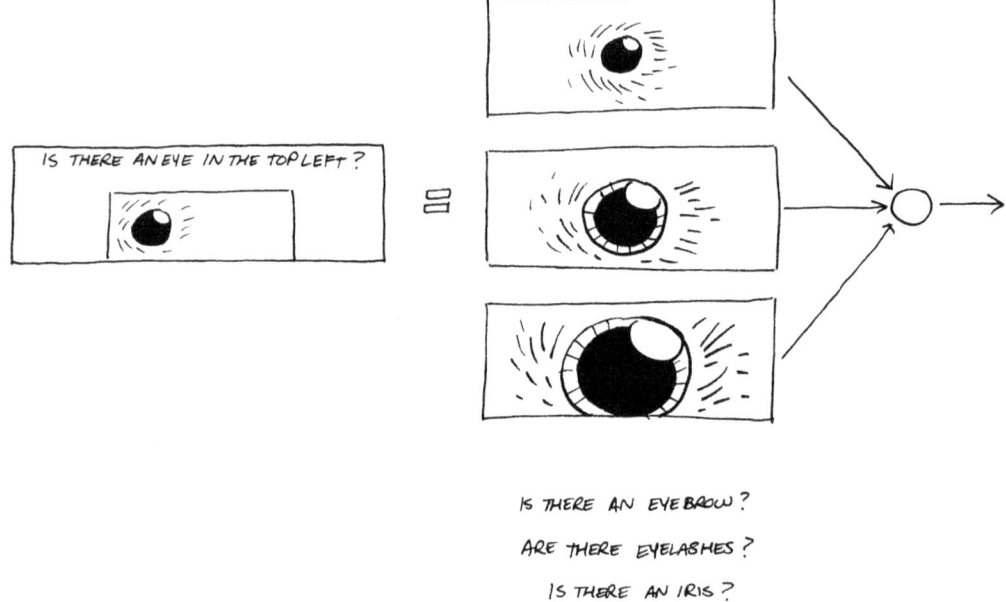

Figure 13.5 A neuron tasked with finding the eyes

Then each of the neurons in the first hidden layer connects to each neuron in the second hidden layer (of 20 neurons), creating another 400 connections. The neurons in the second hidden layer may try to associate the patterns found in the first layer with features of the 10 different breeds. It may find that the ears look like those of a Doberman, whereas the fur length is characteristic of a German shepherd and the coloring is characteristic of a Labrador retriever.

Each of the 20 neurons in the second hidden layer then connects to the 10 neurons in the output layer, creating another 200 connections. Here, the output neurons may look at the characteristics in total and determine the likelihood that the image is of a particular breed of dog. It may conclude that there's an 80% chance it's a picture of a poodle, a 15% chance it's a German shepherd, and a 5% chance it's a dachshund.

Again, this example is oversimplified, but it gives you a general idea of how artificial neural networks operate. The key points to keep in mind are that artificial neural networks contain far more connections than they contain neurons, and it is by adjusting the weights of these connections and the bias within each neuron that the artificial neural network can learn and continue to improve its ability to classify or predict.

Understanding Activation Functions

In the human brain, a neuron collects inputs from different sources, integrates these inputs, and then "fires," sending its output to the other neurons it's connected to. A node in an artificial neural network works much the same way:

1. Collects and weighs inputs from neurons in the previous layer
2. Totals the inputs and adds bias
3. Performs an activation function on the total and "fires" sending its output to the nodes it's connected to

Each neuron in an artificial neural network has an *activation function* that performs a mathematical operation on the sum of its inputs and bias and produces an output.

Different functions produce different outputs, and when you graph the outputs, you get different shapes. The most basic function used in artificial neurons is the *Heaviside step function*, named after its creator. This function outputs 1 (one) if its input plus bias is positive or 0 (zero), and it outputs 0 if its input plus bias is negative. In other words, the neuron either fires or not. When you graph this function, you get something that looks like a step in a stairway, as shown in Figure 13.6. The output can be 1 or 0, but nothing in between.

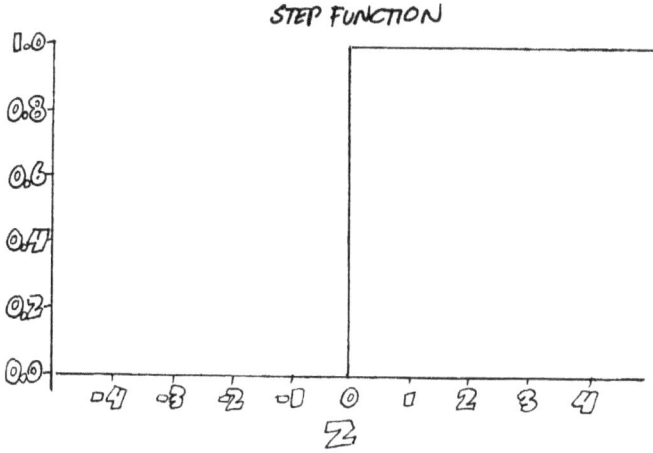

Figure 13.6 The Heaviside step function

The Heaviside step function isn't very useful for ML because it has no sliding scale of outputs. For ML, you want to be able to make small adjustments to weights and biases so the model can approximate a value precisely. With the Heaviside step function, a tiny adjustment to a weight or bias can flip the output from 0 to 1 or vice versa (Figure 13.7).

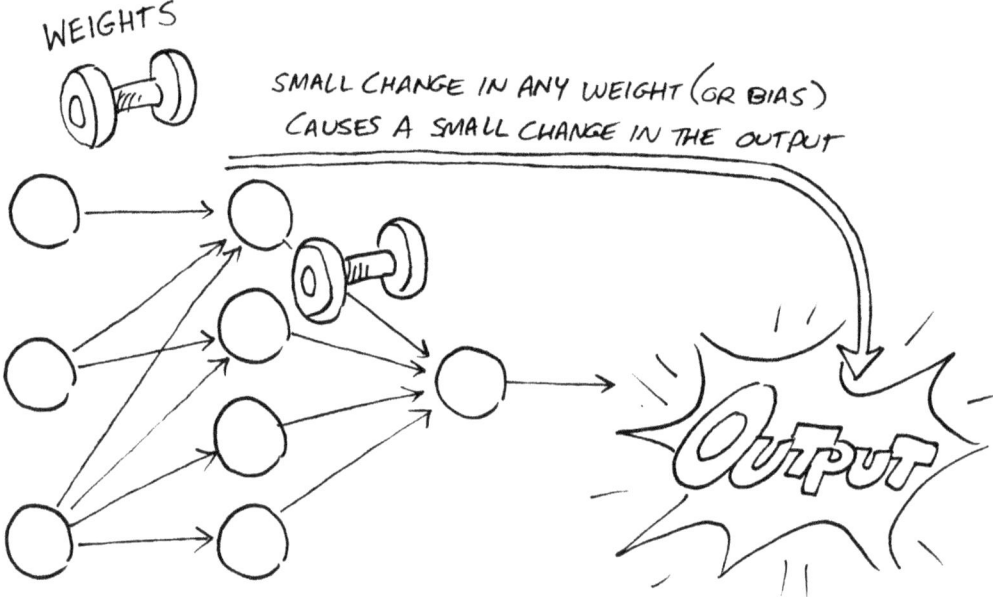

Figure 13.7 Changes in any weight or bias cause a change in the output

To overcome the limitation of the Heaviside step function, artificial neural networks started employing the sigmoid function. When you graph a sigmoid function (discussed in the previous chapter), you get an S-curve like the one shown below. Instead of only outputting a 0 (zero) or 1 (one), a sigmoid function can output any value between 0 and 1. Regardless of the magnitude of the input plus bias or whether it's negative or positive, the sigmoid function's output is between 0 and 1. Think of the sigmoid function as "squeezing down" the input, so it fits between 0 and 1. When you graph this function, the line looks as though it's been squeezed to fit within a frame.

More recently, neural networks started using something called a *rectified linear unit* (ReLU). This function is sort of a combination of the Heaviside and sigmoid functions. Like the Heaviside function, if the input is negative, the neuron produces an output of 0 (zero); that is, the neuron doesn't fire. If the input is positive, the function produces a precise output.

Artificial neural networks use several different activation functions that produce lines of different shapes when graphed. The three activation functions described here are just a few of these functions.

The importance of the sigmoid and ReLU functions is that they enable learning of pertinent features for a given set of inputs. They enable the machine to make small adjustments to weights and biases to make small changes to corresponding outputs.

Adding Weights

Think of a neuron's output as its brightness: the higher the number, the brighter the neuron. In the case of the 625 neurons that compose each of our dog images, each neuron's output ranges from 0 (zero), black to 1 (one), white. Each of these neurons connects to the 20 neurons in the first hidden layer. By adding weights to these connections, any neuron in the first hidden layer can dial up or dial down the connection to shift its focus to different pixels, just as you might shift your focus when looking at the image.

For example, suppose you feed a picture of a dalmatian into the machine, and one of the neurons in the first hidden layer dials up the connections to only those neurons in the input layer that output values of 0.01 or lower. This neuron is likely to focus on the dog's spots and maybe its nose because they're black. Or maybe it dials up the connections to the input layer neurons with output values 0.99 or higher and sees that the dog is mostly white. Another neuron in the hidden layer may dial down connections to input layer neurons with outputs in the range of 0.10 to 0.90 to strip out the background and focus on the outline of the dog, which might reflect its size and shape. Adding different levels of hidden layers may also result in learning different abstraction of features. The first hidden layer may learn basic features such as edges, corners, and colors. The second/higher hidden layers may learn higher order features such as the dog's facial features, tail size, and body build.

Each of these neurons in the first input layer is trying to identify a pattern that's characteristic of the dog in the photo. If you feed it enough pictures of dalmatians, it's likely to start identifying dalmatians.

Prior to training your artificial neural network, you assign random values to the connections. During training and testing, the network dials the connections up or down to improve its accuracy of identifying the different breeds. The network has 12,500 connections between the input layer and the first hidden layer, 400 connections between the first and second hidden layers, and another 200 connections between the second hidden layer and the output layer. That's 13,100 total connections. You can think of this neural network as making 13,100 little decisions.

As you can see, this simple artificial neural network has a lot of dials to turn and ample opportunity to make adjustments. But those aren't the only dials it can turn. It can also add and adjust bias, as discussed next.

Adding Bias

Whereas weights enable an artificial neural network to adjust the strength of connections *between* neurons, *bias* can be used to make adjustments *within* neurons. Bias can be positive or negative, increasing or decreasing a neuron's output. The neuron gathers and sums its inputs, adds bias (positive or negative), and then passes the total to the activation function.

In terms of the sigmoid function graph presented earlier in this chapter, weight affects the steepness of the curve, whereas bias shifts the curve left or right without changing the shape of the curve. Together, weights and biases can be adjusted to shape the output to match the data. For example, suppose you plot points on a graph that form a pattern shaped like an S, but when you input data into your activation function, the S that the function generates is to the left of the data points. You can add bias to shift the S over to the right, so it aligns more closely with the data points, as shown in Figure 13.8.

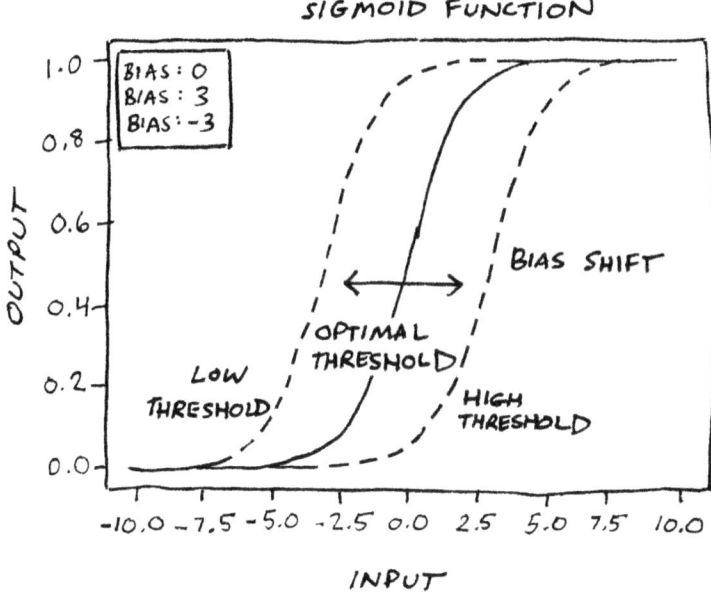

Figure 13.8 Bias shift moving the S to the right so it more closely aligns with the data

Chapter Takeaways

- In an artificial neural network, each node connects to each node in the next layer, creating far more connections than there are nodes.
- Each node sums its inputs, adds bias, and sends the total to the activation function, which produces the node's output.
- An artificial neural network can adjust the weights of connections between nodes to gauge the relative importance of inputs.
- A neuron can add bias (positive or negative) to the sum of the inputs to improve the accuracy of its output.
- An artificial neural network learns by adjusting weights and biases, so the network overall can generate more accurate output.

14

Letting Your Network Learn

In this chapter:

- Understanding how an artificial neural network learns
- Enhancing the accuracy of the output
- Learning through backpropagation of errors
- Fine-tuning your artificial neural network
- Getting up to speed on the chain rule

In the previous chapter, we looked at a simple artificial neural network that distinguishes between 10 breeds of dogs. After this network is trained, validated, and tested, you can feed a picture of a dog (of one of the 10 breeds) into the network, and it will tell you the dog's breed.

Of course, it must learn how to accomplish that feat, and you can help. With supervised learning, you can feed a training set of pictures into the network along with the breed of each dog (called *labels*). The network can then identify patterns in each picture and relate those patterns with the breeds. After training, if you feed similar pictures into the network, it should be able to tell you with some accuracy the breed of the dog in each picture.

However, if you feed dissimilar pictures into the machine, it will struggle. For example, if all the training set pictures were profiles of dogs standing, and you fed the machine pictures of dogs running, lying down, or sitting, it might not do very well classifying the dogs in those pictures. To improve the network's accuracy, you'd have to feed thousands of pictures into the network of the 10 dog breeds in different positions and settings and then tell the network when it made mistakes, so it could improve.

So, with supervised learning, you can interact with the network at the input and output layers to help the network learn, but that tells you very little about *how* the network learns. What's going on in those hidden layers where the network does most of its "thinking"?

Even this basic neural network has thousands of dials to turn to adjust the accuracy of its output. As explained in the previous chapter, this artificial neural network with 625 input nodes, 40 hidden layer nodes, and 10 output nodes has 13,100 connections and 50 biases that can be adjusted to improve the network's accuracy. That's a total of 13,150 adjustments—13,150 dials that can be turned. By turning these dials, the machine learns.

Now no data scientist wants to show up Monday morning facing the task of turning all those dials. In fact, the data scientist probably wouldn't know where to start, what adjustments to make, or how those adjustments would affect other adjustments and affect the accuracy of the network's output.

Fortunately, the network can make these adjustments itself through trial and error. This chapter explains how.

Starting with Random Weights and Biases

When you're setting up a neural network, you have to start somewhere, but you don't want to set all the dials to 0 or 1 because you'd have too much symmetry in the network, making it difficult for the network to learn. You don't want to use the same values for all of the network's connection weights and biases.

In the absence of any prior knowledge, a plausible solution is to assign totally random values to weights and biases. There are various techniques for generating random values, and they all have nerdy names, such as orthogonal random matrix initialization and zero-mean Gaussian. For now, just think of these random values as unrelated weights and biases and that weights use values between 0 and 1.

As you can imagine, a randomly initialized neural network isn't very good at identifying a dog's breed by looking at its picture. In fact, it's not that much better than just randomly throwing pictures of dogs into a line of different buckets. What's important is that these random values provide a starting point that enables the network to adjust weights and biases up and down to improve its accuracy.

As you feed your training data (pictures and labels) into the network, it adjusts the weights and biases to identify a relationship between each picture and label (dog breed), and it begins to distinguish between different breeds. When you feed test data (unfamiliar pictures of dogs) into the network, it may be a little unsure whether the dog in the picture is one breed or another. It may indicate that it's 70% sure it's a German shepherd, 20% sure it's a Doberman, and 10% sure it's a dachshund. When you give the network the correct answer, it readjusts its weights and biases so it can be more accurate the next time.

This is an example of supervised learning. You train the network to identify the relationship between the pictures and the labels (breeds), and then you correct it when it makes a mistake. Through trial and error, the machine learns how to identify the different breeds, even when you show it pictures of different dogs in different positions and settings.

Making Your Network Pay for Its Mistakes: The Cost Function

You probably want your artificial neural network to be more certain than 70% that it's correct. One way to improve its certainty is to use the *cost function*—a mathematical operation that compares the network's output (the predicted answer) to the targeted output (the correct answer) to determine the accuracy of the machine. In other words, the cost function tells the network how wrong it was so the network can make adjustments to be less wrong (and more right) in the future. Essentially, the network pays for its mistakes. The cost is higher when the network is making bad or sloppy classifications or predictions—typically early in its training phase.

Keep in mind, however, that the cost function's output reflects only the overall accuracy of the network. It doesn't indicate specifically which weights or biases need to be adjusted, by how much, or in which direction (positive or negative).

Combining the Cost Function with Gradient Descent

With the cost function, the network knows how wrong it is, but it doesn't have a way to become less wrong. This is where gradient descent comes into play. *Gradient descent* is an optimization algorithm that minimizes the cost by repeatedly and gradually moving the output in the direction of deepest descent. In other words, it works toward reducing the cost, thus increasing the accuracy of the network.

In the case of our dog-breed identifier, the cost function at the output layer signals all the nodes in the hidden layer of how wrong the output was. The nodes in the hidden layer then use gradient descent to move their outputs in the direction of the deepest descent, which results in reducing the cost. As the network learns from its mistakes, the cost declines and the machine becomes more accurate and more confident in its output.

So let's say the output layer has five neurons, but the output values are all over the place. The output neuron for the Doberman activates at 0.40, the German shepherd activates at 0.30, the poodle neuron at 0.25, the beagle at 0.04, and the dachshund at 0.05. So the network is not confident what breed is represented in the picture.

That's not very helpful.

So what you do is find the difference between each wrong answer and each correct answer and then average them. Let's say the picture *was* a Doberman. That means you want to nudge the network in a few places. You want to nudge +0.60 for the Doberman to get it to 1.0. Then you want to nudge the other dog breeds to get to 0. So that's –0.30 for the German shepherd, –0.25 for the poodle, –0.04 for the beagle, and –0.05 for the dachshund.

Then you want to average all your *nudges* to get an overall sense of how accurate your network is at finding different dog breeds.

$$\text{Average nudges } (+0.60 - 0.30 - 0.25 - 0.04 - 0.05)/5 = -0.04/5 = -0.008$$

But remember that this is just one training example. You could go through many training examples with different dogs. So you could end up with several different nudges and averages.

$$\text{Average nudges } (0.01 - 0.6 - 0.32 + 0.16 - 0.25)/5 = -0.04/5 = -0.02$$
$$\text{Average nudges } (0.7 - 0.3 + 0.12 - 0.05 - 0.12)/5 = 0.35/5 = 0.07$$

So then you take the sum and get an overall *cost* function. In this case the overall cost is −0.008 − 0.02 + 0.07 = −0.138. So you will take the sum of these averages until you (in theory) get to 0.

In an attempt to correct itself, the machine adjusts the weights of the connections between nodes to eliminate its mistakes. The goal is for the network to be not only right but also confident in its output.

When I was in graduate school, my wife and I went to a local carnival. At the carnival they had a strange game called Gold Valley that looked incredibly easy to win but was actually quite difficult. It was a large cement structure shaped like a sandbox. In the middle was a little valley painted gold. The goal was to roll your marble into that Gold Valley. Surrounding Gold Valley were numerous rolling valleys that would divert your marble from its goal.

I figured the trick to winning was to identify the widest, deepest valleys and avoid those. Unfortunately, you couldn't really tell how wide or deep they were by looking straight across the top of the structure. You'd have to slice the structure in half to see which valleys were deepest, and that wasn't an option.

I thought I had figured out a couple ways to get a marble into Gold Valley, so I set down my caramel apple and paid for a handful of black marbles.

It might sound strange, but playing Gold Valley reminds me a lot of how neural networks learn from their training data. I didn't have to focus on getting my marble to land in Gold Valley. I just needed to make sure it didn't drop down into the other valleys, especially the widest, deepest valleys. I had to pay for every marble I rolled, so to win the game, I needed to reduce my costs.

Imagine your neural network in terms of this carnival game. The highest costs are associated with the deepest valleys, but you can't tell which of those valleys is deepest. You have to figure out a way to identify the deepest valleys by rolling marbles into the structure. You need to watch them carefully and notice how quickly they descend into the different valleys. Based on your observations, your brain could calculate the relative depths of the valleys.

By doing this one marble at a time, you could eventually map the entire game. You'd know which valleys were deepest and how steeply each one descended. You could then gradually work your way toward steering your marble through shallower valleys that were less likely to divert your marble from reaching its goal.

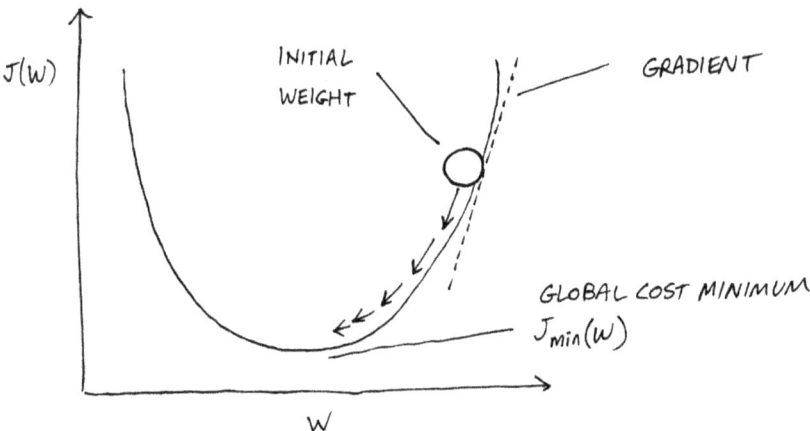

Figure 14.1 Gradient descent

In machine learning, this technique is called *gradient descent* (Figure 14.1). In terms of your neural network, you want it to turn the dials in a way that points the output down the valley with the lowest cost. Unfortunately, the network can't identify the deepest valley, so you roll a black marble through the network by feeding input into the network and seeing what happens at the output layer.

The network compares its output with the right answer, measures the cost, and readjusts the weights and biases. It does this over and over again until it reduces the cost to an acceptable range—usually something close to zero error, but never quite reaching zero. Your network will do this thousands or even millions of times until it's tuned to the highest accuracy at the lowest cost.

Using Backpropagation to Correct for Errors

Your cost function is an average of all the gaps between your network's output and the correct answer, so you don't really get a sense of how well each neuron is performing. Instead, you're just getting an overall view of the network's performance.

You can compare the cost function to the margin of error in polling conducted during election campaigns. A certain poll may have a margin of error of 3 points, meaning the poll's prediction is estimated to be accurate within plus or minus 3 percent. If the poll shows that the race is a tie, one candidate could still win by 6 percent of the vote, and that would be within the margin of error.

Generally, the smaller the margin of error, the more accurate the poll. A poll with a margin of error of 3 points is usually more accurate than a poll with a margin of error of 6 points. Each poll could be wrong, but the one with the smaller margin of error should be less wrong.

A neural network's cost function works in a similar way. Your network is likely to have some margin of error. The goal is to minimize that margin of error and to minimize cost, which it tries to do by adjusting the weights of the connections between neurons. It's not just turning one dial to optimize one connection or one neuron; it's turning as many dials as necessary to optimize the system as a whole and produce accurate output.

One of the challenges with the cost function is that it doesn't really tell you how to improve the system. It just tells you whether or not the network is performing well. To improve the network, you have to adjust the weights of the connections between the neurons. You want your network to learn how to improve its own performance, thus minimizing cost.

So how does the machine know which dials to turn and which direction and how far to turn them? It uses something called backpropagation of errors (or backpropagation for short). *Backpropagation* is the way that a neural network tweaks the weights to minimize cost.

Now imagine standing in front of a control board that had a few hundred little dials like the ones you see in professional sound studios. You're looking at a screen above these dials that has a number between 1 and 0. Your goal is to get that number as close to 0 as possible—zero cost. You wouldn't have to know anything about the data to try to minimize the cost. All you need to do is turn dials and watch the screen.

When you look closely at these dials, you notice that each has a setting from 0 (zero) to 1 (one). Turning a dial clockwise brings the setting closer to 1. Turning it counterclockwise brings the setting closer to 0. Each dial represents a weight—the strength of the connection between two neurons.

Think about how you would turn those dials to make the number on the screen closer to 0. Would you start by setting them all to 1? Would you set them all to 0 and start from there? Would you start with a bunch of random settings?

With an artificial neural network, the dials are turned to random settings at the beginning. Then the network looks for the dials with the greatest weights—the dials that are turned up higher than all the others. It turns all of these dials up a tiny bit to see if that lessens the cost. If that adjustment doesn't work, the network turns them down a little. The network doesn't know anything about the data. It doesn't know that it's looking at pictures of dogs. All it knows is that turning the dials increases or decreases the number on the screen that represents the cost and that it wants to move that number down to 0.

Imagine one dial is set to a weight of 0.01—a light connection. Imagine a pale green connection. Another dial is set to 0.3—a connection that is 30 times heavier. Imagine a darker green connection. Because the second connection is 30 times heavier than the first, adjusting its weight is more likely to affect the output. The more you turn that dial, the more it's likely to influence the cost. If you go from dark green to lighter green, you're more likely to have an impact than if you go from very light green to slightly lighter or slightly darker green.

Backpropagation goes through these dials and turns them up and down to see if it can minimize the cost for the entire neural network.

Let's look at how this might work with our dog breed classifier. Imagine that the output layer identifies 10 breeds: German shepherd, Labrador retriever, Rottweiler, beagle, bulldog, golden retriever, Great Dane, poodle, Doberman, and dachshund. Now we feed a grayscale image of a beagle into the input layer.

This grayscale image is broken down into 625 pixels in the input layer, and that data is sent over 12,500 weighted connections to the 20 neurons in the first hidden layer. The first hidden layer neurons perform their calculations and send the results over 400 weighted connections to the second hidden layer. Those second hidden layer neurons send their output over 200 weighted connections to the 10 neurons in the output layer. So you have your 13,100 dials. On top of that, you also have 50 settings to adjust the bias in the hidden and output layer neurons.

So let's imagine that you have them all randomly set. You send your beagle picture through the neural network, and the output layer delivers its results; it's 0.3 certain it's a German shepherd, 0.8 sure it's a Labrador retriever, 0.5 sure it's a Rottweiler, 0.2 sure it's a beagle, 0.3 sure it's a bulldog, 0.6 sure it's a golden retriever, 0.3 sure it's a Great Dane, 0.3 sure it's a poodle, 0.4 sure it's a Doberman, and 0.7 sure it's a dachshund.

As you can see, our neural network didn't do a very good job. It's equally certain that the image contains a Great Dane or a poodle. It is also reasonably certain that it could be a dachshund, a Labrador retriever, or even a golden retriever. In other words, it has no idea what dog is in the image.

The cost function for this result will be high. You could see that the correct answer is given a 0.2 chance of being right, whereas the incorrect answers are given a 0.3, 0.5, 0.6, or 0.7. So the network has two problems: 1) it's wrong, and 2) it's more confident in all of its wrong answers than in its one right answer.

The neural network needs to use backpropagation to find out how to adjust its weights and minimize the cost. The best place to start is by dialing up the correct answer because it's the right answer, and it has more room for adjustment. That is, you can dial it up more than you can dial down the others. The next priority is to dial down the wrong answers starting with the highest number, so you would start by dialing down the 0.7 (dachshund).

So backpropagation looks at 0.2 and works its way back to the connections to this output neuron to identify which connections have the most room for adjustment, and it dials those up or down. It then looks back to the second hidden layer neurons to see which neurons have the most room to adjust the bias, and it dials those up or down. The network continues to work back through the connections and neurons and continues to adjust until it reaches the input layer.

It's almost as though you're tuning an instrument without actually knowing the notes. As you adjust, you get closer and closer to perfect pitch, at which point the cost is zero.

Tuning Your Network

Remember that getting the correct answer is the highest priority, but it's not the only priority. The network also needs to adjust the weights to reduce the output that's driving the wrong answers. It starts by adjusting the weights and biases of the connections and neurons that feed output to the neurons that are most confident in their wrong answers, and then it moves on to adjust the inputs to neurons that are less confident in their wrong answers.

Keep in mind that the network makes these adjustments not just once for the image of the beagle but for all images in the training data set, which is small. And it continues to adjust as you feed it larger volumes of test data. If you fed the network only the picture of the beagle, you'd end up with a neural network that classifies every image of a dog as a beagle. You need to feed the network more pictures— pictures of dogs of different breeds and pictures of different dogs of the same breed. With every picture you feed into the network, the network uses backpropagation to make tiny adjustments to weights, and it fine-tunes its ability to distinguish between different breeds.

In a sense, as you feed the network a diversity of pictures, it becomes a little less accurate in identifying beagles so that it can do a better job identifying pictures of Labrador retrievers, Rottweilers, German shepherds, poodles, and so on. Your network tries to find the optimal weights and biases to minimize the cost regardless of the breed shown in the picture. The settings may not be the best for any one dog, but having well-balanced settings enables the network to make fewer mistakes, resulting in more accurate classification among different breeds of dogs.

Backpropagation, gradient descent, and the cost function work together to make this magic happen.

Employing the Chain Rule

Backpropagation relies on the *chain rule*—a technique used to find the derivatives of cost with respect to any variable in a nested equation. Admittedly, that's a jargony definition, but that's calculus for you. What's important is that the chain rule can be used to calculate the derivative of cost with respect to any weight in the network. Why is this important? Because it enables the network to identify how much each weight contributes to the cost and whether that weight needs to be increased or decreased to reduce the cost.

Here's how it all fits together:

1. The cost function tells the network how wrong it is.
2. The chain rule enables the network to identify how much each weight contributes to the cost (error) and how much each needs to be adjusted.

3. Gradient descent tells the network the direction each weight needs to be adjusted to reduce the amount that weight contributes to the error.

4. Through backpropagation, the network adjusts the weights of the connections and the bias of each neuron one layer at a time from the output layer back through the hidden layers to the input layer.

5. The network again works forward with these changed weights; the output of the neural network is matched with the target output, and the errors are backpropagated. This process is continued until convergence is reached.

With backpropagation, the network first adjusts the weights of the connections between the output layer and the second hidden layer and determines how those adjustments affect the output. It then adjusts the connections between the second hidden layer and the first hidden layer and determines how those adjustments influence the output. Finally, it adjusts the connections between the first hidden layer and the input layer and determines how those adjustments affect the output.

In other words, the network turns the dials, starting with the dials closest to the output and working back through the network, testing the output after every adjustment and before making the next adjustment. Using this technique, the network is able to reduce errors by fine-tuning the weights and biases one level at a time.

Keep in mind that the network tries to identify the dials that have the most room for adjustment. A big twist of a dial is more likely to have a greater impact on the output. Usually, these dials are closely connected between the layers, so the strengths of connections have a cumulative effect on the output.

Think of backpropagation and the chain rule almost like four megaphones lined up in a row. Even the quietest noise in the first megaphone might lead to a roaring sound when you get close to the last megaphone in the output layer. That's why a series of strong connections is likely to have a big impact on cost. Through backpropagation, the network can mediate the cumulative effect by adjusting dials along the entire series of connected neurons.

Batching the Data Set with Stochastic Gradient Descent

As you can imagine, backpropagation consumes a lot of processing power to analyze the images in your training set, adjust the weights and biases, and then go back and modify these weights and biases to determine the negative gradient for the cost function. And the network repeats the process, through numerous iterations, to fine-tune its accuracy.

To alleviate this processing burden, especially when dealing with massive data sets, data science teams will break down the data set into smaller ones—a technique referred to as *stochastic gradient descent* (*stochastic* means random). For example, with our dog breed classifier, instead of feeding the network 1,000 pictures of dogs, we would shuffle the pictures to introduce some randomness and then divide them into 10 batches of 100 pictures each. We'd then run each batch through the network so the network would have fewer pictures to process at one time and, more importantly, far fewer adjustments to make at one time.

The benefit is that the network can process 100 pictures a lot faster and consume significantly less processing power than if it had to process all 1,000 pictures at once. Because of this, stochastic gradient descent is especially useful for massive data sets that the network can't store in its memory at any one time. One drawback is that the neural network will be highly accurate for each batch but far less accurate for the other batches. Another drawback is that you have to do 10 training sessions instead of feeding the network all 1,000 pictures in a single session.

Think about stochastic gradient descent in terms of your own brain. You'd probably expend a lot less energy and get everything done faster if you had 10 batches of 10 to-do lists than if you had one list of 100 items. With a hundred items, you'd be running around like the proverbial chicken with its head cut off. With 10 lists of 10 items each, you're less likely to become overwhelmed; you focus on only 10 items at a time.

The key thing to remember is not to be overconfident with the results from each of these batches. You can get accurate results pretty quickly with a smaller batch of the training data, but you still need to run all the data through the network.

Chapter Takeaways

- A neural network starts with random weights and biases to avoid having too much symmetry.
- The cost function makes the neural network pay for its mistakes. To lower the cost, the network must improve its performance.
- Gradient descent is an optimization algorithm that minimizes the cost by repeatedly and gradually adjusting the weight of a connection until it delivers an output with minimal error.
- The chain rule enables the network to identify how much each weight contributes to the cost and whether that weight needs to be increased or decreased to reduce the cost.
- With backpropagation, cost ripples through the neurons and connections from the output layer back through to the input layer so the network can make adjustments along the entire chain of neurons that produces the inaccurate output.
- With stochastic gradient descent, you break down a large set of training data into smaller batches of data and train the network using one batch at a time. This approach lightens the processing load on the neural network.

15

Using Neural Networks to Classify or Cluster

In this chapter:

- Deciding whether classification or clustering is better suited to the problem you're trying to solve or the question you need to answer
- Understanding the relationship between classification and supervised learning
- Understanding the connection between clustering and unsupervised learning
- Identifying practical uses for classification and clustering

People don't build artificial neural networks to engage in whimsical thought. They build them to solve specific problems, answer questions, or identify connections in large volumes of data that point the way to solutions.

Prior to building an artificial neural network, you need to figure out what you want it to do. You need to start with its purpose. When you have a purpose in mind, you then need to decide on the capability that will serve that purpose best. Ask yourself, "Am I looking at a classification problem or a clustering problem?" Those are the two things that artificial neural networks do best: classify and cluster. Here's how you choose:

- **Classify:** If you have labeled data, you probably want to use classification with supervised learning. The labels are the classes into which you want the data placed. Our dog-breed identifier network uses classification. The labels are the breeds, and the network classifies each picture as being a dog of a certain breed.
- **Cluster:** If your data is unlabeled, you probably want to use clustering with unsupervised learning. With clustering, an artificial neural network identifies patterns in the data and groups the data based on these patterns. It's up to you

to extract meaning or insight from the clusters. After the machine has done its job, you need to ask, "Why did the machine cluster the data as it did?" The answer to that question can reveal valuable insights.

In this chapter, you gain a deeper understanding of classification and clustering and the differences between them.

Solving Classification Problems

With a classification problem, you already have predefined classes and then train the machine to determine in which class each input item belongs. To start the training, you feed the machine test data that contains the class labels and examples of items from each class. With our dog identifier network, we would feed it the names of the ten dog breeds (German shepherd, Labrador retriever, poodle, and so forth) and one or more pictures of dogs in each category. In other words, we give the machine the label "German shepherd" and feed it a picture of a German shepherd, we feed it the label "Labrador retriever" and give it a picture of a Labrador retriever, and we do this for all 10 breeds. When we're done, the machine has some idea of how the labels are related to the pictures.

Next, we feed the machine test data. The test data consists of pictures of dogs of different breeds, and the machine needs to figure out the breed. If the machine is wrong, we give it the right answer so it can adjust the weights and biases. It might raise the weights and biases for the correct answer and lower them for the wrong answer(s). During this validation step, the machine is fine-tuning its ability to identify the different breeds; it's learning.

Classification is one of the most common ways to use an artificial neural network. Email providers use machine learning (ML) neural networks to classify spam messages. They feed the machine classifications of email messages, such as Spam, Not Spam, and Maybe Spam. When you receive an email message, the spam checker examines the message to identify characteristics of each class, and then it takes the appropriate action. It might automatically delete spam, send anything that's not spam to your inbox, and send anything that may be spam to your inbox and mark it "SPAM" so you can decide whether to delete it or read it.

Credit card companies also use classification and supervised ML for their fraud detection. The human trainer will give the machine the labels, something like Fraud, Not Fraud, and Maybe Fraud, and then feed it transactions representative of Fraud and Not Fraud. The machine may be set up with three output nodes (one for each class). If a transaction has a high level of details characteristic of fraud, the Fraud neuron fires to cancel the transaction and suspend the card. (You probably experienced this if you ever tried to use one of your credit cards when you were traveling out of town without notifying your credit card company in advance.) If a transaction has fewer details characteristic of fraud, the Maybe Fraud neuron fires to notify the cardholder of suspicious activity. If the transaction contains even fewer details (or no details) characteristic of fraud, then the Not Fraud neuron fires, and the transaction is processed.

An artificial neural network can identify patterns in structured data or unstructured data. *Structured data* is highly organized, such as data in tables, spreadsheets, and databases. *Unstructured* or *semi-structured* data is much less organized, such as the text in a document or the body of an email message and the data that comprises images, audio, and video. Some law enforcement agencies use neural networks for facial recognition. Banks will also use neural networks to classify the written text on your checks. That way you can just take a picture of your check with a smart phone and upload it to your bank. Classification can also help with transcribing voice into text.

All tools are the product of machine learning—the process of gathering massive amounts of data, finding patterns in that data, and using those patterns to classify newly inputted entities. Just about anything can be identified using classification—handwritten text and numbers on a check, spoken words, fraudulent transactions, unwanted email, and so on. A human creates these classifications, and then the network will do its best to assign each input to the right class.

Typically, you have each neuron in the output layer assigned to one class. So if you wanted to identify a number on a check, you'd have 10 neurons in the output layer, each representing a number from 0 (zero) to 9. The activation functions in the hidden layer would work together to calculate the probability of a pattern on the check being one of those numbers, and the output layer would indicate whether the pattern was most likely a 0, 1, 2, 3, 4, or some other digit up to 9.

Whether you're using an artificial neural network for facial recognition, spam detection, natural language processing (NLP), or some other task, the network sees the task as just another application of classification. It may appear that the network is doing something really different, but it's essentially doing the same thing in a different manner in each of these applications—classifying inputs.

Next, you'll see what an artificial neural network can do when input data isn't labeled.

Solving Clustering Problems

Supervised learning is terrific, but it doesn't fit every challenge. For starters, you won't always have access to massive amounts of labeled data. Maybe you won't have a million pictures that are accurately labeled with the breed of dog in each picture. Other times you won't be interested in classifying your data into human-created categories. Maybe you'll want the neural network to cluster data to identify patterns that you would never think to look for.

In such cases, unsupervised learning is the better choice. With unsupervised learning, you let the neural network cluster your data into different groups. To understand the difference between supervised and unsupervised learning, imagine demonstrating the difference to a class of preschool students who can't tell the difference between dogs and cats. You bring in 200 photographs, half labeled and half unlabeled. The 100 labeled photographs consist of 50 pictures of dogs and 50 pictures of cats. The 100 unlabeled photos are pictures of a variety of zoo and farm animals.

For supervised learning, you set up two boxes: one labeled "Dog," the other labeled "Cat." You take five dog pictures and five cat pictures and train the students on how to tell the difference between the two. You might point out the prominent whiskers on cats, the fact that their ears are triangular and erect, and that that their heads tend to be round. You point out that dogs tend to have longer snouts, bigger noses, droopier ears, less prominent whiskers. Then you take five more pictures of dogs and five more pictures of cats and lead the students through the process of identifying them and placing them in the correct boxes. You correct them if they make a mistake. Then you shuffle the remaining 80 pictures and give them to the class to sort into the two boxes. Each time they get one wrong, you correct them. By the end of the exercise, they're pretty good at telling the difference between dogs and cats.

Now you're ready to demonstrate unsupervised learning. You give the class the 100 photos of assorted zoo and farm animals, and you tell the students to sort the photos and stack them in groups of pictures that are like one another. They now have pictures of horses, zebras, giraffes, flamingos, snakes, cows, sheep, lizards, lions, various fish, chickens, elephants, and so on. They also have different backgrounds—farm, zoo, jungle, plains, ocean, and so on. If the students ask questions, you simply tell them to do their best finding pictures that look similar and placing them in different stacks.

With this demonstration of unsupervised learning, you have no idea how the students will group the pictures. There are no wrong answers. Students may group zebras and horses together because they have a similar shape; giraffes and flamingos because they both have long necks; all animals with four legs, those with two legs, and those with no legs; animals that live on farms, zoos, or plains and those in water; pictures that are more green, yellow, blue, or red; and so on. They may even create abstract categories, such as pictures that make them happy or sad or pictures that make them laugh. They may have no idea of how to label the stacks; they're just looking for similarities.

So you can see that there are advantages to each approach. Classifying is great if you know what you're looking for and can teach the machine the relationship between the label and whatever you happen to be classifying. Clustering is a more powerful tool for gaining insight—for seeing things in a different way, a way you may never have otherwise considered. One of the biggest advantages of clustering is that there's a lot more unlabeled data than labeled data. It's much easier to find a million random images than it is to find the same number that are tagged and labeled.

Clustering has numerous applications in a wide variety of fields. Here are a few examples of how clustering may be used:

- In biology, clustering of genetic patterns can provide insight into how different organisms are related in terms of evolution.
- In medicine, clustering can analyze patterns of antibiotic resistance among different bacteria. It can also be used to identify patterns in x-ray images that signal a higher risk of certain diseases.

- Businesses may apply clustering to *market segmentation*—to aggregate prospective buyers into different groups so the business can more effectively target its marketing efforts.
- In social networks, clustering can be used to identify "similar" communities within the social network and to introduce members who have shared interests.
- Search engines use clustering to more accurately rank search engine results.
- Law enforcement can use clustering to identify areas that have a greater frequency of certain types of crime or to analyze online communications for patterns that may be related to a potential terrorist attack.
- Educational institutions may use clustering to identify conditions that may place students at a greater risk of poor performance.

When you're trying to decide which approach to take—classification or clustering—first ask yourself what problem you're trying to solve or what question you need to answer. Then ask yourself whether the problem or question is something that can best be addressed with classification or clustering. Finally, ask yourself whether the data you have is labeled or unlabeled. By answering these questions, you should have a clearer idea of which approach to take: classification with supervised learning or clustering with unsupervised learning.

Chapter Takeaways

- Classification is best when using labeled data, you know what the classes are, and you can teach the machine to assign each input to one of the known classes.
- Clustering is best when you have a massive volume of unlabeled data and want the machine to identify patterns you're not yet aware exist.
- To choose between classification and clustering, look at the problem you're trying to solve or the question you're trying to answer and ask yourself whether you're looking at a classification problem or a clustering problem.
- Use supervised learning for classification problems.
- Use unsupervised learning for clustering problems.

16

Key Challenges

In this chapter:

- Getting a sufficient amount of quality data
- Avoiding the common mistake of mixing training data with test data
- Adopting a curious mindset
- Choosing the right tools

Given the potential of machine learning (ML), you can expect some challenges. In the previous chapter, we discussed one of the biggest challenges—deciding how to use a specific ML technique. Whether classification or clustering is best and whether supervised or unsupervised learning is most appropriate are not always clear-cut choices.

This chapter introduces you to other challenges you need to overcome—challenges that pose difficult questions, such as: How do I gain access to the data I need? How do I avoid the most common mistakes? and How do I know whether I'm using the right tool (ML or another available tool) for the job? This chapter provides the guidance you need to answer these questions.

Obtaining Enough Quality Data

Even the most basic artificial neural networks don't do a terrific job learning from a small to moderate amount of data. If you think about how most humans learn, you probably don't have to go through millions of images to figure out what a camel looks like. You probably can nail down that skill with a photo or two, even if they're different species.

Modern neural networks don't have nearly that level of efficiency. You have to feed the network millions of images and have it fine-tune the parameters (weights and biases) until it successfully identifies the animal. You might have to use images from several different perspectives and angles to give the network all the data it needs to master the task. Even such basic training takes considerable time.

The good news is that once the network is set up, it can often do a much better job than humans can identifying different images. It just takes a long time to get there.

To overcome this limitation, a few high-tech organizations and universities are trying a slightly different approach. They're starting to use something called *capsule networks*—compact groups of neurons that can extract more learning from smaller data sets. Hopefully over time, these capsule networks will improve a machine's ability to recognize patterns in smaller data sets. As of this writing, these networks are still very much in the experimental phase for most organizations.

Until capsule networks and other advances are made, you need a lot of data, so one of the key challenges of ML is finding the data you need in terms of both quantity and quality.

Many organizations believe that they can't start reaping the advantages of ML until they've collected the data they need. While you can certainly use data you've collected, that's not always necessary. You can find plenty of data, both free and fee-based. Free sources include government databases such as the US Census Bureau database and the CIA World Factbook, medical databases such as Healthdata.gov and NHS health and Social Care Information Centre, Amazon Web Services public data sets, Google Public Data Explorer, Google Finance, the National Climactic Data Center, the *New York Times* and university data centers. Many organizations that collect data, including Acxiom, IRI, and Nielsen, also make their data available for purchase. As long as you can figure out which data will be helpful, you can usually find a source.

Keeping Training and Test Data Separate

With supervised learning, you start with a training data set—one that contains the labels and the object that each label represents. You're showing the machine examples of how the labels relate to the objects. Then you feed the machine a larger validation data set without the labels to gauge how well the machine does at classifying unfamiliar objects. You tell the machine when its classification is wrong and when it's right, and the machine fine-tunes its skill. Note that the validation data set is part of the larger training set, and its sole purpose is to fine-tune the parameters of the network. The test data set is used only to measure the final performance of the trained network.

In an attempt to improve the results of their models, inexperienced data science teams may combine the training and test data. By doing so, they're actually feeding the machine some of the answers. Although this approach improves results, the improvement is only superficial. It actually impairs performance because the machine doesn't adjust the weights and biases as it should. It's sort of like a student cheating on a test; the student may do well on the test, but that doesn't prove he learned anything.

The moral of this story is this: Don't mix test data with training data. Keep them separate.

Carefully Choosing Your Training Data

When it comes to learning, machines can err in the same way humans do. If you feed a machine training data that's not representative of the test data, you may think it learned well when it actually didn't. Imagine training students on how to multiply. Suppose you teach them multiplication tables up to 12 × 12 and then put problems on the test such as 528 × 627. They're not going to perform very well. In the same way, you want your training data to be representative of the data you'll use during and after testing.

Be careful, as well, not to add your own bias when selecting data. For example, if you're developing a model to predict how people will vote across the country and you feed the machine training data that contains voting data only from white, middle-aged women living in Tennessee, your model will do a poor job of predicting the outcome of a national election.

Taking an Exploratory Approach

Although supervised ML can certainly be used to answer specific questions and solve specific problems, many organizations overlook the exploratory potential of unsupervised learning. They never think of using an artificial neural network to identify patterns they don't even know exist. As a result, they underutilize this valuable tool.

Avoid the temptation to look at ML as just another project. You don't want your data science teams merely producing reports on customer engagement, for example. You want them to also look for patterns in data that might point the way to innovative new ideas or to problems you weren't aware of and would never think to look for.

Choosing the Right Tool for the Job

ML is a powerful tool, but it's not the only tool. Sometimes you can find out what you need to know more easily by looking at a table or a graph or by talking to people in different departments. Don't assume that ML is the best tool for answering every question or solving every problem.

Chapter Takeaways

- For an artificial neural network to learn, you need to feed it good data—and a lot of it.
- Don't use your training data as part of your test data. If you do so, the network will perform better on the test but won't make the needed adjustments; it won't learn as well and will perform poorly on newer, unseen examples.
- Choose training data that reflects the data you'll need the neural network to eventually classify or cluster.
- Don't let your personal bias influence your choice of data.
- To fully exploit the power of machine learning, be willing to let the neural network explore your data via unsupervised learning.
- Look for simpler ways to answer questions and solve problems before turning to an artificial neural network for answers.

Part IV
Putting Artificial Intelligence to Work

17 Harnessing the Power of Natural Language Processing..181

18 Automating Customer Interactions 193

19 Improving Data-Based Decision-Making..199

20 Using Machine Learning to Predict Events and Outcomes.................................207

21 Building Artificial Minds...219

17

Harnessing the Power of Natural Language Processing

In this chapter:

- Understanding natural language processing (NLP) basics
- Seeing NLP applied to customer service
- Checking out the top NLP tools

One of the most interesting areas in artificial intelligence (AI) is *natural language processing* (NLP), which is a combination of *natural language understanding* (NLU) and *natural language generation* (NLG). With NLU, a system receives and interprets written or spoken input. With NLG, a system can respond to the message it received by delivering its own message in written or spoken output. When combined, NLG and NLU are collectively referred to as NLP.

NLP is the foundation of AI chatbots, virtual assistants, and virtual agents—software applications that engage in online or telephone conversations with users through text or text-to-speech, typically to automate customer or technical support to some degree. If you have ever obtained customer service or technical support over the phone or by visiting a company's website, you answered a robocall, or you interacted with Siri or Alexa, chances are good that you have talked with a chatbot, virtual assistant, or virtual agent. Here's how the three differ:

- A *chatbot* generally asks a lot of questions in a structured process to identify what a user needs or wants. It's not geared to engage in unstructured conversations.

- A *virtual assistant* can carry on a conversation with the user and perform tasks for the user, such as placing a phone call, setting an alarm or reminder, or scheduling an appointment.
- A *virtual agent* is like a chatbot, but typically with an animated character to take the place of a person.

When you engage in conversation with a chatbot, virtual assistant, or virtual agent, you may feel as though it is a two-step process—the software listens and replies. However, NLP breaks down the process into a number of steps. For example, suppose you ask, "What will the weather be like today?" The first step the virtual assistant takes is to receive the spoken (audio) input. Next, it runs it through a speech recognition system and converts the audio into text. It then uses its natural understanding to convert the text into something more suitable for a search engine to understand; for example, it might extract the keywords *weather*, *will*, and *today* and translate them into "today's weather forecast" and, if your phone has geolocation enabled, it will extract your phone's location and add that to the search.

The virtual assistant then enters the search phrase it created into a search engine, such as Google—for example, "today's weather forecast for Portland, Oregon." After the search engine pulls up the result, the virtual assistant then uses NLG to read the result and tell you today's weather forecast for Portland, Oregon. Your smart phone might respond, "It will be sunny and 73 today with clouds moving in at two o'clock this afternoon and a 70 percent chance of rain starting at four o'clock p.m."

So, to you, NLP may seem like a simple process—you ask a question about the weather, and you get an appropriate response. But to the AI system, the NLP involves numerous steps.

Although most people are most consciously aware of using NLP via their smart phones, many organizations use it to alleviate the burden of providing customer service and tech support to a high volume of customers. For example, NLU can be used to read and interpret incoming e-mail messages and send out automated replies to common questions or, for more unique questions or concerns, redirect the message to the person in the organization most qualified to respond to it.

NLP can also be used to review documents, such as financial reports, extract highlights, and then produce a summary report that explains the significance of any changes in key figures, such as revenue or profit. The NLP may also be programmed to extract certain figures and chart them to provide deeper insight.

People often think that the greatest challenge with creating chatbots and virtual assistants is speech recognition because they often see on a daily basis how their smart phone struggles to understand what they say. However, it's actually the NLU and NLG aspects that typically pose the greater challenges because they're having to process more complex information.

With speech recognition, the challenge is getting the app to "hear" accurately, and that is certainly a key first step in enabling an app to understand. However, with NLU and NLG, the app must extract meaning from the words and phrases fed into the system, which is much more difficult. Language is filled with structural inconsistencies, and many people exaggerate or use metaphors. It's very difficult for an AI system to understand what you mean when you say that you've "been waiting forever" or that you're "deeply disappointed," and you wouldn't want your system responding by saying something like "I'm glad you're enjoying your product; please stay on the line to take a brief survey."

In this chapter, I take a deeper dive into NLU and NLG and introduce you to some of the tools of the trade for creating your own NLP applications.

Extracting Meaning from Text and Speech with NLU

Natural language understanding (NLU) involves extracting meaning from spoken or written statements or questions. While speech recognition focuses on accurately translating spoken words into text, NLU goes one step further by interpreting the meaning of statements or questions.

Now, it might be easier to talk about AI systems as reading and writing instead of understanding and generating, but even though the end result might be the same, the NLP involves something very different from what you do when you read and write.

Imagine a simple conversation that you might have with a friend or colleague. Suppose a new Indian restaurant opened close to where you work. One day a coworker asks, "Did you and Susan try that new Indian restaurant?"

You reply, "Actually, it was a little too spicy."

Your coworker asks, "Will you go back?"

You say, "I don't know."

From a human perspective, this is a basic exchange, but from an AI perspective, it's complicated. The first challenge is that you need to understand a lot of the context. When your coworker asks you if you "tried" the new restaurant, she's asking if you went there for the first time. (She's not asking if you tried to get there or whether you tried to start a new Indian restaurant.)

When you respond that it's too spicy, you're implying that yes, you've been to that restaurant, and you're adding your opinion of the food—that it's spicier than you like. An AI system would have to reason that you wouldn't be able to know that the food was too spicy unless you had eaten at the restaurant.

Finally, when your coworker asks whether you'll go back, your answer is a little irregular. You say you "don't know." But in this case, your answer doesn't mean that you don't know what your coworker asking. Instead, it means that you don't know whether the food was good enough for you to return to the restaurant. If the AI system didn't understand your meaning when you said, "I don't know," it might respond with something like, "Would you like me to repeat the question?"

Remember that the AI system is looking only at data and patterns. Making sense of this simple exchange would require a great deal of underlying data. The AI system would need to know what "trying" a restaurant means in this context. It would need to know that if you said the food was spicy, you had been to the restaurant. It would need to know that you "not knowing" whether you'll go back is actually your judgment about the food's flavor and not that you don't know what your coworker is asking.

In many ways NLU is really the most challenging component of NLP; for it to carry on a sensible conversation with a person, it first needs to understand what that person is saying.

Delivering Sensible Responses with NLG

"Natural language generation is a sophisticated way for artificial intelligence to generate very natural sounding text." I must confess, I didn't write that first sentence. A natural language generation (NLG) application wrote it for me in response to my question, "What is natural language generation?"

Although NLG applications can produce text similar to what a person might write or say, the *process* of writing is very different for an AI system. The system doesn't write in the same way you might have learned in a creative writing course. The computer sees writing as a data challenge and not a creative process.

An AI system looks for patterns in data, so in this case, the system finds the most common phrases that match the keywords in my question. To respond to my question, the AI system first had to understand what I said. It had to know that by starting with the words "What is...," I would be asking for a definition of the word or phrase that followed. So, my question could be reworded as a command, "Define 'natural language generation'." The AI system then checked its search index of millions of web pages to find information relevant to the phrase "natural language generation."

You can almost think of NLG as a super-powered search engine. In this example, the AI system searched for a phrase and then searched deeper within those results. Using the data it gathered—text that matched what it interpreted I was looking for—it assembled a suitable response starting with the phrase "Natural language generation is...." It even matched its definition of "natural language generation" with existing definitions in its search results to ensure its definition would be unique.

Now, the system just generated this one sentence. But most people use this technology to generate paragraphs and even articles. Right now, NLG works best for product reviews, weather forecasts, and even news stories. It excels at combining data from different sources and then presenting it in a unique way.

The Associated Press uses NLG to publish articles about a company's quarterly earnings and profit—summaries published four times a year to report the company's performance. NLG works well in this application because it can draw data from several different sources. The NLG system combines these data sources and adds some text to write a story; for example, "Microsoft released its third quarter earnings report today. Earnings increased 3% over last quarter, which exceeded analysts' expectations by 1%. Microsoft's share price rose 5% in afterhours trading. The company said that it was not affected by supply chain issues with China."

As you can see in this example, the AI system combined data from Microsoft's earnings report, data regarding what analysts had been expecting, and data about Microsoft's share price in afterhours trading to generate a story that provides investors with the insight they need to make a well-informed decision of whether to buy or sell shares in Microsoft.

You've probably read several short stories written this way and not even realized they were generated in milliseconds by an AI system.

If you're thinking about using this technology for your organization, a good first step is to consider the different data sources you'd like to combine and how you could use those sources to tell a story. Maybe you'll create automated executive briefings or informative blog posts. Or, as you'll see in the next section, you can even use it to better communicate with your customer.

Automating Customer Service

As NLP technologies and techniques advance, their capabilities become more sophisticated. You may have noticed this yourself if you have engaged in a robocall recently. In the past, you could easily tell whether you were talking to a computer or a person. Now some systems are so sophisticated, you have a tough time telling the difference. Even if you try to throw the system a curve ball by asking whether it's a person, it has a response that will make you wonder.

Due to the increasing sophistication of NLP systems and the increasing cost of paying customer service representatives and technical support personnel to handle phone calls, NLP is becoming a more attractive option for companies. Through NLU, the system can take the call and figure out what the customer needs, and through NLG, it can provide the answer and, if it cannot come up with the answer, redirect the call to someone in the organization who's more qualified.

NLG can do what any customer service or tech support person would do—look up the answer or solution in the organization's data sources and formulate a response based on that information. If you have a large volume of pertinent data, it's not too difficult to imagine an NLG system doing the heavy lifting.

Imagine you just bought a new flat screen television, and you're not sure how to connect it with a certain online streaming service, such as Netflix or Hulu. You head to the manufacturer's website and search for "How do I connect my TV to Netflix?" The AI system extracts the keywords "connect," "TV," and "Netflix" to determine the general information being requested, but the data sources have instructions that differ for different models, so it responds with something like, "Thank you for your message. We have a number of television sets that can connect to Netflix. What is the model number of your television set? The model number is affixed to the back of the unit near the power cord."

Even in the simple exchange, you have the AI system searching through a product catalog to verify that certain television sets support Netflix, while others do not. The system is sophisticated enough to request a model number and provide the details the customer needs to quickly and easily find the model number. When the customer responds with the model number, the system has all the information it needs to look up instructions. It can locate the user's manual, skip to the page for programming streaming services, and present the instructions. Or it may find the necessary information on the Netflix website or in a discussion forum.

The more data this NLG system has access to, the more useful the response. You might get a message back that a firmware update is available for your TV model and you must download and install the update before you can connect to Netflix. The system may then ask if you need help installing the update.

An NLP service may also be sophisticated enough to reach out to customers to prevent problems. For example, now that the system knows you're watching Netflix on your television set, it can monitor for any changes in the Netflix service that might affect your ability to stream your favorite shows. If Netflix makes such a change, the NLP system can compose and send you an email or text message indicating that you must perform certain steps if you want to continue using Netflix.

For NLP systems, every interaction is a data challenge, and the more relevant data it has, the better it functions. With every customer interaction, it has more data to fine-tune its operation. It may even gather data directly from your television set to figure out how you use it and identify any problems you're having navigating its menu or watching shows. It can then use this data to send you more relevant and accurate customer service messages.

Reviewing the Top NLP Tools and Resources

NLP is a popular area in the AI arena, so you can find plenty of tools for creating your own NLP systems. Some of these tools are commercial products available through software vendors, and others are open-source tools, which the developers make available for free.

A great open-source product is the Natural Language Toolkit (NLTK), which is available for download at www.nltk.org along with instructions on how to install and use it and a list of frequently asked questions (FAQ). NLTK is written in Python, so you need some background in Python to use it effectively. (It supports both versions of Python, but I recommend Python 3.4 going forward.) The website also contains a link to an active discussion forum, where you can learn more about NLTK from other users. NLTK uses an Open Source Apache license, which means you could use it freely to learn and to create your own applications.

If you decide to use NLTK or just want to play around with it to learn how NLP works and get some experience with it, I strongly recommend you read *Natural Language Processing with Python*, by Steven Bird, Ewan Klein, and Edward Loper, the creators of NLTK. This book is available for free online at www.nltk.org/book. This book contains valuable information, instructions, and code samples that the authors refer to as *recipes*.

Other notable open-source NLP development tools include the following:

- Python tools
  - SpaCy (spacy.io)
  - TextBlob (textblob.readthedocs.io/en/dev)
  - Textacy (pypi.org/project/textacy)
  - PyTorch-NLP (pytorchnlp.readthedocs.io/en/latest)
- Node tools
  - Retext (www.npmjs.com/package/node-nlp)
  - Compromise (www.npmjs.com/package/compromise)
  - Natural (www.npmjs.com/package/natural)
  - Nlp.js (http://www.npmjs.com/package/node-nlp)
- Java tools
  - OpenNLP (opennlp.apache.org)
  - StanfordNLP (stanfordnlp.github.io/CoreNLP)

- Apache Spark tools
  - Spark NLP (nlp.johnsnowlabs.com)

The following sections highlight NLP tools and resources that focus specifically on NLU and NLG.

NLU Tools

NLU is more challenging than NLG. In fact, it is considered an *AI-hard problem*—an extremely challenging computational problem. The process of breaking a question or statement into its component parts and describing their syntactic and semantic roles is much more difficult than outputting statements or questions when the syntactic and semantic schemes are predetermined by the system generating the response.

To help them develop their own conversation bots, several of the leading companies in this area have opened their cloud-based NLU tools to developers and engineers. Four companies are leaders in NLU—Amazon with Alexa, Apple with Siri, Google with Google Assistant, and Microsoft with Cortana. In their paper "A Comparison and Critique of Natural Language Understanding Tools,"[1] Massimo Canonico and Luigi De Russis compared and critiqued the following six main NLU cloud platforms personalized and trained by developers:

- Google's Dialogflow
- Facebook's wit.ai
- Microsoft's LUIS
- IBM's Watson Conversation
- Amazon's Lex
- Recast.ai

They wanted to see which platform was best at understanding the intended meaning of language input—which one worked best in terms of NLU. They concluded that Watson Conversation was best at understanding the intended meaning of various statements and questions. This paper came out in 2018, so the results might be

---

1 Canonico, Massimo, and Luigi De Russis. "A comparison and critique of natural language understanding tools." Cloud Computing 2018 (2018): 120. Harvard.

different today, but if you're choosing an NLP development platform, I encourage you to read this paper to learn how to test different platforms yourself.

Some of the best tools for developing NLU applications are available through the companies that are leading the industry in NLP development. NLU tools include the following:

- IBM's Watson Assistant (cloud.ibm.com/catalog/services/watson-assistant)
- Google's Dialogflow (cloud.google.com/dialogflow)
- Facebook's wit.ai (wit.ai)
- Microsoft's LUIS (www.luis.ai)
- Amazon's Lex (aws.amazon.com/lex)
- SAP Conversational AI (cai.tools.sap)

In their paper, Canonico and De Russis didn't evaluate these tools. They evaluated only the AI conversational platforms built using these tools and then personalized and trained by developers.

NLG Tools

As I mentioned in the previous section, NLG is easier than NLU, but it's still a challenge. NLG is sort of like an automated reference librarian, looking up and pulling relevant data from a variety of sources and stitching it together with other words and phrases to generate and deliver a meaningful and relevant response.

Several tools are available for developing NLG applications. One of the most popular open-source NLG tools is SimpleNLG, a project launched by university professor Ehud Reiter from the University of Aberdeen in Scotland. He later founded a company called Arria, which maintains a commercial NLG platform.

SimpleNLG is a realization engine for Natural Language Generation. It tries to produce natural-sounding text. To get started with SimpleNLG, go to github.com/simplenlg/simplenlg, scroll down to the Getting Started section, and click the link for the tutorial. SimpleNLG is a Java library. You just download the zip file, and you can import it and start using this Java class immediately.

Professor Reiter's blog at ehudreiter.com is a good source of NLG information and additional resources. He also co-authored a book on NLG called *Building Natural Language Generation Systems*, which is a great guide for novice NLG developers.

Reiter also helped start a company called Arria (www.arria.com), which is one of the top commercial NLG platforms. It has a product called NLG Studio (www.arria.com/studio/studio-overview)—a robust, easy-to-use design tool that "gives users (from novice to expert) the ability to automatically generate, from complex data sources, superbly written, natural-language reports that you would believe were written by a human expert." Arria's focus is taking structured data that you might get from a corporate database and then combining it with natural language. For example, you could create an NLG application that would pull a nice chart produced in Microsoft SQL and Excel and generate statements that describe the data.

A competing platform from Automated Insights called Wordsmith (automatedinsights.com/wordsmith) does something very similar, generating stories that sound as though they were composed by a human author. The Associated Press uses Wordsmith to transform raw data into narratives for some of its news releases.

Narrative Science is another company developing NLG applications that transform business data into narratives. This Chicago-based company started out using NLG to create stories that summarized sporting events. Since then, it has moved away from sports journalism and more into corporate reporting. Its main product is called Quill (narrativescience.com/quill), which transforms corporate data into stories and embeds those stories on whatever business intelligence dashboard a company uses. Quill uses NLG to explain complex data visualizations to managers and executives.

Each of these platforms has its own area of expertise. Quill focuses more on readability, whereas the other two products focus more on explaining the data. Which NLG platform is best generally depends on your use cases.

Chapter Takeaways

- Natural language processing (NLP) encompasses natural language understanding (NLU) and natural language generation (NLG).
- NLP is the foundation of *AI chatbots*—software applications that engage in online or telephone conversations with users.

- Chatbots are popular tools for automating customer service or technical support.
- NLU is the more difficult challenge in NLP because the application must understand the literal and figurative meaning of statements and questions along with the context in which they are communicated.
- Numerous tools, both open-source and commercial, are available for simplifying the development of NLP, NLU, and NLG applications.

18

Automating Customer Interactions

In this chapter:

- Adding speech recognition to NLP
- Enabling AI systems to converse in spoken language
- Exploring tools for building virtual agents

Natural language processing (NLP) can understand written communications and compose its own articles and stories, but NLP is being used increasingly to converse with people in spoken language. To accomplish this feat, NLP requires additional functionality in the form of speech recognition and text-to-speech synthesis.

Let's focus on *automated speech recognition* (ASR), which is closely related to NLP. They're not identical, but they do work closely together to facilitate natural language understanding (NLU). ASR converts spoken language into text, and NLU extracts meaning from that text. Much like NLP, speech recognition is considered a major data challenge. ASR needs to account not only for differences in voice quality, volume, and intonation, but also background noise.

To make sense of spoken language, ASR relies on similarities in the pronunciation of words. When you speak, your vocal cords create precise audio output in the form of sound waves, which travel through the air like ripples on the surface of a pond (see Figure 18.1). These waves form smooth, continuous curves and are often referred to as *analog signals*. Computer systems receive the sound waves and convert them into digital signals (also shown in Figure 18.1).

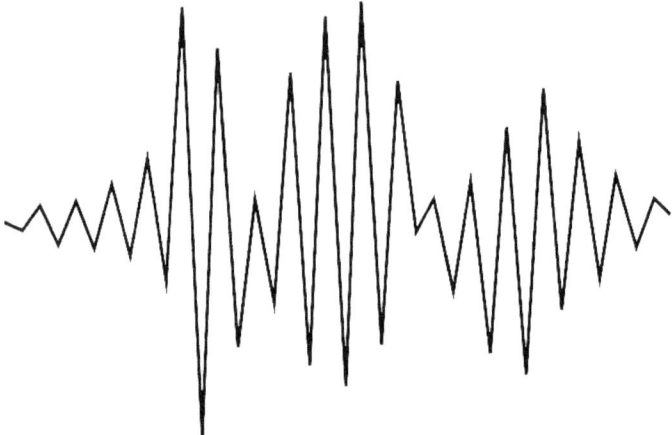

Figure 18.1 An Audio Waveform

Whether the audio wave is analog or digital, it forms a pattern of peaks and valleys that convey data. It turns out that audio waveforms contain accurate digital data, even across different voices. This explains how we can identify words and phrases regardless of the person saying them. Whether you or I say something like, "This is an audio waveform," the wave pattern will be similar; the peaks and valleys will pretty much align. Through the use of machine learning, computers can learn to match these patterns with specific words and other utterances.

To improve accuracy and speed, ASR often uses a statistical model called the *hidden Markov model* to predict the probability of subsequent words based on what was previously said. For example, the system might examine the waveform, determine that the first three words spoken are, "This is an…," and based on the hidden Markov model predict that the next word is most likely to be a noun or an adjective and not a verb. (People don't usually say something like, "This is an eating.") Because the system predicts that the next word will be a noun or an adjective and not a verb, it can reduce the range of possibilities, thereby avoiding having to search through all the verbs in the English language to find the right word. As a result, the speech recognition executes faster and more accurately than it would have without the hidden Markov model.

Now remember that speech recognition is still different from NLP. Here the artificial intelligence (AI) system is simply trying to recognize the sounds you make while speaking. NLP, specifically NLU, is required to extract meaning from the words and phrases. That's why speech recognition has been around so much longer than NLP. It's much easier for a system to convert sound to text than to understand the intended meaning of a statement or question.

Choosing Natural Language Technologies

When you combine NLU, natural language generation (NLG), and ASR, you end up with an AI system that can converse with people via text and speech. In fact, the best known chatbots and virtual assistants—Siri, Cortana, Google Assistant, and Alexa—rely on a combination of all three of these AI language technologies along with text-to-speech synthesis to function.

When you talk to any of these virtual assistants, you might think that you're interacting with an application built with a single technology. In reality, these virtual assistants rely on all these technologies working together to create a seamless experience.

However, when you're thinking about these concepts in your business, you need not take an all-or-nothing approach; you can treat each technology as a separate AI system. With this approach, you can allocate resources to the AI system(s) that will play the biggest role(s) in the desired application. In other words, you avoid spending time, money, and expertise on technologies you don't need.

For example, Amazon encourages businesses to use its virtual assistant, Alexa, to help book conference rooms. To enable the virtual assistant to perform this task, you don't need to invest much in ASR because audio requests for conference rooms contain a narrow selection of words—an employee will state the name or group reserving the room, the conference room number, the date the room is needed, and the start and end times of the meeting. You could even eliminate the need for ASR by requiring employees to use a text-based chatbot to enter their requests.

To create this conference-room scheduler, you don't need to invest much in NLG, either, because the virtual assistant will merely confirm the reservation or indicate that the room is unavailable and suggest another room or other dates or time blocks.

You would invest most of your resources in NLU because that's the biggest challenge. Once the system understands the employee's request, it merely needs to pass along the details to a scheduling system. The system may simply email a confirmation to the person requesting the room.

When you're planning to build your own AI chatbot or virtual assistant, take the same approach to identify the biggest challenges and choosing areas to allocate resources. Will your system be spending the most time listening, understanding, or generating responses or content (articles or stories)? By answering that question, you can focus your design and resources on the technologies that matter most.

Review the Top Tools for Creating Chatbots and Virtual Agents

Chatbots and virtual agents often combine NLU, NLG, ASR, text-to-speech synthesis, machine learning, and automated decision-making. Building chatbots and virtual agents used to require a robust skillset, but several companies now offer sophisticated online tools that simplify the process.

One such tool is Microsoft's Power Virtual Agents (powervirtualagents.microsoft.com/en-us), which enables you to build a virtual agent simply by creating a map of questions and possible responses. You don't need to know how to write code, develop complex models, or train your AI system. All the complexity is handled behind the scenes. You can create virtual assistants to automate customer service, sales, human resources, and other functions that serve users externally or internally.

Another company called Artificial Solutions features a platform called Teneo (www.artificial-solutions.com), which uses a series of algorithms to do something it calls "conversational AI." Using Teneo, you can create a custom chatbot that enables customers to type or speak their questions and then responds via text. As with Microsoft's Power Virtual Agents, Teneo requires no programming knowledge or experience.

Another company called IPSoft has a slightly different approach to providing automated customer service. Instead of allowing you to create your own chatbots or virtual agents, you hire digital employees from IPSoft to build a digital workforce. Digital employees "take on high-volume and repeatable tasks for IT Service Desk and other functions, so human employees can concentrate on higher-value jobs." The DigitalWorkforce.ai page on IPSoft's website (www.ipsoft.com/digitalworkforce) has a cool demonstration that invites you to interview its top digital employee, Amelia (see Figure 18.2).

Figure 18.2 Interview Amelia, a digital employee

You can interview Amelia by typing your questions or by clicking Chat and speaking your questions. Of course, after you hire a digital employee, it will respond to commands and perform common tasks. For example, if you forgot your password to log in to an account, you can say something like, "Amelia, I need to reset my Google password." Amelia will access the Google login page, ask for your username and the new password you want to use, and then perform the steps necessary to reset your password.

Amelia acts pretty much like a human assistant, although she's limited to certain types of work, including account management, performing tasks using Office 365, ticket management, Wi-Fi management, procurement requests, and messaging. Because she has access to the backend data, she can also do some real-time automated decision-making.

This is a nice demonstration of how you can hire a digital worker to perform some of the more mundane work.

Chapter Takeaways

- Automated speech recognition (ASR) can be added to natural language processing (NLP) to enable an artificial intelligence (AI) system to interpret spoken statements, commands, and questions.
- To improve speed and accuracy ASR often employs a statistical model called the hidden Markov model to predict the probability of subsequent words based on what was previously said.
- AI chatbots, virtual assistants, and virtual agents combine natural language understanding (NLU), natural language generation (NLG), ASR, and text-to-speech synthesis to converse with people via written and spoken language.
- Not all AI communication applications require the use of all four technologies (NLU, NLG, ASR, and text-to-speech synthesis), or they may rely on some more than others.
- The easiest way to build custom chatbots, virtual assistants, and virtual agents is to use an online tool developed to simplify the process.

19

Improving Data-Based Decision-Making

In this chapter:

- Automating the decision-making process
- Weighing the pros and cons of automated decision-making systems
- Keeping tabs on Internet of Things (IoT) devices
- Automating customer communications

Imagine you're at the airport getting ready to catch a flight to Phoenix to attend a friend's graduation party. You're a loyal customer, so you fly the same airline. When you arrive at the airport, you start to worry. You see people gathering in front of the arrivals and departures monitors. You follow the crowd, look up at the screen, and see that your flight has been canceled due to inclement weather.

Almost immediately, you get a text on your phone informing you that you've been booked on the next flight. You also receive a smart code with a coupon for one of the airport restaurants. All of this happens in a matter of seconds because you didn't have to get on the phone or wait in line to speak to an agent who then spent additional time booking you on another flight and possibly bringing in a supervisor to help. Everything happens in an instant because your airline uses an artificial intelligence (AI) technology called *automated decision-making*.

Remember that AI systems do well when they have access to tremendous amounts of data. Using that data, the airline can build a system that makes instant decisions and performs tasks in a fraction of the time it would take a human customer service agent.

The automated decision-making system probably evaluated your customer loyalty and used that information to prioritize which customers to rebook first. Then it performed some probability analysis to determine the likelihood of your new flight departing on time. For that, it may have used data sources from the National Weather Service, looked at historical trends of flight delays, and checked its internal data source to check on the future availability of planes at this airport.

Finally, it created a restaurant coupon based on the probability that you might like something to eat before your next flight. To determine whether to offer a coupon, the system may have calculated the probability that you would have sufficient time to eat before your flight. It may have checked the airport to find available restaurants and checked your credit card history (assuming you allowed that) to determine the types of food and restaurants you prefer.

An automated decision-making system like this would use a combination of statistical techniques. One of the most important is *real-time data gathering*—pulling currently available data from a variety of sources, such as the National Weather Service, the airport's database, and your credit card company's database. It may also pull data from the airline to determine whether your original flight was a direct flight or involved connecting flights.

Data analysis may also be used in decision-making to answer questions that enable the system to make better decisions, such as: How long is the average flight delay in similar conditions? Which airport restaurants do the most business when inclement weather delays numerous flights? and What percentage of travelers book their next flight with us after experiencing a flight delay?

Another commonly used statistical technique used in decision-making systems is *trend analysis*, which involves examining large volumes of data to identify patterns and make predictions based on those patterns. For example, trend analysis may look at a graph to determine whether the average duration of flight delays has been increasing or decreasing over the past two hours to predict how long a flight will be delayed or the likelihood it will be canceled.

An AI system may use both data and trend analysis to forecast different outcomes. What's the likelihood that you'll arrive close to your original arrival time? What's the likelihood that your next flight will take off without a delay?

Remember that the AI system sees this as a data challenge. Then it looks for data and patterns in that data, so it can more accurately predict future outcomes.

In many ways, statistical analysis makes an AI system uniquely qualified to make real-time decisions. A human customer service agent may be friendlier, but it would be nearly impossible for a person to weigh all these different statistical outcomes to provide you with timely information, accurate estimates, and quality service. So it would be harder for a live agent to come up with the solution that has the highest probability of retaining you as a satisfied customer.

AI systems can automate the decision-making process to improve both the quality of decisions and the efficiency of making those decisions in a variety of business and financial contexts. For example, in the world of finance, AI systems often perform better than humans at deciding which stocks to buy and sell and when.

Choosing Between Automated and Intuitive Decision-Making

Automated decision-making systems can manage many tasks better than human customer service agents because they can evaluate a larger volume of more diverse data in less time than is humanly possible. However, humans are more intuitive and creative, so instead of approaching AI decision-making systems as replacement for humans, think of using them to enhance how human workers perform their jobs and as a tool for performing mundane, repetitive tasks, so human workers can engage in higher-level work that involves innovation and creative thinking.

In most organizations, people make two types of decisions—analytical and intuitive. *Analytical decisions* are based on data, patterns, statistical analysis, and logic. So with a canceled flight, an AI system can use data about the airport, the flight schedule, and even the weather. Then it makes an analytical decision on how to rebook a flight.

However, sometimes businesses don't have the data they need to make a particular decision or choose the right course of action in a certain situation. For instance, in March 2020 many airlines were forced to shut down not because of weather, but because of a global pandemic. Airlines never had to shut down before due to a pandemic, so no relevant data was available to analyze. As a result, many of the AI systems underperformed in the crisis.

As a result, customer service agents needed to resolve many of the problems using their own analytical/rational thinking and through a more *intuitive decision-making process*.

When choosing between a human and an AI system, keep in mind that AI systems, processing data analytically, generally outperform humans when they have plenty of historical and current data to inform their decisions. In contrast, humans generally outperform AI decision-making systems when historical data is limited and more creative and intuitive thinking is required to solve problems.

Regardless of the business you're in, you generally want a healthy mix of analytical and intuitive decision-making, but that mix may be weighted more heavily on one side or the other. Which is weighted more heavily depends on the types of decisions being weighed and on the data on which those decisions are based. In a business that relies heavily on data-based decision-making, AI systems can play a larger role. For example, a parcel delivery service such as UPS or FedEx could really benefit from an automated decision-making system. These companies have massive amounts of data on delivery times and routes.

Businesses that rely more on innovation to compete are likely to benefit more from creative and intuitive thinking. For example, whereas marketing and advertising can certainly benefit from historical data, decisions about how to approach an advertising campaign or establish a brand require more intuition than analysis.

For many decisions, a combination of analytical and intuitive decision-making can produce the best results. In these cases, an AI decision-making system may be able to provide the information and insight that inspires human innovation.

Gathering Data in Real Time from IoT Devices

Automated decision-making systems work best when they have access to massive amounts of data, and a great source of data are devices that are part of the *Internet of Things* (IoT). The IoT is a network of computers and mechanical and digital machines that can communicate with one another across the network. For example, newer thermostats in homes enable owners to adjust the temperature via an app on their smart phone. A sensor on an oil well can monitor the vibration of the motor used to pump the oil and signal maintenance personnel when the pump needs to be serviced.

Many IoT devices generate real-time data that can be collected and analyzed to inform the decision-making process. For example, chances are good that the electricity gauge on the side of your home is an IoT device that communicates readings back to your electric company for billing purposes. This data can also be analyzed to identify trends and predict spikes in electricity use. Large electric companies or a consortium of companies can gather this data from the home on a block, in a neighborhood or city, or even across states and feed it through an AI decision-making system, which can analyze the data and offer suggestions on how to build the next generation of smart grids.

Using data collected from "smart" meters, an AI system can instantly identify patterns of electricity usage and route more power to different parts of the grid in real time to better serve customers' needs while preventing surges and other fluctuations in power. The system could also be used to monitor home energy use and automatically notify customers of any sudden and significant changes in their energy use, which could indicate a problem with their heating and air-conditioning system or other issues.

Newer IoT meters can even identify individual appliances in someone's home. At some point they might be able to cut power to outlets if they detect an appliance is malfunctioning and at risk of short circuiting.

So if you're thinking about using AI in combination with IoT devices, carefully consider which IoT devices could provide useful data and which data would be the most useful for enabling data-based decision-making. Remember that AI systems perform best with massive amounts of data and that they're great at making analytical decisions that don't require a lot of creativity.

Also consider how data from the IoT devices may be able to be combined with data from other sources, especially historical data, to provide deeper insights and improve decisions. Analyzing real-time data isn't always enough. For some purposes, real-time data must be combined with historical data to identify trends that help predict future events or outcomes. Accurate predictions greatly simplify the decision-making process, whether those decisions are made by an AI system or a human being.

As always, the quality of data improves the AI system's speed and accuracy, which results in better and faster decisions.

Reviewing Automated Decision-Making Tools

With AI-powered automated decision-making, you are essentially replicating or augmenting the abilities of the best decision makers in your organization. You may also be improving decisions and consistency in the decision-making process because automated systems are not subject to human error or bias.

You won't find many tools on the market for creating AI-powered automated decision-making systems, but there are a few. One is Rulex (www.rulex.ai), which uses *inference* (drawing conclusions based on data) and simple predictive if-then logic rules to automate many of the decisions otherwise made by business and operations personnel in several areas, including these:

- Network management
- Supply chain planning
- Public utility control
- Plant operations
- Loan approval
- Service dispatch
- Screening job applicants
- Security management
- Public safety

Rulex examines past decisions that resulted in positive outcomes, figures out the logic behind those decisions, and uses that logic to evaluate new data to make optimum predictive decisions.

Rainbird (https://rainbird.ai/) is another AI-driven solution—an automation platform that scales complex decision-making, reduces human error, and lessens reliance on limited human expertise. It is an authoring platform that provides a graphical user interface (GUI) that makes it easy for nonprogrammers to encode the business's logic. Rainbird claims that its decision-making applications can make decisions 100 times faster and 25 percent more accurate than an organization's smartest employees. In addition, because the decision process is formalized in code, a business can look back and understand how a decision was made.

Rainbird is built on an open architecture, so it can connect to and gather data from a wide variety of external data sources, which can improve the accuracy of decisions and enable the system to make data-based decisions that may not have otherwise been possible due to limitations in the business's internal data sources. One area in which Rainbird excels is in fraud detection and prevention. One of its clients is a large international credit card company that reported a savings of 60 percent in processing costs after automating decisions in its back-office operations.

ACTICO is another company that provides software for developing automated decision-making systems that can 1) improve decisions and 2) automate decisions. Businesses use the decision-making systems they develop through ACTICO to do the following:

- Mitigate risks
- Achieve and maintain regulatory compliance
- Prevent fraud
- Enhance customer engagement (through chatbots, for example)
- Optimize operations

Chapter Takeaways

- AI-driven automated decision-making systems typically make better decisions significantly faster than their human counterparts.
- Businesses use automated decision-making systems to make better, faster decisions and to replicate or augment what the smartest people in their organization do.

- Automated decision-making works best with analytical decisions, when the system can identify patterns in data or logic in previous good decisions and base its decisions on that historical data and logic.
- People are generally better at making decisions that require intuition and creativity, and no historical data is available to guide the decision.
- Devices that make up the Internet of Things collectively produce large volumes of data that can provide valuable insights and help inform the decision-making process.
- You can find a few tools for building AI-driven automated decision-making systems, including solutions from Rulex, Rainbird, and ACTICO.

20

Using Machine Learning to Predict Events and Outcomes

In this chapter:

- Building machine learning platforms
- Identifying practical business applications for machine learning
- Steering clear of unethical practices regarding data
- Checking out some machine learning tools

Natural language processing (NLP), automated speech recognition (ASR), and artificial intelligence (AI)-driven automated decision-making are very different technologies, but they are all developed with the help of the same technology: machine learning (ML).

All these technologies rely on the ability to identify patterns in large volumes of data and learn from those patterns. With NLP, the system identifies patterns in the way people communicate. With ASR, the system looks for patterns in the way people pronounce and string together words. With AI-driven automated decision-making, the system looks for patterns in data or in the logic used to make successful decisions in the past. Based on the patterns the system identifies in the data or logic, the system can make projections or predictions about future outcomes or events and even choose a course of action.

All these systems rely on massive data sets and sophisticated pattern matching, which is what ML is all about. As defined in Chapter 7, "What Is Machine Learning?", *machine learning* is a branch of artificial intelligence that involves the development of systems whose performance improves from experience without being explicitly programmed to perform a task. An ML application consists of a set of algorithms that identify patterns in large volumes of data. These algorithms typically label the data so that it can be classified or clustered.

Google and Bing use ML to classify web pages. So, when you type the word *cat* into a search engine, it searches its massive database to see which web pages it labeled with the keyword *cat*. These search indexes use numerous algorithms to classify billions of web pages based on keywords. The algorithms function a bit like giant label guns, tagging web pages the same way you might label the spices in a spice rack to make them easier to identify.

But again, even though one system classifies web pages and the other tries to make decisions or understand language, the underlying concept is similar; data is being labeled and categorized based on the ML's classification or clustering algorithms.

Think of ML as a key ingredient or component of AI that specializes in pattern matching and labeling. These patterns and labels can then be fed into larger AI applications that use the patterns and labels for various purposes—to understand and respond to users, to write articles or stories, to predict outcomes, to make decisions, and so on.

However, much like any other key ingredient, ML can be mixed with other technologies or used on its own. Later in this chapter, we'll take a look at various ways ML can be used alone and with other AI technologies in business applications.

Machine Learning Is Really about Labeling Data

Before an ML application can do anything useful, it needs to identify patterns in data sets and label the data according to the patterns it identifies. An ML application must be trained to accurately label data. As explained in Chapter 8, "Different Ways a Machine Learns," four training methods are used in ML:

- **Supervised learning** involves showing the machine the connection between data and labels, such as the connection between a picture of a dog and the word *dog*. Supervised learning is best for classification.
- **Unsupervised learning** involves feeding data into the machine and letting it classify the data based on similarities and differences it notices; for example,

suppose you feed the machine a stack of animal photos. It could classify them by animal type; color; shape; whether the animals have fur, feathers, or scales; and so on. Unsupervised learning is best for clustering and when you want to see what a machine may think are similarities in data sets.

- **Semi-supervised learning** is a cross between supervised and unsupervised learning. It involves providing the machine with some overall direction and lots of data and letting the machine work out the details.
- **Reinforcement learning** involves giving the machine a task to perform and rewarding its performance. With each reward, the machine improves at performing the task.

Imagine that you start a business that requires sorting through tons of trash to separate out the recyclable material. Thousands of pieces of garbage might be carried down the conveyor belt in a matter of seconds, and the ML algorithm needs to identify each piece.

From a data perspective, this is a standard classification problem. In this example, you can use supervised training to teach the system what's recyclable and what's not. You might have separate piles of aluminum, plastic containers, and paper (all recyclable), along with piles of food waste and garden clippings (not recyclable). Each pile would serve as a training data set, and you would use the items in each pile to train the system to tell the difference between recyclable and nonrecyclable items.

As you can imagine, unsupervised learning wouldn't be very useful for a recycling plant. With unsupervised learning, the system could cluster items based on color, for example, in which grass clippings, green plastic bottles, and green aluminum cans would all end up being treated the same.

Unsupervised learning would be best for discovering patterns in data sets that humans might not notice; these might be patterns in symptoms of patients who have the same illness or patterns in the chemical composition of different medications that might reveal a use for a medication that researchers would never think of.

When you're thinking of how to apply ML to solve a problem, consider the nature of the available data and the problem you're trying to solve. These considerations will help guide your choice of algorithms and training methods to use.

Looking at What Machine Learning Can Do

Business leaders are always looking for new technologies that can help the business perform better, faster, and more efficiently. They often want to adopt the technology before they have a clear idea of how they can use it in the context of their business operations. Taking a look at different use cases for a technology can often provide the clarity business leaders need and spark ideas for applications of it. The following sections reveal several practical applications of ML.

Predict What Customers Will Buy

One of the most valuable insights a business can extract from its data is a prediction of what a customer will buy or do. You could use various traditional methods to make such predictions, such as conducting a survey or a focus group, but those methods are costly and time-consuming and may not provide the volume of data needed to make an accurate prediction. These methods are also susceptible to bias and human error.

With ML and large volumes of relevant, quality data, you can have a computer conduct the analysis and make highly accurate predictions for a fraction of the cost. For example, Netflix has gobs of data on what its subscribers watch, and it analyzes this data along with data from other sources to determine the types of movies and series that are likely to be popular with viewers. Amazon analyzes each member's purchase history to choose which products to advertise to members based on their past purchases and preferences. Some businesses purchase access to anonymized credit card data so they can analyze spending patterns to develop ideas for products that are likely to attract buyers.

When you're thinking of implementing ML in your business, consider how you might be able to use it to serve your customers better and increase sales in the process.

Answer Questions Before They're Asked

ML is adept at identifying problems and opportunities before anyone is aware of them and at answering questions before anyone in the organization thinks of asking them. It performs this magic by—you guessed it—identifying patterns in large volumes of data.

For example, suppose you built an ML application that gathered all social media data about your business and analyzed that data to identify patterns. The application would then summarize the data and present it in a weekly report to let executives know how people who engage in social media feel about your company and its products and services.

You could use supervised or unsupervised ML to train the system, depending on what you decided you wanted the system to do. With supervised learning, you might classify customer feedback using specific labels, such as "satisfied," "dissatisfied," "disgruntled," and "interested." You might even identify which users have the most influence. You would then create a training data set for each mood, grouping messages that users posted by mood. During training, the machine would identify patterns in the messages that match up with the different moods.

Supervised learning would be great to monitor and gauge how people feel about your company in relation to the moods you chose to identify. However, it would fall short for anything posted about your company that didn't fall into one of those mood categories, such as discussions about what customers need that's not being provided by your company that could lead to an innovative product idea.

Unsupervised learning would do a better job of revealing patterns in data nobody at your company would have ever imagined looking for. With unsupervised learning, you would just feed the social media data into the system and have it identify patterns in the data and cluster the posts according to those patterns. You could then examine the clusters to find out why the system clustered the posts as it did. One cluster may reveal a pattern of support for the company's community outreach efforts, another may reveal an unmet customer need, and another may reveal an issue many customers are having with a specific product. You may even discover that a celebrity used your product, which provides a marketing opportunity to build on that free press.

In some ways, an unsupervised ML system has much more flexibility, but that comes at a cost. Unsupervised learning is more susceptible to "noise" in the data, resulting in numerous small clusters that are difficult to interpret. Some posts may even appear to be clustered randomly.

As you think about how to integrate ML into your business, consider the pros and cons of both supervised and unsupervised learning and try to determine which approach would be best for the desired application.

Make Better Decisions Faster

In 2016, the famous computer scientist Geoffrey Hinton said, "People should stop training radiologists, now. It's just completely obvious that within five years deep learning is going to do better than radiologists." A few seconds later he corrected himself. He said it might take ten years. He believed that ML systems could do a much better job of spotting anomalies in X-rays, so radiologists would no longer be needed. The reason he gave is that deep learning systems can look at millions of X-rays within minutes and use vast amounts of data to fine-tune their ability to spot patterns. The human brain just doesn't have the capacity for that.

The ability of ML to analyze vast amounts of diverse data makes it well equipped to play a key role in AI-powered automated decision-making systems. For example, an automated decision-making system that can identify patterns in X-rays could "decide" whether surgery is necessary or recommended. It could then recommend this to a surgeon, who would make the final decision. It would be like getting a second opinion.

Depending on how you would want this radiologist robot to function, you could build it using supervised or unsupervised learning. With supervised learning, you would train the system to recognize patterns. For example, you could gather thousands of X-rays of spines of patients who needed back surgery and feed them into the system to create a connection between the patterns in these X-rays and a label such as "Positive for back surgery." You could also feed the system thousands (or millions) of X-rays of healthy spines to train the system on their connection with a label such as "Negative for back surgery." Of course, you could make the radiologist robot even more sophisticated by training it on a host of different patterns in spine X-rays that would be associated with every spinal diagnosis that could be made from examining X-rays.

The advantage of such a system is it can make instantaneous decisions. It might even be included as part of the X-ray machine. Also, if you believe Professor Hinton, it could be much more accurate. The machine could see tiny abnormalities that would be nearly impossible for a human radiologist to identify. A possible disadvantage is that the system could overlook an abnormality that's not linked to a known diagnosis. Of course, you could mitigate this disadvantage to some degree by training the system to refer any patterns that don't match a known condition and don't match X-rays of healthy spines to a human radiologist or surgeon.

As an alternative, you could develop the radiologist robot using unsupervised learning, allowing the machine to decide how to cluster X-rays according to the patterns it detects. Then a radiologist or surgeon could examine the clusters and try to figure out why the machine clustered the X-rays as it did. The clusters may match up with known spinal diagnoses, and they may not, perhaps leading to the discovery of a previously unrecognized condition.

Most of the work in this area (using ML in automated decision-making systems) is done using supervised learning. The developer has a list of classifications and a training data set for each one and trains the system to make the connection between patterns in each data set and its corresponding class. After the training session, the system can identify patterns in any new input and figure out the class to which it belongs.

Of course, there are pros and cons to replacing human experts with machines, but I'll let the human experts and the proponents of AI and ML debate the issue. The point I want to make in this section is that ML can play a key role in all sorts of AI-driven automated decision-making applications, but what's important is that you decide how much control you want to leave in the "hands" of the system.

Replicate Expertise in Your Business

In the 1982 film *Blade Runner*, the Tyrell Corporation designs and builds *replicants*—bioengineered beings nearly identical to humans but with superior strength, speed, agility, and intelligence that varies depending on the model. We're a long way from that, assuming it's even possible, but AI bots have been developed to replicate human expertise and, in some cases, perform the same tasks as their human counterparts.

If you have recently applied for a loan or credit card online, you probably have already interacted with an AI bot and perhaps never even realized it. Many banks and credit card companies advertise a 30-second decision for loans and credit card accounts, and they usually deliver on that promise. How do they do it so quickly? By using a machine-learning AI-driven automated decision-making system. The system quickly reviews the applicant's credit report and any other relevant data it has access to, compares it to a set of criteria, and approves or denies the request accordingly.

What they're really doing behind the scenes is making educated guesses or predictions about your ability to make payments. Assuming the loan or credit card application is approved, the system will calculate the maximum loan or credit limit based on detailed financial information about the applicant. Banks and credit card companies don't want to approve an applicant for an amount that he or she would be unable to make the payments on.

The latest generation of automated credit-approval systems isn't limited to a credit score or credit report. These systems may examine your employment history, payment history, recent purchases, insurance claims, changes in marital status, and even your social media data. Because they're looking through so much more data, they can usually predict outcomes more accurately and at a much lower cost than is possible by a human loan officer.

Because systems such as these give more accurate results at a lower cost, they're now being used for many different types of decisions. Some businesses are using automated decision-making systems to screen out job applicants. Some universities use similar systems to screen candidates for admission.

If you're thinking about using a system like this in your organization, start by considering your data. The most common system is one that classifies people based on established criteria. Many of these systems use supervised ML to separate the chaff from the grain, so to speak, placing people in one group or the other. Either you're credit worthy or you're not. Either you're likely to succeed at this school, or you're not. Either you're likely to get in a car accident in the next six months, or you're not.

If you have decisions that can be made based on any sort of classification, a machine learning AI-driven decision-making program may be able to automate the process, thereby replicating or augmenting the expertise in your organization.

Use Your Power for Good, Not Evil: Machine Learning Ethics

If you read comic books or watch any superhero movies or TV shows, one of the common themes is characters with superpowers choosing whether to use those powers to benefit society or to benefit themselves to the detriment of others.

Likewise, ML is a powerful tool that can be used for good or evil, and because it wields much of its power inside the confines of a black box, developers are often unaware of the harm their AI-driven automated decision-making systems cause.

ML algorithms have the power to decide whether a person gets a loan or not, who gets into a certain school and who doesn't, who gets a job, who pays more in health insurance, and so on. A machine makes these decisions that can have a big impact on peoples' lives. But on what criteria are these decisions made? What really makes a person a quality employee? Which factors are most likely to lead to a student's success in school, and how is "success" defined? Should we be loaning money on the basis of a person's historical data?

ML often has a limited scope and perspective. It just looks at the data. It doesn't consider a person's background or mitigating circumstances that may have influenced a person's behavior. It may not fact-check the data. It may not have data that reflects the person's character traits. As a result, it may not render a fair judgment. The ML system may conclude that students from more affluent neighborhoods are more successful in college and, as a result, reject a superior candidate from a poorer neighborhood. It may find that more affluent people are more likely to make their loan payments and reject a younger person who's just getting started but has great prospects.

If the system has any inequality built into it, including biases passed along by the trainer or the selection of training data, the AI system can magnify it and include that magnified bias in making future decisions. Any inequality baked into the system might get amplified.

Imagine that you work for a software development company. Your executives decide they want to use an ML automated decision-making system to rate employment applications. So you gather up the employment applications your company has on record for your top 500 employees. Then you use this data to train your ML algorithm to identify candidates who have submitted applications that are a close match.

Now suppose that out of those 500 top employees, only 150 of them are women. When you train your system to rate new employees, it learns (from the data you feed it) that women are less likely to do well in your organization. That means it will rate applications from female candidates lower.

The lesson here is that when you're building out these automated decision-making systems, you have to be careful about the data you use to train the system. Biased training data bakes bias into the system, which is unfair and unethical. In fact, the

European Union has enacted a "right to explanation," which grants people the right to know the criteria and logic a system uses when making decisions about them.

Review the Top Machine Learning Tools

ML is one of the richest areas in artificial intelligence because so much data is available. Most companies are still struggling with what to do with just the data they've collected internally, not to mention data they can pull from other sources. Lack of data is no longer the challenge. The challenge is in figuring out how to extract business value from all that data. ML enables companies to meet that challenge.

The good news about ML is that it's been around for a long time, so a variety of tools and services are available to help companies take advantage of this technology. Individuals, businesses, and universities have been developing tools for decades, and most of them are easily accessible and free to use.

Now, remember that ML is the technology used to build much of the functionality into AI systems, so as soon as you get a handle on ML tools, you can use them to build systems around natural language processing, speech recognition, and automated decision-making.

If you're just getting started with ML, one of the best resources is scikit-learn (scikit-learn.org/stable)—an ML implementation in Python. It's built on numerous Python projects, and it's open source. You can even use it in your own ML projects because it's protected under the very permissive Berkeley Software Distribution (BSD) license. (By the way, "scikit" is short for "science kit" and is pronounced *sy-kit*.)

The reason this is such a good resource to start with is that it enables you to work with a variety of ML algorithms, including algorithms for classification, clustering, and even regression. And you can actually use scikit-learn on the top cloud-based ML platforms from Microsoft and IBM, among others.

Many large tech companies feature cloud-based ML as a service (MLaaS) solutions. These platforms handle most of the infrastructure issues, including data preprocessing and model training. The big four are these:

- Amazon SageMaker (aws.amazon.com/sagemaker)
- Microsoft Azure Machine Learning (azure.microsoft.com/en-us/services/machine-learning)

- IBM Watson (www.ibm.com/watson)
- Google Cloud AI (cloud.google.com/products/ai)

Amazon describes SageMaker as "a fully managed service that provides every developer and data scientist with the ability to build, train, and deploy machine learning (ML) models quickly." As you might expect, SageMaker connects up with a lot of Amazon's other cloud services, so you can upload your organizational data to an Amazon cloud data warehouse and then use SageMaker's ML algorithms to analyze that data.

Microsoft's ML platform, which is part of its Azure cloud services platform, is aptly called Azure Machine Learning. It is a cloud-based service used to build, test, and deploy ML solutions. To simplify the creation of ML models, Microsoft offers Azure Machine Learning Studio (studio.azureml.net)—a drag-and-drop tool that can be used to build ML models and publish them as web services. With Machine Learning Studio, "you can build, train, and track highly accurate machine learning and deep-learning models in an Azure Machine Learning Workspace."

Like Microsoft, IBM has a cloud-based platform for deploying ML models and a drag-and-drop studio for creating them. IBM Watson Machine Learning is the platform that "enables data scientists and developers to accelerate AI machine-learning deployment." This platform uses a concept IBM call *pipelines*. You can pipeline in different data sources and analyze the data using ML. You can also stream data in from other sources. With IBM Watson Studio, you can prepare data and build ML models using open source codes (such as those available through sci-kit) or visual modeling.

Google Cloud AI comprises three separate products: *AI Hub* is a hosted repository of plug-and-play AI components. AI building blocks simplify the process of adding sight, language, conversation, and structured data to AI applications. AI Platform is a code-based data science development environment that enables data scientists and developers to take projects from ideation quickly to deployment.

These commercial services and tools are similar and different in many ways. They all support classification and regression algorithms, but only Amazon and Microsoft support clustering. Microsoft Azure Machine Learning Studio is the only one that supports anomaly detection and ranking. Azure ML Studio and Google Cloud AI support recommendation, whereas Amazon SageMaker and IBM Watson do not. Also, AI solutions offered by Amazon, Google, and IBM Watson all feature built-in algorithms, whereas Microsoft Azure requires you to bring your own. Most of them have the flexibility to use frameworks like scikit-learn. And, as you'll see in the next chapter, they all support the popular TensorFlow framework—a free and open-source software library for dataflow and ML development.

Chapter Takeaways

- Machine learning is the foundation of most artificial intelligence systems, including NLP, ASR, and automated decision-making.
- An ML application consists of a set of algorithms that identify patterns in large volumes of data.
- ML algorithms typically identify patterns in data and use those patterns to classify or cluster data.
- ML is centered on labeling data using labels provided by a trainer (in supervised learning) or labels based on clusters the system creates (in unsupervised learning).
- ML systems can perform many tasks traditionally performed by humans, including tasks that require making predictions and decisions and answering questions.
- When developing ML systems, choose your data carefully to avoid baking bias into the system.
- A great open source resource for building ML models is scikit-learn.
- The four big commercial machine learning as a service (MLaaS) solutions are Amazon SageMaker, Microsoft Azure Machine Learning, IBM Watson, and Google Cloud AI.

21

Building Artificial Minds

In this chapter:

- Creating artificial neural networks that can learn on their own
- Differentiating between automated and intelligent computer systems
- Adding layers to your neural network to enable deep learning
- Putting your neural network to work performing practical tasks
- Getting up to speed on the top tools for building deep learning solutions

One challenge with machine learning (ML) systems is that they can be processor intensive, especially when they need to examine data measured in petabytes—a little over a thousand terabytes or a million gigabytes. This challenge isn't a new one; as far back as the early 1940s, computer scientists were trying to develop ways to meet that challenge by expanding the power of computers.

What they came up with is something called an *artificial neural network*, which is fashioned to mimic the physiology of the human brain. The brain consists of neurons (nerve cells) that form a complex, three-dimensional network. Each neuron serves as an independent processor, and the neurons communicate with one another across the network via electrical and chemical signaling mechanisms. This 3D network enables humans to make split-second decisions. Think about all the calculations your brain needs to make when you're performing a simple task, such as loading your dishwasher, and how quickly it performs those calculations and choreographs all the physical movements.

An artificial neural network is structured and functions in a similar manner, but instead of using biological neurons, it uses computer processing units called *nodes*. These nodes are arranged in layers with all nodes in one layer connecting to all nodes in the layer above and below it, creating an intricate network of nodes. Each accepts input, performs a calculation on that input, and passes the output along to one or more other nodes. Working together, the network can learn and perform operations such as classification and clustering. (See Part III, "Artificial Neural Networks," for more about how artificial neural networks are constructed and how they function.)

Unlike most ML applications that are trained to perform a specific task via supervised or unsupervised learning, artificial neural networks learn by trial and error. They learn from making mistakes, and they operate on probabilities. That's why when you look at the results of artificial neural networks, they're typically displayed as a likelihood or probability of being correct. For example, in facial recognition, the neural network will return a result such as, "This has a 98.6 percent chance of being a certain person."

The system processes the data and optimizes itself in real time. In the beginning, an artificial neural network may be right only a small percentage of the time. However, over time, with practice, performance improves, just as it does with humans. When you first implement a deep learning system, monitor the system carefully and have a human expert double-check the results until the system achieves a level of accuracy and confidence in the results that are satisfactory for its application.

Despite their potential drawbacks, neural networks deliver five key benefits over less sophisticated ML networks:

- **Distributed processing:** Processing tasks can be divvied up and distributed across nodes to significantly increase the overall speed at which results are calculated. Instead of having one processor doing everything, you can spread the load.
- **Organic learning:** Neural networks can learn on their own without being trained—that is, without being fed predetermine data and logic gleaned from experts.
- **Nonlinear processing:** With nonlinear processing, a neural network can take shortcuts to reduce the computation required to find a solution.

- **Fault-tolerance:** The neural network can re-route communications to bypass any nodes that are down, thus preventing system failures.
- **Self-repair:** Neural networks can help diagnose, repair, and recover from node malfunctions to maintain proper function.

Deep learning artificial neural networks can expand the capabilities of ML significantly. They enable artificial intelligence (AI) systems to sift through massive volumes of diverse data to quickly and easily identify complex patterns.

Separating Intelligence from Automation

At the 1939 World's Fair, one of the most popular attractions was a 250-pound robot named Elektro. He dazzled audiences while smoking, blowing up balloons, and even telling jokes. Many consumers believed they were just a few years away from having their own Elektro who could clean the house and do the dishes.

However, as impressive as Elektro was, he had a serious limitation: he was automated, not *intelligent*. When you pressed a button, he could blow up a balloon, but he didn't have the ability to decide when to blow up a balloon or figure out how to get more balloons if he ran out. He had no ability to learn new skills or even become better at what he did know how to do.

Fast forward to today, and you still witness this lack of clarity around the difference between automation and intelligence. Some of the ambiguity is intentional. Many software and hardware vendors eagerly pitch their products as being artificially intelligent when they're not. In fact, as a customer you probably see this all the time. Your tax software may advertise that it uses AI to check your returns. But the system isn't really discovering new ways for you to save on your taxes. It's simply following routine automation on well-established tax code.

Another source of confusion is the growing field of *robotic process automation* (RPA), which involves the use of software and ML to train computers to handle high-level routine tasks. The software observes how a human does a job and tries to repeat the same steps in the same sequence. These systems are sometimes presented as applications of AI, but they're really just standard automation. The software bots do exactly what they're shown, almost like an old-style tape recorder. They never learn or adapt.

In their book *Artificial Intelligence: A Modern Approach, Fourth Edition* (Pearson, 2020), Stuart Russell and Peter Norvig draw a clear distinction between automation and AI by explaining that unlike automated systems, AI extends "the reach of the designer into unknown environments." In other words, an essential quality of an AI implementation is that the system can learn and improve without input or guidance from a human trainer.

One of the first questions you should ask when you're planning to build an ML system or artificial neural network is whether you need it to be intelligent or automated. Do you need a system that can learn on its own or one that merely replicates an ability to perform a task it can be programmed or trained to do? If you need an automated system, basic ML or programming can handle the job. On the other hand, if you need a system that can learn and adapt, a system that can extend "the reach of the designer into unknown environments," you probably need to build a deep learning artificial neural network.

Adding Layers for Deep Learning

In the world of ML, being deep matters. Bigger networks generally perform faster and are better at spotting patterns in data. Depth is usually measured in nodes and layers.

As explained in Chapter 12, "What Are Artificial Neural Networks?", artificial neural networks have at least three layers:

- An input later into which data is fed
- One or more hidden layers, which process the data
- An output layer, which presents the result of the processing

An artificial neural network with multiple hidden layers is often referred to as a *deep learning artificial neural network* (or just a *deep learning network*) because it is multiple layers deep.

Industry leaders in ML, including Google and IBM, have really embraced deep learning. In fact, Google built a deep learning network that learned how to win a high score on a popular video game. Later, using the same technology, Google built a deep learning network that learned how to become a master at playing a strategic board game popular in China called Go. Go is thought to be so complex that the number of legal positions for pieces on the board (a 19-by-19 grid) greatly exceeds that of atoms in the known, observable universe. Clearly, for a bot to master this game, it would need to process a massive amount of data.

Why would Google spend so much time figuring out how to build machines that could beat most of their employees at video and board games? Because it can use the same technology to better understand user and customer behavior and sell its technology to its customers who want to do the same. And that's valuable. If a Google-built AI system can predict with 95 percent certainty that a certain customer will buy a specific product and is willing to pay a certain amount for it, that has incredible commercial value.

And if Google can build a deep-learning network that can learn how to master complex games, then building a system that can understand and predict how a customer will act or what the customer will buy is a relative snap. Regardless of the application, the underlying technology is the same.

Considering Applications for Artificial Neural Networks

Before you decide to build a neural network, you have a few considerations to make, such as the following:

- Where can an artificial neural network benefit my business? Look at areas of your business where people are generally required to make decisions based on gut instinct. Deep learning networks can often acquire this same skill while delivering better and more consistent decisions.

- What specifically do we want the neural network to do? In the following sections, I highlight a couple of common applications for artificial neural networks.

- What data do we need to feed into the neural network to enable it to learn how to do what we need it to do? Do we have that data internally, or do we need to obtain it? If we need to obtain external data, who collects such data?

- What tools are available for creating the type of deep learning network we need? See the later section, "Reviewing the Top Deep Learning Tools."

In the following two sections, I present a couple of common applications of deep learning artificial neural networks to illustrate how this technology can be useful in business.

Classifying Your Best Customers

A few years ago, I worked for an organization that handled vast amounts of credit card data. The entire business centered around analyzing customer purchases and recommending promotions based on each customer's interests. When customers logged in to check their charges or pay their bill, they had the option to add a digital coupon to their credit card, maybe 10 percent off their order at a certain restaurant. By adding the coupon to their credit card, eating at the restaurant, and paying with the credit card, they'd get the discount.

More importantly for the company creating these promotions, they could charge businesses for these promotions. They could charge a fee if the customer added the coupon to her card and maybe another fee if the customer visited the business and made a purchase.

To perform this function, an ML system would need to analyze mountains of data. Each customer may have dozens of transactions each month. The major credit card companies have tens of millions of customers. Over time, that could represent billions or even trillions of transactions and several petabytes of data. The system would need to analyze all that data to identify patterns that would help predict what would appeal to each customer based on purchase histories, analyze this customer's purchase history, compare it with those patterns, and then decide which two or three promotions would be most likely to trigger this customer to add the promotion to her card. And it would need to do this in the blink of any eye.

Executing this task would require more than one to two processors working alone or in series, so the business created a deep-learning artificial neural network.

Remember, data alone isn't necessarily valuable. In this instance, the data consisted of a list of mundane transactions linked to anonymous customer IDs. What made the data valuable was the analysis of it and the application of that analysis to make accurate predictions about customer behavior. Figuring out where a customer shopped and what he bought in the past is easy. The real challenge is to predict new places the customer might go and what the customer is likely to try.

To predict which promotions a customer was likely to respond to favorably, the system probably used a combination of unsupervised and supervised learning. It would need to cluster users based on their spending habits, label the clusters, and then classify customers using these labels. The system could also cluster customers into two groups—those who are likely to try something new and those who aren't—and then create labels for classifying customers according to that criterion. The system would then be able to choose which promotions to present each customer based on that customer's purchase history and likelihood of being willing to try something different.

Such a system could also use reinforcement learning, rewarding the system each time a customer added a coupon to his card and each time he redeemed a coupon so that the system could fine-tune its predictions. Over time, the system would become better and better at microtargeting promotions to the customers most likely to respond favorably to them.

Recommending Store Layouts

Imagine that you work for a big-box retail organization with many brick-and-mortar locations. You want to examine video footage of all these stores to figure out how people shop, so you can maximize the total dollar value of goods the average customer purchases. This would be a great application for a deep-learning AI system because it would need to analyze large volumes of data, including video footage of customer movements throughout the store, what each customer purchased, and the amount paid for each item. No human could possibly ingest all this data, analyze it, and come up with any data-based recommendations on how to reorganize the store to increase sales revenue.

In contrast, an artificial network would excel at the task, ingesting and processing the data, analyzing it, and possibly experimenting with different store layouts to determine a layout that would work best, at least theoretically. It might even be able to produce visuals that show how different store layouts would likely perform.

When you're in the process of deciding on a type of AI system to use, consider the pros and cons of deep learning and artificial neural networks. If you have the resources and expertise to build an artificial neural network and you can afford to have the system make mistakes as it learns, this deep learning is likely to outperform systems that don't rely on deep learning in terms of both speed and accuracy.

Analyzing and Tracking Biometrics

Are you one of those people who remembers someone's face better than you remember his name? That's not unusual. In fact, from a young age, most humans are excellent at tracking faces. Each person's face is a little bit different. Eyes, noses, lips, and ears all vary slightly from person to person. All of these details are data that the brain ingests and processes, enabling people to instantly determine whether someone looks familiar or not and to identify a friend, family member, or coworker.

Artificial neural networks can learn to perform the same feat through the analysis of *biometrics*—physical or behavioral human characteristics that can be converted into digital data and used to identify a person or grant access to systems, devices, or data. Biometrics include fingerprints, DNA, facial features, voice quality, signature, physical movements, engagement patterns (with websites, social media, or other individuals, for example), typing cadence, and so on. *You* might not think of your face, fingerprints, voice, or physical movements as data, but to an artificial neural network, they're all just numbers and probability.

Imagine dialing into a company's customer service line and becoming increasingly frustrated because the system is leading you on what seems like an endless trail to nowhere and provides no option for speaking with a customer service rep. As your frustration grows, your voice sounds more strained, and maybe your breathing becomes irregular. An AI agent could warn a supervisor that there's an unhappy customer on the line.

An AI system can examine biometrics as it would any other type of data. It can compare *your* voice with voices from hundreds of thousands of other customer support conversations and learn, over time, the changes in voice patterns characteristic of disgruntled customers.

Facial recognition is a common use of artificial neural networks and one of the more controversial uses of biometrics. Remember that ML and AI systems excel at analyzing large volumes of data. These systems can collect and analyze video from thousands of digital video cameras, identify individuals through facial recognition, retinal scans, or even body movement, and use that data to track an individual's movements, record their behaviors, and even predict what they'll do next. If this sounds suspiciously like Big Brother is watching, that's exactly what these artificial neural networks are capable of and why many people are justifiably concerned over how they are and will be used. Of course, these AI systems can be used for good, such as locating a missing person or solving a murder, but they can also be used to silence anyone who disagrees with an oppressive regime.

During the 2019 to 2020 coronavirus pandemic, many healthcare workers were given biometric rings. These rings could transmit their body temperature and other data to ML systems, which were able to process the data in real time and predict the likelihood of an outbreak at the hospital. If everyone in the world were required to wear one of these rings, health organizations could probably do a much better job of tracking the spread of the virus, identifying problem areas-+ and predicting where new outbreaks would occur, and notifying the public.

However, even in hospitals, only a few healthcare workers wore the biometric rings. Among the general population, at least in democratic countries, compliance would be even more of a challenge, and perhaps rightfully so. We have no idea how the data collected could be used. For example, if insurance companies were to access the data, perhaps they would use it to jack up the premiums of certain individuals who show signs of potential future illness or accidents.

If you're thinking about building an artificial neural network to analyze biometric data, consider what you would want the network to do, what data would be needed to enable the network to perform that task, and the possible ethical implications of building and using such a system. Consider both how the network could help you deliver value to customers and how it could be used to their detriment.

Reviewing the Top Deep Learning Tools

Deep learning is one of the most interesting areas in AI, so a number of tools are available for creating deep-learning artificial neural networks. These tools are in the form of deep learning frameworks. A *deep learning framework* is an interface that enables developers to quickly and easily build and deploy deep learning AI models using a collection of prebuilt components.

One of the most popular deep learning frameworks is TensorFlow. Created by the Google Brain Project in 2011, TensorFlow is an end-to-end open source ML framework for developing, training, and deploying ML models. You can use it with most of the cloud-based ML services, including Amazon SageMaker, IBM Watson, and Microsoft Azure. TensorFlow is cross platform, meaning it runs on a variety of architectures—servers, smart phones, and even GPUs (graphics processing units). It abstracts much of the hardware using something called the "TensorFlow Distributed Execution Engine." It uses Python as its front-end application programming interface (API) for building applications and high-performance C++ for executing those applications. (Visit https://www.tensorflow.org/ to learn more about TensorFlow and to start using it to build and deploy your own deep learning models.)

Another framework you might want to consider is the Microsoft Cognitive Toolkit (CNTK)—an open-source toolkit for commercial-grade distributed deep learning. A competitor to TensorFlow, CNTK is another low-level deep learning framework used to build and deploy deep learning models. CNTK seems to have an edge over TensorFlow with respect to processing speed, creating models that are production ready, and supporting CPU and GPU computation. TensorFlow scores higher in terms of ease of use, community support, and mobile deep learning. However, the two frameworks are in continuous development, so the comparison can differ by the time you read this. (Visit docs.microsoft.com/en-us/cognitive-toolkit for additional details about CNTK and to get started using it.)

Another popular tool is Keras—an open-source neural-network library written in Python. You can run Keras on top of TensorFlow or CNTK (and other low-level deep learning libraries) and use it as a higher-level API to simplify the process of building deep learning models. It is modular, extensible, user-friendly, and designed to enable fast experimentation. (Visit https://keras.io/ to find out more about Keras.)

If you're using your deep learning artificial neural network to identify objects (image processing), check out another deep learning framework called Caffe, developed by Berkeley AI Research or BAIR and a community of contributors. (Visit caffe.berkeleyvision.org for more about Caffe.)

If you are just getting started with building your own deep learning artificial neural networks, I encourage you to start with TensorFlow and Keras. As you gain more experience with ML algorithms, Python, and C++, you can begin to do more customization. In addition to simplifying development and deployment, TensorFlow is one of the most popular frameworks for building deep learning networks on almost all the popular cloud services. You can also run them on your own server, smart phone, computer, or other computational device. It abstracts away most of the technical challenges you get with building these networks and provides the flexibility to run your deep learning artificial neural networks on top of a lot of your existing technology.

Chapter Takeaways

- An artificial neural network is a computerized version of a human brain consisting of computational nodes that communicate across several layers of the network.
- Unlike most machine learning applications that are trained to perform a specific task via supervised or unsupervised learning, artificial neural networks learn by trial and error.
- Google has built deep learning artificial neural networks that have learned to play (and win) video games and strategic board games.
- Before you start building an artificial neural network, determine where it can benefit your business most, what you want the network to do, what kind of data is needed to enable it to learn the task, and what tools you want to use to build it.

- A *deep learning framework* is an interface that enables developers to quickly and easily build and deploy deep learning AI models using a collection of prebuilt components.
- TensorFlow and CNTK are two of the leading low-level deep learning frameworks.
- You can run Keras on top of TensorFlow or CNTK to further simplify the process of building and deploying deep learning artificial neural networks.

Index

A

accuracy, model, 127–128
ACTICO, 205
activation functions
   definition of, 149
   Heaviside step function, 149–150
   ReLU (rectified linear unit), 149–150
Acxiom, 176
agents, virtual, 181, 196–197
AI (artificial intelligence) applications. *See also* artificial neural networks; ML (machine learning); NLP (natural language processing)
   automated decision-making, 199–205
      data analysis, 200
      intuitive decision-making compared to, 201–202
      overview of, 199–201
      real-time data gathering, 200, 202–204
      tools for, 204–205
   automatic translation, 77
   choosing approach to, 57–59, 61–63
   customer interaction, automation of, 186–187, 193–197
      analog signals, 193
      ASR (automated speech recognition), 193–195
      chatbots and virtual agents, 181, 196–197
      customer classification, 224–225
      customer purchases, prediction of, 210
      hidden Markov model, 194–195
      NLG (natural language generation), 181, 184–186, 190–191, 195–196
      NLU (natural language understanding), 181, 183–184, 189–190, 193
   definition of, 3–4
   expert systems, 13, 35–37, 46
   heuristic reasoning, 14–15, 19
   human intelligence compared to, 3–4
   IoT (Internet of Things), 50–51
   learning versus memorization in, 15–18
   pattern matching, 5–6, 12, 19
   prediction of events and outcomes, 207–218
      anticipating questions, 210–211
      automated decision-making, 212–213
      customer purchases, 210
      data labeling, 208–209
      replication of expertise, 213–214
   robotics, 45–48
   strong AI, 11–13
   testing, 6–8
   weak AI, 11–13
AI (artificial intelligence), history of
   artificial intelligence planning, 14–15
   expert systems, 13
   general problem solver, 8–11
   perceptrons, 135
   symbolic systems, 13
   Turing test, 6–8
AI (artificial intelligence) planning, 14–15
AI Hub, 217
AI-hard problems, 189
Alexa, 19, 48, 53, 189, 195
algorithms, 115–123, 128. *See also* artificial neural networks
   bias-variance trade-off, 115–118
   choosing, 120–121
   classification, 120, 169–172
   clustering, 120, 172–174
   decision-tree, 97, 99–101, 120
   definition of, 71, 96–97
   ensemble modeling, 121–123
   fitting model to data, 119–120
   Google, 31
   k-means clustering, 104–107, 120
   k-nearest neighbor, 97, 101–104, 120
   naïve Bayes, 97, 110–113, 119–120
   prediction/estimation, 120
   regression analysis, 108–110, 120
   selecting approach to, 123
AlphaGo, 92–93
Amazon
   Alexa, 19, 48, 53, 189, 195
   AWS (Amazon Web Services), 176
   Lex, 191
   SageMaker, 216, 217
Amelia (IPSoft), 196–197
analog signals, 193
anticipating questions, 210–211
Apache Spark tools, 189

Apple
  iMessage, 49
  ML (machine learning) used by, 77
  Siri, 12, 19, 48, 53, 189
applications. *See* AI (artificial intelligence) applications
Arria, 190
Artificial Intelligence (Russell and Norvig), 222
artificial neural networks, 24–26, 143–153
  activation functions
    definition of, 149
    Heaviside step function, 149–150
    ReLU (rectified linear unit), 149–150
  advantages of, 133–135, 220–221
  approaches to, 133–134
  backpropagation, 160–165
  bias, 132, 141–142, 156–157
    bias-variance trade-off, 115–118
    definition of, 152–153
    positive/negative, 152
  chain rule, 164–165
  challenges of, 175–178
    data quality and quantity, 175–176
    selection of training data, 177
    separation of training and test data, 175–176
  classification, 169–172
    algorithms for, 120
    classification problems, 95, 97–99, 169–172
    customer classification, 224–225
    regression analysis and, 41–42
  clustering, 29–30, 169–170, 172–174
    algorithms for, 120
    with artificial neural networks, 169–170, 172–174
    clustering problems, 96
    k-means clustering, 104–107, 120
  cost function, 158–160
  deep learning, 222–229
    applications for, 222–229
    frameworks for, 228–229
    tools for, 223–228
  definition of, 219
  disadvantages of, 59
  error in, 132–133
  exploratory approach to, 177–178
  feeding data into, 143–145
  gradient descent
    cost function and, 158–160
    stochastic, 166
  intelligence versus automation in, 221–222
  layers, 24–26
    hidden, 131, 145–148
    input, 145
  nodes, 131
  overview of, 131–133
  perceptrons, 135–138
    feedforward, 136
    Mark 1 Perceptron, 27–30
    multilayer, 138
    single-layer, 138
  sigmoid functions, 139
  sigmoid neurons, 138–141, 144–145
  tuning, 163–164
  weights, 137–138, 149, 156–157
  when to use, 62
Artificial Solutions Teneo, 196
ASR (automated speech recognition), 193–195
Associated Press, 185
Automated Insights Wordsmith, 191
automated speech recognition (ASR), 193–195
automation
  automatic translation, 77
  customer interaction, 186–187, 193–197
    analog signals, 193
    ASR (automated speech recognition), 193–195
    chatbots and virtual agents, 181, 196–197
    customer classification, 224–225
    customer purchases, prediction of, 210
    hidden Markov model, 194–195
    NLG (natural language generation), 181, 184–186, 190–191, 195–196
    NLU (natural language understanding), 181, 183–184, 189–190, 193
  decision-making, 199–205, 212–213
    data analysis, 200
    intuitive decision-making compared to, 201–202
    overview of, 199–201
    real-time data gathering, 200, 202–204
    tools for, 204–205
  intelligence versus, 221–222
  phone system analogy, 36–37
Azure Machine Learning, 216, 217

B

backpropagation, 29, 37–38, 160–165
bagging, 121–122
Berkeley AI Research (BAIR), 229
Berkeley Software Distribution (BSD), 216

bias
    in artificial neural networks, 132, 141–142, 156–157
    bias-variance trade-off, 115–118
    neural networks and, 152–153
    positive/negative, 152
big data, 20, 30–32, 53–59. *See also* ML (machine learning)
    choosing approach to, 57–59, 61–63
    concept of, 53–59
    data mining
        definition of, 55–56
        machine learning compared to, 55–57
        transitioning to machine learning, 56–57
    data scientists, role of, 54–55
binary classification, 95, 97–99
Bing, ML (machine learning) used by, 208
biology, clustering in, 173
biometric analysis, 226–228
Bird, Steven, 188
boosting, 121–122
Brain Project (Google), 228
BSD (Berkeley Software Distribution), 216
Building Natural Language Generation Systems (Reiter), 191
business intelligence tools, 56, 62

C

Caffe, 229
Canonico, Massimo, 189
capsule networks, 176
cars, self-driving, 46–48
chain rule, 164–165
chatbots, 196–197
Chinese room experiment, 10–11, 20
CIA World Factbook, 176
class predictor probability, 111–112
classification
    algorithms for, 120
    classification problems, 95, 97–99, 169–172
    customer classification, 224–225
    regression analysis and, 41–42
Cloud AI, 217
clustering, 29–30
    algorithms for, 120
    with artificial neural networks, 169–170, 172–174
    clustering problems, 96
    k-means clustering, 104–107, 120
CNTK (Cognitive Toolkit), 228
combinatorial explosion, 11

"A Comparison and Critique of Natural Language Understanding Tools" (Canonico and De Russis), 189
Compromise, 188
Cortana, 12, 48, 189
cost function, 158–160
customer interaction, automation of, 186–187, 193–197
    analog signals, 193
    ASR (automated speech recognition), 193–195
    chatbots and virtual agents, 181, 196–197
    customer classification, 224–225
    customer purchases, prediction of, 210
    hidden Markov model, 194–195
    NLG (natural language generation), 181, 184–186, 190–191, 195–196
    NLU (natural language understanding), 181, 183–184, 189–190, 193

D

Dartmouth Summer Research Project on Artificial Intelligence (1956), 3
data, 74–77, 107, 175–176
    analysis of, 200
    classification, 169–172
        algorithms for, 120
        classification problems, 95, 97–99, 169–172
        customer classification, 224–225
        regression analysis and, 41–42
    clustering, 29–30, 169–170, 172–174
        algorithms for, 120
        with artificial neural networks, 169–170, 172–174
        clustering problems, 96
        k-means clustering, 104–107, 120
    definition of, 71
    feeding into neural networks, 143–145
    fitting model to, 119–120
    labeling, 37, 84, 89, 208–209
    mining
        definition of, 55–56
        technology used in, 56
        transitioning to machine learning, 56–57
    quality and quantity of, 175–176
    real-time data gathering, 200, 202–204
    semi-structured, 171
    structured, 171
    test versus training, 85, 127
        definition of, 75
        selection of, 177

separation of, 175–176
training sets, 21, 38
unlabeled, 89
unstructured, 171
validation, 75
data scientists, role of, 54–55
data security, ML (machine learning) in, 23
De Russis, Luigi, 189
decision-making, automated, 199–205, 212–213
data analysis, 200
intuitive decision-making compared to, 201–202
overview of, 199–201
real-time data gathering, 200, 202–204
tools for, 204–205
decision-tree algorithms, 97, 99–101, 120
deep learning, 29–30, 31–32, 222–229
applications for, 222–229
biometric analysis, 226–228
customer classification, 224–225
store layout recommendations, 225–226
frameworks for, 228–229
DeepMind project, 5, 31–32, 92–93
dependent variables, 83–84
Dialogflow, 189, 190
DigitalWorkforce.ai page, 196–197
distributed processing, 220

E

education, clustering in, 174
EKG (electrocardiogram) sensors, 50–51
Elektro, 221
ensemble modeling, 121–123
entire search space, 14
entropy, 101
errors
in artificial neural networks, 132–133
backpropagation of, 29, 37–38
estimation algorithms, 120
ethics of machine learning, 214–216
Excel spreadsheets, 62
expert systems, 13, 35–37, 46
expertise, replication of, 213–214
exploratory approach, 177–178

F

Facebook
ML (machine learning) used by, 77
wit.ai, 189–190

fault tolerance, 221
feature-weighted linear stacking, 121–122
feedforward perceptrons, 136
fitting model to data, 119–120
frameworks, deep learning, 228–229
fraud detection, 23, 171
functions
activation
definition of, 149
Heaviside step function, 149–150
ReLU (rectified linear unit), 149–150
optimization, 26
sigmoid, 139

G

general problem solver, 8–11
generalizability, neural networks, 26
Go, 92
GOFAI (good old-fashioned artificial intelligence), 5
Google
AlphaGo, 92–93
Brain Project, 228
Cloud AI, 217
DeepMind project, 5, 31–32, 92–93
Dialogflow, 189–190
Finance, 176
Google Assistant, 189
Maps, 14–15
ML (machine learning) used by, 23, 77, 208
Public Data Explorer, 176
search algorithms, 31
gradient descent, 39–41
cost function and, 158–160
stochastic, 166

H

healthcare, ML (machine learning) in, 23
Healthdata.gov, 176
Heaviside step function, 149–150
heuristic reasoning, 14–15, 19
hidden layers, neural network, 24–26, 131, 145–148
hidden Markov model, 194–195
high overlap of data, 107
Hinton, Geoffrey, 28–29, 212
history of AI, 6–8
artificial intelligence planning, 14–15
expert systems, 13
general problem solver, 8–11

machine intelligence, 19–22
ML (machine learning), 19–22, 27–30, 67
perceptrons, 135
symbolic systems, 13
Hulu, 186–187
human intelligence, AI compared to, 3–4
hyperparameters, 71, 119

I

IBM Watson, 5, 189, 190, 217
iMessage, 49
imitation game, 6–8
independent variables, 83–84, 109
inductive reasoning, 89–90
inference, 204
input layer, neural network, 24–26, 145
input variables, 109
intelligence. *See also* AI (artificial intelligence) applications
   versus automation, 221–222
   definition of, 3–4
intelligent quotient (IQ), 4
interconnected symbols, 9–10
Internet of Things (IoT), 50–51, 202–204
interrogators, in Turing test, 6–8
intuitive decision-making, 201–202
investment, ML (machine learning) in, 23
IoT (Internet of Things), 50–51, 202–204
IPSoft, 196–197
IQ (intelligent quotient), 4
IRI, 176

J

Java tools, 188
Jeopardy, IBM Watson on, 5

K

Keras, 229
Klein, Ewan, 188
k-means clustering, 104–107, 120
k-nearest neighbor, 97, 101–104, 120
*k*NN. *See k*-nearest neighbor

L

labeling data, 37, 84, 89, 208–209
language processing. *See* NLP (natural language processing)

law enforcement applications, clustering in, 174
layers, artificial neural networks
   hidden, 131, 145–148
   input, 145
learners, 71
learning, memorization versus, 15–18
Lex, 191
limiting the search space, 14
linear problems, 28
linear regression, 109–110
LinkedIn, ML (machine learning) used by, 77
Loper, Edward, 188
LUIS, 189–190

M

machine intelligence. *See* AI (artificial intelligence) applications
machine learning. *See* ML (machine learning)
majority voting, 121
Maps, Google, 14–15
Mark 1 Perceptron, 27–30
marketing
   market segmentation, 174
   ML (machine learning) in, 23
McCarthy, John, 3
medicine, clustering in, 173
memorization, learning versus, 15–18
Microsoft
   Azure Machine Learning, 216–217
   CNTK (Cognitive Toolkit), 228
   Cortana, 12, 48, 189
   LUIS, 189–190
   Power Virtual Agents, 196
   Skype, 49
Minsky, Marvin, 27
ML (machine learning). *See also* artificial neural networks; data
   advantages of, 20
   algorithms, 115–123, 128
      bias-variance trade-off, 115–118
      choosing, 120–121
      classification, 120, 169–172
      clustering, 120, 172–174
      decision-tree, 99–101, 120
      definition of, 71, 96–97
      ensemble modeling, 121–123
      fitting model to data, 119–120
      k-means clustering, 104–107, 120
      k-nearest neighbor, 97, 101–104, 120
      naïve Bayes, 97, 110–113, 119, 120

prediction/estimation, 120
regression analysis, 108–110
selecting approach to, 123
application of, 77–78
automated phone system analogy, 36–37
backpropagation, 29, 37–38
big data, 20, 30–32
challenges of, 175–178
    data quality and quantity, 175–176
    selection of training data, 177
    separation of training and test data, 175–176
classification of problems in, 95–99
components of, 71
deep learning, 29–30, 31–32, 222–229
definition of, 55–56
ethics of, 214–216
expert systems versus, 35–37
gradient descent, 39–41
history of, 27–30, 67
learning process, 71–74
MLaaS (ML as a service), 216
model accuracy, 127–128
overview of, 19–22, 67–71
practical applications of, 22–24
prediction of events and outcomes, 207–218
    anticipating questions, 210–211
    automated decision-making, 212–213
    customer purchases, 210
    data labeling, 208–209
    replication of expertise, 213–214
questions to ask before implementing, 125–126
regression analysis, 41–42
reinforcement learning, 91–93, 209
selecting approach to, 123
semi-supervised learning, 79–81, 89–91, 123, 209
supervised learning, 21, 37–38, 46
    challenges of, 80
    classification, 41–42, 169–172
    definition of, 123, 208
    dependent variables, 83–84
    independent variables, 83–84
    labels in, 37, 84
    overview of, 79–81, 83–85
    regression analysis, 41–42
    training sets, 38
technology used in, 56
tips and guidelines for, 125
tools for, 216–218
training versus test data in, 85, 127, 175–176
transitioning from data mining to, 56–57

unsupervised learning, 21, 37–38, 46, 79–81, 86–89, 123, 172–174, 208–209
when to use, 62, 178
MLaaS (ML as a service), 216
models
  accuracy of, 127–128
  algorithms, 128
  bias
    bias-variance trade-off in, 115–118
    neural networks and, 152–153
    positive/negative, 152
  definition of, 71, 75
  ensemble modeling, 121–123
  fitting to data, 119–120
  hidden Markov model, 194–195
  noise in, 119–120
  overfitting, 119–120
  signal in, 120
  training versus test data in, 85, 127
    definition of, 75
    selection of, 177
    separation of, 175–176
  underfitting, 119–120
multiclass classification, 95, 97
multilayer perceptrons, 138

N

naïve Bayes algorithm, 97, 110–113, 119–120
Narrative Science Quill, 191
narrow AI. *See* weak AI (artificial intelligence)
National Climactic Data Center, 176
Natural, 188
natural language generation. *See* NLG (natural language generation)
natural language processing. *See* NLP (natural language processing)
Natural Language Processing with Python (Bird, Klein, and Loper), 188
Natural Language Toolkit (NLTK), 188
natural language understanding. *See* NLU (natural language understanding)
negative bias, 152
Netflix, 186–187
networks, capsule, 176
neural networks. *See* artificial neural networks
Newell, Allen, 8
NHS Health and Social Care Information Centre, 176
Nielsen, 176
NLG (natural language generation), 181, 184–186, 190–191, 195–196

NLG Studio, 191
NLP (natural language processing), 36, 48–50, 62–63, 181–191
  automatic translation with, 77
  customer interaction, automation of, 186–187, 193–197
    analog signals, 193
    ASR (automated speech recognition), 193–195
    chatbots and virtual agents, 181, 196–197
    customer classification, 224–225
    customer purchases, prediction of, 210
    hidden Markov model, 194–195
    NLG (natural language generation), 181, 184–186, 190–191, 195–196
    NLU (natural language understanding), 181, 183–184, 189–190, 193
  overview of, 181–183
  tools for, 187–191
Nlp.js, 188
NLTK (Natural Language Toolkit), 188
NLU (natural language understanding), 181, 183–184, 189–190, 193
Node tools, 188
nodes, neural network, 131
noise, definition of, 119–120
nonlinear processing, 220
Norvig, Peter, 222

O

online searches, ML (machine learning) in, 23
online software development, ML (machine learning) in, 23
OpenNLP, 188
optimization function, 26
organic learning, 220
output layers, neural network, 24–26
overfitting, 119–120

P

parameters, 71
pattern matching, 5–6, 12, 19, 210–211
perceptrons, 135–138
  feedforward, 136
  Mark 1 Perceptron, 27–30
  multilayer, 138
  single-layer, 138
Perceptrons (Minsky), 27
personalized marketing, ML (machine learning) in, 23

physical symbol system hypothesis (PSSH), 9–11
pipelines, 217
planning, artificial intelligence, 14–15
Pong, 91
positive bias, 152
posterior probability, 112
Power Virtual Agents, 196
prediction algorithms, 120
prediction of events and outcomes, 207–218
  anticipating questions, 210–211
  automated decision-making, 212–213
  customer purchases, 210
  data labeling, 208–209
  replication of expertise, 213–214
predictors, 109
prior probability, 112
probability
  class predictor, 111–112
  posterior, 112
  prior, 112
PSSH (physical symbol system hypothesis), 9–11
"Purring Test" 32
Python, 56, 188, 216, 228
PyTorch-NLP, 188

Q

Q-learning, 92–93
quality of data, 175–176
quantity of data, 175–176
questions, anticipation of, 210–211
Quill, 191

R

R language, 56
Rainbird, 204–205
real-time data gathering, 200, 202–204
reasoning
  inductive, 89–90
  transductive, 90
Recast.ai, 189
rectified linear unit (ReLU), 149–150
refrigerators, smart, 50
regression algorithms, 120
regression analysis, 41–42, 108–110
regression problems, 96, 98–99
regressors, 109
reinforcement learning, 91–93, 134, 209
Reiter, Ehud, 190
replication of expertise, 213–214

Retext, 188
robotics, 45–48
    AI applications for, 45–48
    Elektro, 221
    RPA (robotic process automation), 221–222
Rosenblatt, Frank, 27–28, 31, 135
RPA (robotic process automation), 221–222
Rulex, 204
Russell, Stuart, 222

S

SageMaker, 216, 217
Samuel, Arthur, 20, 27, 67
Sanchez, Julian, 32
SAP Conversational AI, 190
scikit-learn, 216
search space, 14
Searle, John, 10
self-driving cars, 46–48
self-repair, 221
semi-structured data, 171
semi-supervised learning, 79–81, 89–91, 123, 134, 209
sigmoid functions, 139
sigmoid neurons, 138–141, 144–145
signal, 120, 193
Simon, Herbert A. 8
SimpleNLG, 190
single-layer perceptrons, 138
Siri, 12, 19, 48, 53, 189
Skype, 49
smart devices. *See* IoT (Internet of Things)
social networks, clustering in, 174
SpaCy, 188
spam messages, detection of, 74–75, 170
Spark NLP, 189
speech processing. *See* NLP (natural language processing)
spreadsheets, 62
stacking, 121–123
StanfordNLP, 188
stochastic gradient descent, 166
store layout recommendations, 225–228
strong AI (artificial intelligence), 11–13
structured data, 171
supervised learning, 21, 37–38, 46, 133
    challenges of, 80
    classification, 41–42, 169–172
    definition of, 123, 208

dependent variables, 83–84
independent variables, 83–84
labels in, 37, 84
overview of, 79–81, 83–85
regression analysis, 41–42
training sets, 38
symbolic AI, 9–10
    memorization in, 15–18
    symbol matching
        general problem solver, 8–11
        PSSH (physical symbol system hypothesis), 9–11
symbolic systems, 13
synapses, 24

T

tax return software, 19
Teneo, 196
TensorFlow, 217–218, 228
test data, 85, 127, 175–176
Textacy, 188
TextBlob, 188
thermostats, smart, 50
tools. *See also individual programs*
    for automated decision-making, 204–205
    for ML (machine learning), 216–218
    for NLG (natural language generation), 190–191
    for NLP (natural language processing), 187–191
    for NLU (natural language understanding), 189–190
traditional programming, 74
training data, 85, 127
    definition of, 75
    selection of, 177
    separation of, 175–176
    training sets, 21, 38
transductive reasoning, 90
translation, automatic, 77
trendlines, 109
Turing, Alan, 6–8
Turing test, 6–8
Twitter, ML (machine learning) used by, 77

U

underfitting, 119–120
unlabeled data, 89

unstructured data, 171
unsupervised learning, 21, 37–38, 46, 79–81,
    86–89, 123, 134, 172–174, 208–209
US Census Bureau database, 176

V

vacuum cleaners, robotic, 46
variables, 83–84, 109
variance, 115–118
virtual agents, 196–197
virtual assistants, 182
visualization tools, 56

W

watches, smart, 50
Watson (IBM), 5, 189–190, 217
weak AI (artificial intelligence), 11–13, 19–22
weights, adding to neural networks, 137–138,
    149, 156–157
wit.ai, 189–190
Wordsmith, 191

X-Y-Z

Yahoo! 31
YouTube, ML (machine learning) used by, 77

Photo by izusek/gettyimages

Register Your Product at informit.com/register

Access additional benefits and **save 35%** on your next purchase

- Automatically receive a coupon for 35% off your next purchase, valid for 30 days. Look for your code in your InformIT cart or the Manage Codes section of your account page.
- Download available product updates.
- Access bonus material if available.*
- Check the box to hear from us and receive exclusive offers on new editions and related products.

*Registration benefits vary by product. Benefits will be listed on your account page under Registered Products.

InformIT.com—The Trusted Technology Learning Source

InformIT is the online home of information technology brands at Pearson, the world's foremost education company. At InformIT.com, you can:
- Shop our books, eBooks, software, and video training
- Take advantage of our special offers and promotions (informit.com/promotions)
- Sign up for special offers and content newsletter (informit.com/newsletters)
- Access thousands of free chapters and video lessons

Connect with InformIT—Visit informit.com/community

Addison-Wesley • Adobe Press • Cisco Press • Microsoft Press • Pearson IT Certification • Que • Sams • Peachpit Press

www.ingramcontent.com/pod-product-compliance
Lightning Source LLC
LaVergne TN
LVHW080311260326
834688LV00038B/1062